Have a Cigar!

Have a Cigar!

The Memoir of the Man Behind Pink Floyd, T. Rex, The Jam and George Michael

BRYAN MORRISON

Edited by Barry Johnston

Quiller

For Greta

First published in the UK in 2019
by Quiller, an imprint of Quiller Publishing Ltd

British Library Cataloguing-in-Publication Data
A catalogue record for this book is available from
the British Library

ISBN 978-1-84689-308-7

Design by Guy Callaby

Printed in the Czech Republic

Quiller
An imprint of Quiller Publishing Ltd
Wykey House, Wykey,
Shrewsbury SY4 1JA
Tel: 01939 261616
Email: info@quillerbooks.com
Website: www.quillerpublishing.com

CONTENTS

COME IN HERE, DEAR BOY, HAVE A CIGAR

YOU'RE GONNA GO FAR, YOU'RE GONNA FLY HIGH

Roger Waters, 'Have a Cigar'

INTRODUCTION

This book is the extraordinary memoir of the music publisher, entrepreneur and co-founder of the Royal County of Berkshire Polo Club, Bryan Morrison. He wrote the original manuscript in 1991, intending it to be published the following year to coincide with his fiftieth birthday.

He signed a book deal with a publishing company, was paid an advance, and a ghost writer was appointed to work on the manuscript. However, when Bryan read the publisher's rewritten version of his story, he felt that it no longer reflected his own style or his personality, so he handed the money back to the publisher and cancelled the contract.

After that, the manuscript stayed mainly in a locked drawer at the home of Bryan's son Jamie Morrison and, as time went by, it seemed the moment to publish it had passed. But Jamie always wanted his father's story to be told, and after the death of his mother, Greta, in August 2018, he approached Andrew Johnston, the managing director of Quiller Publishing, to see if he might be interested in publishing the book. Andrew showed the manuscript to me, because I am a book editor and I also worked in the music business for nearly twenty years, and we agreed that it was a unique insight into the golden age of British pop music.

For the first time, Bryan Morrison reveals the true stories behind his music publishing business and his close and personal relationships with legendary rock stars such as Syd Barrett of Pink Floyd, Marc Bolan of T. Rex, Paul Weller of the Jam and George Michael of Wham! He also reveals why the Pretty Things were banned for life from New Zealand, how he became involved with the Kray twins, and received death threats after Robin Gibb left the Bee Gees, not to mention his experiences with U2, the Sex Pistols, Haircut One Hundred, Gary Glitter, and many others.

The original manuscript has been edited for publication, and the dates and facts checked where possible, but this is Bryan Morrison's personal memoir. There may be more stories that he left untold, possibly to protect his own reputation and that of his friends and colleagues, or perhaps he was saving them for a later volume. But as Bryan looked back on his life at the age of fifty, these are his candid and outspoken memories of a truly extraordinary career of success, and occasional failures, in the worlds of music, art, design, fashion and polo.

Barry Johnston, May 2019

PROLOGUE

The most difficult serpent to catch in English polo goes by the quaint name of the Archie David Cup. Of all the tournaments, this competition is probably the most difficult to win, because of the sheer number of players it attracts. During the eighties, up to sixty low goal teams would enter the Archie David, which is a straight knockout tournament. Six tough rounds, often in mud up to the hocks of the horses, sometimes so hard you could make bricks out of it.

My mentor and good friend Major Ronald Ferguson had played in this competition more than twenty times in as many years and never even made it to the semis. Somehow, I had made it to the finals in 1983, but lost to another great polo mate Galen Weston. I vowed then I would never enter again. The pain of losing was too great.

Months later, I was asked the inevitable question. Did I want to have one more try in 1984? The answer, of course, was yes. Looking in my diary for that April, I noticed one very important date, which was with one of the gods of the American music business Al Teller, the president of Columbia Records, and it was in New York at 4 p.m. on a Friday.

Dick Leahy, my partner in Morrison Leahy Music, had fixed a meeting to try to kick ass in the States for Wham!, who were fast becoming one of the biggest acts around the world with the exception of the USA. We hoped to change this with the release of their next single, 'Wake Me Up Before You Go Go'. At the time, I hadn't anticipated that anything would get in the way of this date with destiny at the CBS headquarters in midtown Manhattan, known as Black Rock.

I entered the Archie David with my four-man polo team and the first four rounds were tough, but we managed to progress all the way to the semi-finals, which were to take place two days later on a Thursday.

It was my assistant Cora, the next morning, who pointed out that there was going to be a bit of congestion in my calendar.

'Bryan, how can you play on Thursday? If you win, you've got to play the final on Saturday and you have that really important meeting in New York on the Friday.'

I was torn between business and pleasure. It seemed insoluble. We discussed my dilemma for hours before finally coming up with a solution. If we won on Thursday, I would take Concorde to New York on Friday morning, have the meeting and return Friday evening. Tickets were reserved in case the improbable happened.

It rained for most of Wednesday and the sight of a very wet and muddy polo field greeted us on that Thursday afternoon. It was a match in which every yard of terrain was fought over. By the end we were hanging onto our saddles in near exhaustion, frantically stabbing at a ball that seemed to sink forever deeper into the ruts and holes of the field.

The last minute or two of the game seemed like an eternity. We were a goal up and literally hanging in there, then the bell and the whistle sounded, and we were in the final of the Archie David. The only problem now was that I had barely forty-eight hours to get to New York, have my meeting, return and play the final.

At 11 a.m. the next morning, I was in the Concorde departure lounge at Heathrow. I had travelled once before on Concorde in the late seventies and what a wonderful example of man's ingenuity it was. The only significant difference between this trip and the first was that on the previous occasion we had been served Dom Perignon from the outset, even at the check-in, and it had continued flowing while on board, as had the caviar. Now it was plain Moët (nothing wrong with that), plus a tiny pot of caviar. The thrill, however, was the same.

Some three and a half hours later, we were standing outside Kennedy Airport waiting for one of those absurd stretch limos. The limo wafted us towards what must be one of the most amazing sights in the world, the colossus of Manhattan, with its granite skyscrapers and the deep canyons of the streets below. I have been to New York a hundred times, but the swift transition from London to the Big Apple on this visit left me in awe.

We stopped off at my lawyer's office, had a quick wash and brush-up, shot over to the Stage Star Deli for a delicious sandwich, and forty-five minutes later we were in Black Rock for our meeting. A tough three hours of bargaining took place over the immediate future of Wham! Finally, a deal was concluded to all of our advantages, and before you could say 'Jack Robinson', we were back in the limo heading for Kennedy.

The rain, which had started as a light shower an hour or so earlier, had by now developed into a deluge. The traffic was chaotic. People huddled in doorways and traffic ground to a virtual stop. Madison Avenue was a nightmare, and all the time the clock was ticking. If I missed the 7.30 flight, there was going to be no final for me on Saturday.

Thirty minutes before departure, the limo swung into Kennedy, we jumped out and charged over to the check-in. I had decided to forgo my usual mode of travel and splash out on a first-class sleeper seat, given that I would need as much rest as possible before the big game the next day. Hopefully I would get at least five hours of sleep.

I informed the fresh-faced stewardess that I would not be requiring any refreshments, that all I wanted was to go to sleep, and then it happened. The words 'Brysey!' and 'Morry!' I looked up and there was the band U2. That was it. In that second, I knew it was going to be party time whether I liked it or not and, actually, I quite liked it.

I was one of the first in the music business to try to sign U2 to a publishing deal back in 1978. The deal had been virtually agreed, until I took out their manager Paul McGinnis to lunch in Dublin. For reasons lost to me now, we started having a political debate that became an argument and an extremely heated one at that. The upshot was that I never did sign the band who, then and now, I consider to be one of the greatest. But as they say, that's rock 'n' roll.

Anyway, we partied on that 747 for an hour or two, until eventually, I decided that as much fun as it was, sleep was still the imperative. I had just snuggled down for a few hours' kip when a rather emotional sounding captain came across the intercom and said that due to an exceptional tail wind, we were most certainly going to make the crossing in under five-and-a-half hours, and let's not forget that we were on a Jumbo.

I was now down to a couple of hours of shut-eye if I was lucky. It turned out to be about one hour. My wife, Greta, met me at Heathrow and drove me home, where I tucked into a large portion of eggs and bacon.

By one o'clock, the adrenaline was starting to kick in. At 3.15 p.m. the ball was thrown in and one hour later I lifted the Archie David cup. We had done it.

Another dream had come true.

1

HOW IT ALL BEGAN

Life for me started like many of my generation during the Second World War, on the edge of poverty, but my upbringing was typical of thousands of families. I was born on 14 August 1942 in Hackney, in the East End of London. We had two rooms in a cramped flat and all the 'Nos'. No car, no money, no inside loo, no garden, no heating, no hot water, no fridge – you get the idea. What my sister and I did have in abundance was masses of love from our parents, Joe and Diana. My mum was the greatest. If you believed her stories about our experiences during the war, at least three V1 rockets landed on our street, and each time she threw her body over mine to protect me, which she obviously must have done, as I am still here.

Three eggs a week was the ration, not per person, but for the whole family, which was only the two of us until 1947. Dad was still fighting the Japanese in Burma, so three eggs wasn't that bad. These small treasures were kept in what I can only describe as a cold box. It stood on four legs and had a door with a mesh covering on it. It didn't create ice, as it had no electricity, but it was where you stored milk, if you could get it (the only milk we drank was the powdered kind), margarine in small quantities and, of course, those precious eggs.

What Hitler failed to do in his bombardment of London, this little bugger achieved. A neighbour called my mother downstairs, and while she was gone only a minute or two, on her return she found her son scrambling three broken eggs on a scrappy old linoleum floor. She had queued for hours to obtain those three little gems, and now all that was left were three broken shells and a hell of a mess. I have it on good authority that she crumpled to the floor and cried for over an hour. Not just over the eggs, but the circumstances of her life at that time.

When my dad returned, the bedroom was shared by all four of us: me, my sister, Jan, and Mum and Dad. Nothing particularly unusual about that either. The walls, even in summer, had a smell of wet plaster. In the winter, the walls would freeze and I would watch small rivulets of water meandering their way from ceiling to floor. This, all the doctors believed, was the root cause of the chronic asthma that I suffered throughout my childhood.

Other than bombs raining down night and day, the first five years were pretty uneventful. I have no recollection of ever hearing a bomb, or spending many a night sleeping down in the tube stations. The war ended in Europe and I remember faintly the biggest occasion in all our lives, the VE party held in our grimy little street; the bunting and colour brightening this impoverished place for possibly the first time in its life.

Most of my early memories centre on the things that appeal to all of us in our formative years – Christmas Day, when there was fruit in the bowl and chicken to eat, and Guy Fawkes Night, with guys to be made and pennies to be collected.

After 1947, my old man was back from the war and gainfully employed in an accountancy practice, so our lot started to improve slowly. Within a year or two, he had decided to take his family out of the East End for hopefully a better life.

At the age of seven, I left my primary school in Shacklewell Lane, in Hackney, and moved to the wide-open spaces of Chingford in Essex. My new school in this desirable suburb was called Chase Lane. I mention it for two reasons only, neither of which has affected my life. Many years later, I was to discover that two celebrities were also alumni of this innocuous seat of learning. They were David Beckham, who requires no introduction, and Michael Nyman, now one of England's greatest classical musicians and composers.

How David Beckham ever learnt to play football at this school is amazing, because to the best of my memory, there were no football fields in Chase Lane, only a tarmac playground. I could be mistaken about this, as it was a long time ago now.

From here, having failed my eleven-plus exam miserably, I was on my way again to another great educational institution, Wellington Avenue Secondary School, where I was to spend the next four years in the junior remove. I can hear you wondering, what is the junior remove? Well, basically, it was a polite title for the group of kids who were backward or with anti-social behaviour, so most of my mates had been locked up in a borstal detention centre, or had lost arms and legs falling off motorcycles, before they were seventeen.

My reason for being there was much simpler. I was a mess. At thirteen years old, I could barely write. Arithmetic was a word with no meaning. My days in class were spent staring into the middle-distance, watching chalk dust floating slowly around the teacher's blackboard. In one year alone, we had twelve teachers, each one replacing the other, unable to cope with the rabble sat in front of them. I certainly learnt nothing and the other kids probably didn't either. However, one man thought that this skinny, frightened little kid had something going for him, even if it was well hidden.

At fifteen, I was due to leave with absolutely no qualifications, when Dave Wallace suggested that if I were to stay on an extra year, he would give me special tuition, and I should try to take at least two GCE O levels, so this I did. By some mistake, I ended up with five.

During this period of enlightenment, I achieved two things that possibly gave a clue as to my future as an entrepreneur. Firstly, I discovered that the local fish and chip shop needed newspapers, bundles of them. A bundle was enough newspapers to create a fifteen-inch-high stack, for which they paid me three pence. The funny thing was that I worked at this trade for weeks on end, collecting discarded newspapers from houses up and down the street, then trudging a quarter of a mile to deliver them. Tough as it was, it definitely lit the entrepreneurial flame.

My second business, which I started aged about fifteen and a half, happened after my mum and dad had given me a Christmas present of some plaster of Paris and rubber moulds of various animals. One of the moulds was a panda. It stood about three and a half inches high. I soon set to it and produced a small plaster panda. I painted its ears black, as well as its arms and legs. He was beautiful. A day or two later, one of my mates asked me to show it to his mother, which of course I did.

'But it's beautiful,' she declared, echoing my sentiment. 'I have to have one of these!' So she did. The next morning, she was the proud owner of a plaster panda and I was two shillings richer. This definitely beat delivering to the fish and chip shop. Within days I went into full production and a week or two later I had an army of pandas in various states of drying, half-painted and glazed, lined up on the coal bunker in the back garden. With the success of these tiny statues, I decided to expand my line, and so the pandas were joined shortly by a bullfighter and – horror of horrors – three flying ducks. Three mates became my salesmen at a commission of six pence per item. They sold in droves and, without knowing it, I had started my first business.

I became besotted by music at the age of fifteen. I remember sitting in front of a small black-and-white television in early 1957 watching *Sunday Night at the London Palladium*. There was an American singer on the show by the name of Guy Mitchell, and a light suddenly switched on in my head. His big hit was 'Singing the Blues'. I felt a surge of excitement for this new music, which I had never heard before. I recall turning to my father and saying to him, 'That's what I want to do one day. I want to be in music.' His response was typical of his generation. 'Don't be silly,' he said. 'That's one business it is impossible to get into.'

This feeling was only to be surpassed a few weeks later, when I was sitting high up in the cheap seats at the Dominion Theatre on Tottenham Court Road, watching Bill Haley and his Comets. It was his first UK tour after his smash hit 'Rock Around the Clock', and his live show hit me like a steam hammer. When the double bass player threw himself onto his instrument, legs pointing upwards into the air, this was to become my inspiration some six years later. It drove me to persuade Viv Prince, the drummer of my first band, the Pretty Things, to leave his drums during a number and to crawl across the floor, beating a tattoo as he went, and encouraging the bass player onto his knees as well.

This was the first of many hundreds of rock 'n' roll gigs that I was to attend in the next decade or two. My other musical influences were the artists of the late 1950s, with wonderful records such as 'Oh Carol' by Neil Sedaka, and 'Everyday' by Buddy Holly, who I could have died for, but before them, of paramount importance, was Al Jolson, who sang songs like 'Swanee' and 'I'm Sitting on Top of the World'. He died in 1950, when I was eight years old, and he was the first and last artist that I ever worshipped. Indeed, on his death, I cried for days and was totally inconsolable.

The other major influence in those days was a gentleman by the name of Mike Todd, who was married to the film star Elizabeth Taylor. He was a great showman and film producer, who made my imagination swoop and swirl. Each new creation, each new production, such as the film *Around the World in 80 Days*, was achieved by a promoter of consummate ability. Here was a master.

Having left school at sixteen with no academic achievements other than the obligatory O levels, I set out to take on the real world. The first thing I had to do was to earn a crust and it was barely a crust that was forthcoming. I spent that first summer doing nothing but finding and collecting golf balls on a municipal golf course in Chingford, then selling them back to the hapless golfers; or walking hand in hand in the local park with a girl called Nicolette, going home and listening to my pop records. Like any kid, music was the lynchpin of life.

Sadly, a man's life cannot be all fun and frolics; I needed a proper job, or so my mother told me. I had to become a contributor to the family income, and she decided that London was the place to go. So, one morning we both took the Central line from Loughton to the West End, where we alighted at Bond Street station. She set off down New Bond Street with me trailing behind her, when lo and behold, there was an advertisement in a shop window.

It was for one of the great purveyors of photographic equipment, Wallace Heaton Ltd, and, after a successful interview, they were to become my first employers. However, this is where the glamour stopped. The job of stockroom assistant was simple. I was pinned down in the bowels of the earth, surrounded by a multitude of cardboard boxes, each one containing Rolleiflex, Leica and Pentax cameras, alongside rows of enlargers standing together like a satanic wood, and surrounded by reams of enlarging paper, print paper, bottles of developer and fixer.

On receiving the order from the front desk, or from one of the salesmen two floors above me, I would lug the camera or instruments up to the awaiting customer. Of course, this action also worked in reverse: what goes up, had to come down. When the daily delivery arrived, the goods were taken down to where they were stored, checked and racked. All this, including train fare, for a measly wage of £3.50 a week.

There was a method in my madness; for some reason I was quite taken with the idea of becoming a photographer. Believing there was no way of getting into the music industry, it seemed that I had fallen into a job that had a certain amount of creativity, and all I had to do was go upstairs with the photographers and study their craft (well, it seemed a good idea at the time). Indeed, but for one small incident, this would have been the case. Promotion came quickly and before too long I was up on the third floor in the print drying and glazing room. It was my task to take the wet prints from their vats into the processing room, where they were placed on large, heated, polished silver drums to produce either a plain or glazed print.

At odd times during the day, I was invited downstairs by the 'big boys' into the studios, where the whole plate cameras, tripods, backdrops and light meters cluttered the floor in a profusion of polished wood and beautiful craftsmanship. As the spring and summer approached, the pace and my

21

interest quickened. Then one day I was offered the position of assistant photographer.

However, there were certain stipulations and other pieces of knowledge to be acquired before achieving this exalted position. I would have to spend at least six months in the darkroom processing and printing films, and would also need to take the City & Guilds course in photography, but, with a bit of luck, I would be fully fledged within twelve months.

Sure enough, six weeks later, I was told to start the next day in the darkroom. The promotion had found its way to my doorstep. The next morning was a blistering hot summer's day, followed in sequence by another and yet another. As each day passed, the recurring thought was of the horror of being lost in that darkroom for the rest of that glorious summer. Tempting as the prospect was of becoming a photographer, I handed in my notice and this promising career faded before me like a sepia print left too long in the sun.

So, with only a post office account stamped South Moulton Street and the £50 that I had saved, I took a few months off. The time was spent dreaming of the future. I was nearly seventeen years old and I yearned to do something more creative with my life. How, I wondered, could I turn my love of music into some kind of paid activity?

My other interests were the making of films; art, drawing and sculpture; and acting. I'd been particularly keen to try to get into RADA, but had met with increasing opposition from my parents. At around this time, I noticed that the BBC had put an advert in the papers looking for trainee film cameramen, and this seemed to me to run parallel with my photographic interests. The course was for a year, the wages were an amazing £12 a week, and the potential glamour of the whole thing was unquenchable. It sounded just the kind of thing I needed, so I applied. After all, hadn't I spent many hours taking still photos, as well as holiday films on a rather antiquated second-hand Bolex cine camera? I had the perfect pedigree.

A week or so later, a very formal letter arrived from the BBC, commanding me to attend an interview at Broadcasting House, time and date supplied. I arrived at the appointed hour and was ushered into a large, airless waiting room, only to find several other persons awaiting their fate.

'Morrison!' The word rang round the room.

'Yes, sir,' I stuttered, feeling increasingly tense.

'Follow me,' he said, with about as much charm as a wet tea towel.

We entered into a huge, wood-panelled boardroom consisting of twelve chairs and a highly polished boardroom table. A large picture hung behind the chairman (I think it was of a past director-general). A dozen pink faces turned towards me as I was seated at the end of the table. I was immediately reminded of that wonderful Victorian painting about the English Civil War, *And When Did You Last See Your Father*, where a timid little Royalist boy is being grilled by a panel of stern-faced Parliamentarians. At once I sensed disaster was about to unfold, and was quickly proven right. The first question they asked me gave it away.

'Do you use 35mm or 8mm film?'

'Oh no,' I replied, 'I buy a box of film from the chemists.'

Let me assure the reader that all our annual licence fees were being very well looked after, at this time at least, and these twelve 'just men and true' were not about to hand out £12 a week unless you knew exactly what you were talking about and, unfortunately, I didn't.

'Thank you, Morrison, we'll be in touch.'

The letter duly arrived advising me that I was not the stuff of which film cameramen are made. Years later, when I went frequently to the studios of both the BBC and ITV to see their various rock 'n' roll shows, my eyes would dwell on these cameramen and my thoughts would turn to what might have been. Once again, the hand of fate had thrown the dice. Fortunately, it was a double six.

Meanwhile, there was a more pressing problem that I had to contend with; that of making money. The fifty quid had by now been frittered away.

● ● ●

Bill Haley and his Comets embarked on their first British tour in February 1957. They arrived at Southampton from New York on the liner Queen Elizabeth *and were greeted by about five thousand cheering fans, before travelling by train to Waterloo Station in London, where they were met by thousands more fans, who formed such a crush that the press dubbed it 'The Second Battle of Waterloo'. It was the first time an American rock 'n' roll star had ever visited the UK.*

The month-long tour opened at the Dominion Theatre in Tottenham Court Road on 6 February and the demand for tickets was so great that the Daily Mirror *sponsored a special farewell concert at the Dominion on 10 March, and this is probably the show that Bryan attended, as it came after Guy Mitchell's appearance on* Sunday Night at the London Palladium. *Also on the bill were the British singers Dennis Lotis and Alma Cogan, and the Jack Hylton Orchestra. Not exactly rock 'n' roll!*

② WHERE IS MICHELANGELO BURIED?

So I returned to Bethnal Green, back to my old stomping grounds of Victoria Park, the Mile End Road and Hackney. My new job was probably the least creative and demanding pursuit that any man could undertake. It was simply cutting out the little oval rubber inserts that make up the Mason Pearson hairbrush. The factory itself resided by the side of a canal; to say it was Dickensian would be an understatement. In fact, it would be an insult to Dickens.

It retained all the worst and grimiest aspects of the Industrial Revolution. Dirty, dangerous and reeking of decay. To reach my operating position, I had to climb a rickety ladder and walk across what was fondly referred to as a walkway, but was little more than a gangplank. This spanned two huge vats of some seething, bubbling liquid. I always imagined this to be acid, but it probably wasn't.

If the factory inspectors of today had been around then, they would have shut the whole place down. Health and safety were positively disregarded. The corner in which I worked consisted of a large press bolted to an already decrepit floor. A few steel pattern cutters lay on a shelf close by, and rolls upon rolls of thin red rubber lay strewn about. The daily chore was to use the cutters like a cook would do, cutting shapes out of a sheet of flat pastry. One by one, the thunder of the machine cleaved the pattern from the rubber sheet until the sheet became a skeleton of itself.

In the course of a day, I would cut hundreds and thousands of these rubber fillers to feed the world's hunger for hairbrushes. The people who worked there were the salt of the earth, including, I might say, the management. The bookkeeper and wage-packet filler was originally of Jamaican descent, but first generation in England. By stint of effort, he had become the accountant to this hairbrush factory. Some of my fondest memories were spent over lunch in Victoria Park, slicing the crust off the top of a hot meat pie, filling it with HP sauce, and then getting into a heated discussion with this lovely man. He would discuss politics, life, and what being black meant in England in the late fifties and early sixties. He became a very good friend.

Sometimes we used to go to a typical fifties café near the park. Six or seven wooden tables scattered around a wooden floor. The window steamed up, made foggy by the sweat and heat of forty men all arguing about last night's football. A wave of the hand to the waitress, followed by a short, sharp cough, brought you a round of tea and toast in that little café by the park in Bethnal Green.

Day after day I reported for duty, clocked in, climbed the ladder, picked up the rubber bundles and started work. The pay was good; in fact, in relation to my other job it was fantastic. I was now making some £15 a week, but it was mind-numbing. I would look at the produce of my labour and wonder how many heads there must be in the world to be brushed with these tools of my creation.

There was a positive side to the job, though; because the execution of my job was so simple, I had time to think, to plan and imagine. The result of these thoughts was that I decided I wanted to be a painter and sculptor. I wanted to create, to live in a garret and suffer for my art. Remember, I was eighteen years old and every bit a romantic.

I applied to St Martin's School of Art and was accepted in the September of that year. It had the reputation of being one of the best fine art schools in England. Indeed, during my three years at St Martin's, I was taught at various times by the sculptors Sir Anthony Caro and Dame Elisabeth Frink, and the pop artist Peter Blake.

I found myself in an entirely new and riveting world. A world of Bohemianism and mental freedom. The pursuit of these freedoms tore away the last vestiges of inhibition. These were truly some of the most wonderful years of my life. Each day was a new canvas. We built a mythology about our own greatness as painters and radicals. Anti-establishment, with long hair and Levi jeans, an unheard-of commodity in 1961 – we bought them from the GIs at the American bases.

My years at St Martin's, and later the Central School of Art, were filled with art appreciation, drawing, the enjoyment of colour and a growing awareness of the great beauty, both natural and man-made, that had been stored over centuries. 'I will teach you to see, to record visually the images around you,' was the daily mantra. As the history of art was revealed to my lustful eyes, my imagination grew to see the majesties of Velázquez and Vermeer, the draughtsmanship of Picasso, the sheer scale of Michelangelo. To see marble breathe, to feel the pain of Van Gogh, and more and yet more.

I observed every generation moving forward, probing with a brush or pallet; composition, perspective and colour, from the pure human to the tortuous images of Picasso, and even the matchstick men of Lowry. The art of the silversmith Benvenuto Cellini, the potters and architects: all that wealth of creation that has been passed down to us through the centuries. These were our daily rations at art school and we gorged on them.

It was during my time at St Martin's that my entrepreneurial spirit was really born. I became the social secretary of the college and it didn't take me long to realise that not only were previous art school dances unpopular, they also lost money. With great gusto, I set about to remedy this situation. This is where the American showman Mike Todd came in: he had demonstrated that good music and good promotion could produce a more than successful end product, which would encourage the paying public to come back the next time. And they did, in droves, until the monthly dances at St Martin's became nationally renowned.

There was a sense of being the first liberated generation unshackled from the deprivations that the young had endured after the First and Second World Wars. A new generation that was to establish a new youth culture, one that manifested itself in the expression of the Swinging Sixties. It turned the existing demarcation lines of class upside down. Within a few years the aristocracy, who previously would never have deemed to associate with the working classes, suddenly couldn't wait to be part of the action.

I have been asked on many occasions what it was like to have been a part of the Swinging Sixties; the suggestion always being what fun it must have been to break new ground and to turn the world upside down. The reality is that I was unaware of what had befallen previous generations. For me, this was simply the way of life, one that I thoroughly enjoyed. I was never conscious of the impact that these years would have on generations to come. There was not an abundance of sociologists hanging about suggesting that what was happening at that time was unique. They only arrived on the scene years later and dissected it all in retrospect.

In 1962, the Cold War was at its height, and my wonderful Bohemian lifestyle was suddenly under threat. It was an incident of mind-boggling world proportions, which almost led to the destruction of half the planet, and it became known as the Cuban Missile Crisis. Here were two of the mightiest nations in the world, the Soviet Union and the United States, about to wage nuclear destruction over the Caribbean island of Cuba.

One fateful morning in October 1962, I woke up wondering if I would ever see my twenty-first birthday. From that day to this, I have never felt the same sense of finality as I did on that morning. Every news station in the country was broadcasting the same terrifying message: nuclear war was imminent. I rushed to St Martin's and asked the secretary if I could use the telephones in the office, then proceeded to get in contact with all the representatives of the various student unions from all over London. Polytechnics, art schools, universities – they all rose as one. All of them had the same sense of foreboding.

We marched that day, ten thousand strong, on the United States Embassy in Grosvenor Square, chanting all the way the slogans of peace. We were met by a huge police presence. Barricades dominated the square. The anger in the crowd was at boiling point. This was no ordinary protest march; it was a demonstration of survival. A few of us broke free from the pack and charged towards the embassy steps. Why, I don't know, but I was the only one to make it to the huge glass doors that dominated the front of the building.

For some reason it hadn't occurred to me that they would be locked, and I was suddenly isolated, left like a squirming fish on the bank of a river. I was unable to go forward, and in the ten seconds of my isolation outside those doors, I wondered what to do next. As it turned out, I didn't have much choice in the matter, as four large coppers were charging up the embassy steps towards me. I was hoisted bodily by them and tossed back into the seething mass that had now made it to the bottom of the steps.

Afterwards, this episode taught me that if you believe passionately enough about something, it is worth fighting for. A day later, the Soviets conceded defeat and stood down, and the greatest threat to world peace had been averted.

Soon after this incident, a tiny moment happened that was to change my life. It happened during a life class, when artists draw or paint from a live, nude figure. We had stopped for a break. Most of the other students had wandered into corners drinking coffee, or they were staring out of the windows lost in their thoughts.

I wandered around the various easels, looking with more than my usual interest at the morning's offerings, then back to my own. By my standards, this particular drawing was very good, but it wasn't the best. It didn't even rate second or third. And then it hit me. I was quite good as a painter and sculptor, but I just wasn't good enough.

I knew with total clarity that in this year alone, from all the art schools in England, there were probably fifteen or more students with more talent than me. And out of these fifteen or so students, one of them, if they were lucky, might be making a decent living from their art by the time they were forty. The years at college, and in particular the commercial running of the dances, had taught me that what I needed was to combine my creative talent with some other art form or music.

I had no intention of living in a garret when I was fifty years old, or worse, being second best as a painter. I picked up my corduroy jacket, went down to the principal's office and told him I was leaving straight away. In my wisdom, I decided that I would have to put any talents I had as a painter into a more practical artistic direction, and so came up with the idea of taking a course in interior and furnishing design.

England had still not freed itself in 1962 from the post-war yoke of functional, utility furnishing. You had to go back to Hepplewhite or Robert Adam in the eighteenth century to find a piece of well-designed British furniture. The influence of modern design movements such as Bauhaus, not to mention the astonishing developments taking place in contemporary Italian and Scandinavian furniture design, had yet to reach these shores. I saw that there was a gap in the market and thought that I could fill it by enrolling on an interior design course at the Central School of Art.

All the time that my career as an artist was stopping and starting, my entrepreneurial instincts had been bubbling away beneath the surface. During my first summer holidays at St Martin's, I got a job for three months with a small travel company called Riviera Holidays, of which my old man was a director. His partner was an ex-cab driver named Aubrey Morris. They had started the company together following the holidays our two families used to take together in the South of France and Northern Italy. We would set off in an old Ford Anglia and his black taxi-cab, with our GB plates attached. It was a requirement then that your car displayed GB plates.

In the early fifties, it was an exciting event to come across another GBer, as we called them. If we were fortunate enough to see another British car, we would wave and flash them until they stopped, then we'd spend maybe ten minutes asking what the road ahead was like, did they know of any small villages where we could visit, or any cheap restaurants and nice hotels.

Our nightly stays in these towns and villages were hugely amusing, as crowds sometimes as large as two hundred strong would pore over the London taxi for hours. I would sit in a little café watching the multitude exploring an iconic image that they had seen only on grainy black-and-white film, or the odd poster. This was happening not a century ago, but within the past thirty-five years. We were among a few intrepid travellers from the UK, the first of a gigantic wave of people that were about to crash onto Europe.

Beaches in Italy lay empty, with hardly a parasol in sight, and no one on them for mile after mile. Today they are filled a hundred deep, stretching from Sardinia to Sicily. So, in the mid-fifties, these two adventurers started Riviera Holidays, which was later to become none other than Thomson Holidays. For the next two summers, I became one of their couriers. It sounds pretty romantic, and so it was, although the TV shows of recent years have rather tarnished this image.

I would board a train at Cattolica in Italy at about 11.30 on a Saturday morning, with the passengers arriving at about 12.00. As the train departed the station, I would witness the same twenty to thirty Italian Lotharios shedding bucketfuls of tears and shouting heartfelt farewells to the English roses, while the girls were practically throwing themselves off the train in lemming-like displays of unbridled passion. These scenes were repeated week after week. The only part of the jigsaw to stay the same was the boys. Two days after losing the loves of their lives, they would be at the station awaiting our next arrival and eyeing up the newcomers.

Anyway, as our train pulled out of Cattolica, I would be giving it large in my neatly pressed, light blue blazer, with a dashing smile and a feigned interest in the remnants of my fellow passengers' holidays. My job for the next twenty-four hours was to accompany my charges back to Dover or Boulogne. You may think this was not too difficult. However, on one of my return trips from Boulogne to Italy, I did manage to lose two husbands, who between them had seven children and two hysterical wives. I had warned them not to get off the train, as most of the stops were unscheduled, but they saw a vendor selling delicious lasagne, alighted from the train with a few lire, and chased him down.

Seconds later, the train pulled out and they were left on the platform high and dry, with no passports, no money and no sense. It was discovered later that they didn't even know where they were going. On the other hand, I was left with two screaming wives and seven kids. By the time the news reached me, the train was kicking off at eighty miles per hour towards Italy. It took three days to reunite the two families. The husbands were exhausted, but they were only about to start their misery, as the wives took them off to their rooms.

On reaching Boulogne on Sunday morning, I would discharge my wards before picking up another thirty or forty passengers for the return journey to Italy, arriving back in Cattolica at approximately 12.30 on Monday morning. For three months, I spent virtually three days and two nights each week on a train, for a grand total of £7 per week, plus board and lodging.

It was brought to my notice that the price of cigarettes in Italy was about five shillings a pack for UK or US produced fags. Most, if not all, of the cigarettes were smuggled in from Yugoslavia. I had also noticed that all of my passengers arrived clutching their cartons of two hundred cigarettes that they had purchased duty free on the boat. As regular as clockwork, within a week of their arrival in Cattolica, they would run out of fags and then complain about the ridiculous prices being asked locally. Their complaints were understandable, as they were being charged two or three times what they had paid on the boat.

I had an idea, but first I needed to talk to my rather more experienced fellow couriers, there being about ten of them who worked regularly on my train.

'No, Bryan,' I was told firmly, 'don't even think about it. At least three couriers have been caught smuggling on various routes in the last three months and are currently enjoying jail sentences.'

There had to be a way. I figured out that in the dead of night on the Swiss–Italian border, I could purchase as many cigarettes as I wanted at one-shilling and sixpence per pack.

There had to be a way of completing the perfect crime, not that I thought smuggling a few fags was really a crime, but how to do it? That was the puzzle. A week later, I had the answer on the way back from Boulogne having picked up my next party. In the course of my duty, I would visit the various compartments where the passengers were to spend the next twenty-four hours swaying to the motion of a fast-moving train. I'd explain about the heat of the sun, the local cheap wine, how many lire to the pound and don't, under any circumstances, leave the train.

The business part of the day over, I would then go on to explain the plight of the various couriers and reps that worked down there. In particular, the fact that fags were very expensive. 'Would you mind,' I asked, 'if I were to buy some cigarettes at the Swiss border and just stick a packet at the end of your bunks?' I assured them that the customs would have absolutely no problems with someone taking four hundred cigarettes with them to Italy, as there was no hard and fast rule as to what tourists were permitted. As a man, they would look at their stash of two hundred and magnanimously agree.

This was repeated weekly for months. At about 1.30 in the morning, we would arrive at the border, I would make a beeline for the cigarette vendor, and buy up to five thousand cigs for my fifty tourists who were asleep on the train. With great difficulty, I would heave my bulging, large brown paper bags full of contraband onto the train and into my compartment. I then had about thirty minutes before the arrival of Italian custom officers, who would get onto the train for their inspection. In that time, I would take approximately six packets of two hundred, place one on or near a bunk, or in the overhead rack in each compartment. Several compartments later, my night's work was done.

By eight the next morning, I had gathered my contraband back together, loaded it into a suitcase and was now ready to perform the sting. Right on schedule, within five or six days of arriving, my tourists would run out of cigarettes, only to discover the exorbitant prices being asked on the coast. At this time, I would place two or three cartons of two hundred on my lunch or dinner table. Within minutes, one of my travellers would approach and the same conversation would always take place.

'Bryan, you don't have any spare fags, do you? They're bloody expensive on the beach.'

'How much are they?' I would enquire.

'Oh, five or six shillings.'

'Blimey!' I would reply. 'Yes, I do have some spare that I could sell you. Let's say three shillings for twenty, a saving of almost fifty per cent.'

'You're a star, Bryan.' With that a few packs left my table. The word soon spread to his acquaintances. Before you knew it, over the next two days I'd sell the lot. My profit being between £10 to £20 per week depending on the size of my party. On top of this I would also make 500 lire per head by taking clients to the various clubs. All in all, with my salary and the deals I was making, it added up to a tidy thirty-odd pounds per week. Sadly, this was for only a few months of the year.

One evening, I received a call from our head rep, a beautiful Italian girl by the name of Bruna. She asked me to come to her room. Once there, she told me she was dying of flu and that I had to take a coach party to Florence and show them the sights.

'But Bruna, I've never been to Florence,' I explained. 'I know very little about the city!'

'Well, you're studying fine art, aren't you?' was the reply. 'Take this guidebook, study it tonight. The coach driver knows the four or five important sights, just keep your eyes open.'

The first stop was the Ponte Vecchio bridge. The guidebook told me the dates it was erected and all the various edifices built on it. The passengers nodded in confirmation and the first trial was over. The next was the beautiful Basilica of Santa Croce, the largest Franciscan church in the world. Our driver stopped outside and pointed at it. This was obviously my next assignment, so I strode forth into the interior, followed by my hapless tour group.

I had read about one particular picture of the Madonna that I should point out, and also all the dates of the building and its age. We had been in there barely five minutes, when a question was fired from somewhere in the multitude. It was a question that froze me to the spot.

'Bryan, where is Michelangelo buried?'

I didn't have the foggiest idea.

This was it. The game was up. I was going to look totally stupid and shown to be the charlatan that I was. Any tour guide that couldn't answer this question standing in the middle of Florence deserved to be shot. I hung my head in shame, not knowing how I was going to get out of this one. I swear what I am going to recount now is the honest truth. There at my feet, carved into the stone floor were the words: *Qui quiace la tomba di Michelangelo.* Here lies the tomb of Michelangelo.

I was standing on it!

I had been saved. I studied the words for a few more seconds before throwing my head back, turning towards my charges, and had the affront to say, 'I'm glad you asked that question, because below where you are standing is his grave!'

'Wow, fantastic.' Smiles all round. They were confident that they were safe in the hands of an art historian and guide.

The rest of the day sailed by, and as they were disembarking the coach that evening, I received dozens of thank-yous for a thoroughly great day. I had scraped through once again.

● ● ●

Bryan's father, Joe Morrison, had grown up near his friend Aubrey Morris in Bethnal Green, in the East End of London, and they had been at school together. The son of a Jewish baker, Morris had fought against Sir Oswald Mosley's fascist Blackshirt marchers in the notorious Battle of Cable Street in 1936, and later he was evacuated from Dunkirk. The two men set up Riviera Holidays in the mid-fifties, after spotting a gap in the travel market for cheap package holidays in Europe for working-class families.

Later they became the first company to organise air travel for British football fans wanting to watch their teams playing against the big European clubs. Riviera Holidays became so profitable, it was bought out by the Canadian businessman Roy Thomson in 1965, when he merged it with three other travel companies to create Thomson Holidays.

3

OH, YOU PRETTY THINGS

In 1962 I applied to the Central School of Art and, on hearing of my credentials at St Martin's, a place was created for me. This simple decision was to have a dramatic effect over the next thirty years, because on arrival at Central I met and befriended Rodney Kinsman and Lisa, who was later to become his wife. It was this friendship that created the partnership of OMK Design, which today ranks as one of the top modern furniture companies in Europe. In addition to this, I was about to meet my dream of being in the music business.

Accidents of fate do happen.

I was soon back to my old tricks at the Central School, organising dances and events. I faced major opposition from a few students. My reputation had gone before me: they thought I was far too autocratic in the running of the student unions and suspected I was siphoning off a percentage of the profits (as if I would do a thing like that). The truth will out, though, and a small percentage was indeed siphoned off, but only to pay expenses.

I gradually built a team of about six to eight students. As one success after another was racked up and the profits rose, so our expectations climbed. To quote one of Rice and Lloyd Webber's songs from *Evita*, 'And the Money Kept Rolling In'. It soon became mandatory that I took the whole committee for a slap-up dinner in the Universal Chinese restaurant up the road on the corner of Denmark Street.

In 1962, it was one of the few Chinese restaurants that existed, which only raised the excitement of the uniqueness. It was unheard of for any art student to even think about entering this den of Eastern promise, because no one could afford it. The bill once discharged, we were ready to boogie. Me in my Levi's and my most loved possessions: my calf-length, Cuban-heeled, blue Anello & Davide boots – they were the business.

With the success of these events and after much canvassing, I was voted in as the president / social secretary of the student union at the Central School of Art in a landslide victory. My first job, however, was not organising dances, but trying to get the restaurant manager of the college off his arse to produce a decent meal for my fellow students. We had received dozens of complaints from students about the inedibility of the food, sloppiness of its serving, and general cleanliness of the cafeteria.

Armed with these three very salient facts, I set off with Rodney Kinsman (who was now my partner in crime), hoping to have reasonable discourse with the restaurant manager. He refused point blank to consider any of our complaints and when we pointed out it might become necessary to boycott the restaurant, he told me to 'Fuck off'. This, after some discussion, merited some industrial action. We decided on the course to take the next day.

So, it came to pass, the students vs. officialdom, yet another confrontation between the masses and the suits.

'All out strike!' we yelled.

We set up a soup kitchen in the Common Room, and had pickets outside the door of the restaurant, which seated two hundred people. The food sat untouched, simmering in the pans. Within forty-eight hours, the battle had been won, with the total capitulation of the restaurant manager and a couple of free meals for Rodney and me thrown in for good measure.

Sometime later, at one of the dances I organised in the October of 1963, a fellow art student approached me from another college. He had a big shock of long ginger hair and a beard to match. He introduced himself to me as Dick Taylor, and he came out with an expression that amused me, as I'd heard something similar in one of those old Hollywood movies.

'Listen, man,' he said. 'I've got a band that can really cut it, and we'd love to play at your next Christmas dance.'

'Sorry,' I replied, 'but I've already booked the bands for that one.' I seem to remember it was the Bonzo Dog Doo-Dah Band. Rodney Slater, their founder, had been a fellow student of mine at St Martin's and a few years later they would have a hit with 'I'm the Urban Spaceman'.

Seeing the disappointment in Dick's face, I said, 'Give me the name of your band and your address so I can get hold of you and I'll keep you in mind for another dance.'

'The Pretty Things,' he replied.

'The what?'

'That's the name of the band. The Pretty Things.'

'The Pretty Things.' I repeated it twice. I was struck immediately by the uniqueness of this name. It was totally fresh and original, and I felt a certain inexplicable excitement.

'I'll tell you what,' I said, 'I'll give you a fiver plus expenses to come and do the Christmas dance.'

Don't ask me why, because I don't know what made me book that band, but I did. Dick was delighted and said he'd see me in December.

A few weeks later, the big night arrived and the support group took to the stage. They were fantastic and I was mesmerised. They played the blues, R&B, and rock with a passion, and I knew that somehow I had to be involved. As soon as they'd finished, I dragged Dick and the lead singer, Phil May, over to the bar for a chat.

It turned out that Dick Taylor had just left another band he was playing with, a band by the name of the Rolling Stones, simply because he wanted to play the lead guitar in his own band. Both he and Phil were at art school in Erith, Kent, and the other three members were mates of theirs. I was consumed with this band for the next few weeks, I thought about them morning and night, until finally I asked them if I could be their manager.

It occurred to me that on the club circuit alone, they could probably work four gigs a week in London, each one bringing in £15-20 a night, which meant a gross of £60-80 a week.

Their answer came back a week later.

'You're our new manager, Bryan. Get on with it.'

Without realising it at the time, I was about to see the dreams of my youth become a reality. It would be fair to say that I didn't actually understand that I was now on the first step of a very long ladder.

About two months prior to my meeting with the Pretty Things, I had walked out of Central School of Art into High Holborn, where there was a news vendor selling evening papers. Scrawled across the poster on his stand were the words, *Beatles Make Number 1*. It was 'She Loves You'.

This was the off. All around me music was happening, there were newspaper headlines, clubs packed to capacity, and rock 'n' roll was in the air. The starter's gun had been fired and something told me that a new phenomenon was about to dominate the world stage.

My days were spent running from Holborn the short distance to Denmark Street, which was commonly known then as Tin Pan Alley. Although the street measured only about eighty yards in length, this road of crumbling buildings was one of the power houses of world music. It housed the main seven or eight top music publishers of the day, plus a myriad number of smaller publishers, sundry agents and managers.

At one end of the street was Regent Sound, the little studio of the day, which recorded both demos and masters, and about halfway down sat La Giaconda café, the hub where all the musicians, songwriters and publishers would gather to meet each other.

The street was always full of people from the music business, but full is a relative term, because the whole music business was quite small at this time. There were only four major record companies – there were no independents then – only a handful of publishers, and the press and other media boiled down to a few producers on each side. Then, of course, there were the hangers on, even then. It all made for a bustling and electric atmosphere. Without knowing why, you simply knew that something magical was about to happen.

My evenings were spent in the clubs of London trying to sort out gigs for my fledgling band. It reminded me of 'On Broadway', that great song by the Drifters, and its lyric line that talks about the pain and suffering of trying to get a break. I started at the only natural place, which was at the bottom, and spent hours and days talking to promoters in pubs and clubs, social secretaries, and anyone who had a venue, and gradually I began to fill up the date sheet.

One of the gigs I got in the early days was at the famous 100 Club on Oxford Street.

Within three appearances of the Pretty Things, the crowds were spilling out into the street. By coincidence, the owners of the 100 Club also had a fairly successful agency, which booked bands all around the country. It wasn't long before I was called into their office to discuss my first major business deal. My excitement knew no bounds for days before this meeting. My only thought was that this could really be the start of something.

I arrived and sat there in deep apprehension. The music business of the sixties was a jungle and bore no relation to the civilised and sanitised business it now resembles. You had to watch your back in every way.

'Bryan,' they said, 'we want to sign your band to a sole agency agreement.'

This meant that they would, for a period of time, be the exclusive agents for the band. Now if someone wants you exclusively, I figured they would have to pay for it. Then and there, I'd have given my back teeth to have been guaranteed a minimum income of £100 a week. A sum I could only dream about. After all, twenty per cent of £100 (my management commission) meant £20 a week, a king's ransom in 1963, and all this guaranteed for a year.

After the usual toing and froing, I suggested they make me an offer.

'How would £125 a week do?'

I was so shocked at this generous proposal that I sat there stunned. I looked totally blank, while my mind raced with the enormity of what I had been offered.

I stammered, 'Well—'

I was interrupted in mid-sentence, as they obviously assumed I was dissatisfied with the offer. I was only going to enquire how they would pay us; would it be on a weekly or monthly basis?

'Alright,' they said. '£200 a week.'

I was now getting really excited. Without opening my mouth, they had gone from £125, a sum I couldn't conceive of, up to £200. Even in my unsophisticated and youthful state, something told me I was on a winner here. Without even considering what I was saying, I said, 'Make it £250 and you've got a deal.'

They sucked in their breaths as one, gasped at the enormity of the suggestion, but didn't say no. I left that office and meandered down Oxford Street into New Oxford Street and finally Holborn, a walk of about twenty minutes, before parking myself down in the canteen at Central with a cup of tea. I sat there for a couple of hours, convincing myself I had blown it, that I had failed at the first major hurdle.

The next morning, I rang my mother. I used my parents' phone number as my office number, my mother as my secretary, and I would ring her every couple of days to see if she had received any messages. She informed me that the agency had been on the phone and could I go and see them at lunchtime that day.

I did just that and one hour later I was walking down Oxford Street, the happiest man in the world. Here I was still at art school and making more money than I'd ever dreamed of.

A minimum of £50 a week for a year. I thought I'd won the pools.

On the day we signed the contract, I walked down Oxford Street singing 'On the Street Where You Live', from the musical *My Fair Lady*. Like the song says, I was feeling 'several storeys high'.

Events moved rapidly, and within months the Pretty Things had built a name on the London club circuit. Meanwhile, the Rolling Stones were tearing clubs and audiences apart all over London and, in particular, down in

Twickenham. I knew it was all up for grabs as to which of these two bands was going to represent the long-haired rebels of the future. At this time, the Stones had a good lead on us. I now had to secure the band a record deal.

From out of nowhere, I received a call from Jack Baverstock, the A&R man for Fontana Records, who commanded me to attend upon him. The A&R men of the sixties were still viewed as gods. The record companies were few and they were all-powerful, totally dominating the artist in every aspect of his recording career, from the kind of contract that was offered, to what kind of material he should play. However, with the advent of the Beatles, this attitude was starting to break down.

Before the sixties, all but the greatest artists received session fees rather than royalties. This archaic attitude came to an end by the early sixties, but although artists were paid royalties, they were tiny compared with the royalties they are able to command today. The average deal at this time gave the artist no more than three to five percentage points on the wholesale price of the record, which was a pittance, but a lot more than a mere session fee.

On our first meeting, Jack threw a contract on the table in front of me and said in his slight American drawl, 'Get the boys to sign this and we'll make a record.'

There was no negotiating and no advances. We signed our lives away for five years and that was the end of it.

We had a record deal, and an agent who was getting us seven gigs a week – what we needed now was some serious press. Somehow we had to get the name and image of the band across to millions over the whole country. I came to the conclusion that the only way to do that was through a national newspaper.

I contacted Robert Bickford of the *Daily Mail* and, after a great deal of persuasion, he agreed to do a feature on the band. On 3 April 1964, we rushed to the newspaper stands and gleefully pored over the half-page feature that the Pretty Things had been given. From then on, it went totally crackers. Press, radio, TV – everybody wanted a piece of the action with this hot new band.

But wait a minute, fairy stories don't really happen, do they? Could it be that within a few short months, this ragged little art student had a band with a record contract and money pouring in? The answer is a resounding 'No'. Fairy stories do not happen. Some weeks later, Dick and Phil approached me at the Central School with the devastating news, for me at least, that they were now professional musicians whose manager was an art student.

Despite the fact I had helped them get this far, they insisted I should leave the college and take on a partner. They didn't think, and rightly so, that a manager who was still a student could cut the mustard. They wanted someone who was a professional in the music business, and, by the way, they knew just the person. James Duncan.

Faced with this *fait accompli* and having no contract with them at this point, I had to accept the inevitable. All I needed was another six months to complete my course, take my NDD, and at least have something to show for four years of studying fine art – a diploma.

At their suggestion, I met Jimmy Duncan a day or so later. He wasn't my cup of tea, but I had no choice. He was a songwriter of sorts, who had spent the last couple of years living in and around Denmark Street, making La Giaconda café and Regent Sound his home. It now became inevitable for me to make *the* decision. One of my occupations would have to go. After much soul-searching and deliberation, I took the huge step of leaving Central and becoming a full-time manager.

In the spring of 1964, the first Pretty Things single, 'Rosalyn', was released. It had been written by Jimmy and it got to number 41 in the charts. By now, English rock 'n' roll was in full swing, with the Mersey Sound dominating all. Our time on the road gigging hard had proven to be most worthwhile, as the band had grown quite accustomed to doing up to three forty-five-minute gigs per night in clubs as far apart as the Norique in Seven Sisters Road, and the Star Club in Hamburg, made famous by the Beatles.

I was becoming an expert in the art of publicity and almost daily I arranged stunts and situations with the national press. This was the time when rock 'n' roll was big news. The exploits of the big bands were always being splashed across every conceivable newspaper and magazine. I quickly learnt that the more outrageous the Pretty Things were, both in their look and style and their total disregard for the conventions of the day, the more the papers loved it. The more mothers told their daughters not to go to the shows, the more they wanted to. The more society said no, the more youth craved it.

Screaming girls, record companies, promoters and press. Everybody wanted a piece of the action. So this was rock 'n' roll. Next, however, came the Bill Haley factor. I had been observing the Pretty Things at various gigs, and although they were getting a fantastic response from the audience, they never quite tore them apart.

After a gig in Liverpool, they were all in the dressing rooms drinking the by-now traditional rum and coke. I suggested once again that they should try to create mayhem on stage by being completely outrageous and over the top.

'Showmanship,' I urged them. 'In the middle of a number, why doesn't Viv leave his drum kit and play across the floor to the bass player and then beat out a rhythm on his bass guitar? Phil, you could roll across the floor while you're singing!' It was, you see, all planned right down to the last detail. I knew Dick Taylor on lead guitar was immovable. He always stood there like a withering English oak tree lost in his playing and his music.

'Just try tomorrow,' I begged.

They did and mayhem not only ensued on the stage, but the audience of two thousand created a near riot. At one point, the security came under such pressure that a number of girls managed to catch the bottom of Phil May's leg. It was an awe-inspiring sight to see him disappear into this seething chasm, like a sardine being sucked in by a whale. The instant he went in, we all leapt to pull him out, legs and arms flying, and the sight we beheld was unbelievable. In those few seconds in the crowd, he had one trouser leg totally ripped off, his shirt and sweatshirt removed, and he was stripped of his socks and shoes. He became the prince with no clothes.

Having discovered the secret of driving the crowds to a frenzy, after this particular gig we also learnt the need to put up secondary barriers between the stage and the audience, and to double or even triple the number of bouncers. It was game on.

● ● ●

Jack Baverstock was one of the great British A&R men of the sixties. He had originally worked for New Musical Express *and was involved in introducing the Top 20 charts to the UK. In 1958 he had been appointed as the A&R manager for Philips Records' new Fontana label. At first, they released mainly American easy listening and jazz product, such as 'Take Five' by the Dave Brubeck Quartet, but after the success in 1963 of the Beatles and the Mersey Sound, Baverstock started signing up new groups such as the Merseybeats, Wayne Fontana and the Mindbenders, and the Pretty Things, who all scored Top 10 hits in 1964. The label became so successful, with number one hits by the Spencer Davis Group, the Troggs, Manfred Mann, Dave Dee, Dozy, Beaky, Mick & Tich, and the New Vaudeville Band, that by 1966 the label had a record in the Top 10 almost every week of the year.*

After the Pretty Things had a hit with 'Rosalyn', Jack Baverstock booked them into the studio for two days to record an album. According to Phil May, their drummer Viv Prince was so out of it that in the first hour he threw up over his drums and fell off his stool twice. Baverstock was so disgusted that he stormed out of the studio, declaring, 'I'm not working with that bunch of animals!' Session drummer Bobby Graham was hurriedly brought in as a replacement producer, which turned out to be very fortunate, as he was able to fill in for Prince after the drummer tumbled off his stool for a third and final time and lay there unconscious on the studio floor.

4

DON'T BRING ME DOWN

It became more and more evident to me that although the Rolling Stones had more than a head start on the Pretty Things, one massive record could reverse the roles. By this time it was blatantly obvious that the English record-buying public were looking for the good clean boys versus the nasties. The Beatles had already taken the mantle of the former, so we started looking in earnest for 'the song', but no one came up with anything that in my opinion was the big one.

In the summer of 1964, I was sitting having a cup of tea in La Giaconda with the folk singer and songwriter Donovan. We were quite close at the time and I thought he had an incredible talent that was soon to emerge. Sadly for me, by the time we met, he had already committed himself to a management and publishing deal.

On this particular day, I mentioned to him that I was looking for a song for the Pretty Things, but it had to be really special. He said he had just written a fantastic song and would I like to hear it? It is impossible in these pages to play you the music of this song, but the lyrics went like this: 'Please darling Tangerine Eyes, sing a song for me. One that I can hear all the day ...' and it continued in this vein.

I loved it. It was wonderful – the song I'd been looking for.

'I need a demo of it,' I said. Donovan replied he would get it together for me immediately.

Within a couple of days, I played the song to the Pretty Things, but they didn't see it the way I did. A few weeks went by, and I received a telephone call from another publisher, who invited me to come and see him. I duly took a trip to his Denmark Street offices.

'Have a listen to this,' he said, and played me a song that bore more than a passing resemblance to Donovan's 'Tangerine Eyes'. I didn't know how this was possible, but it was even better. It was a brilliant song and a worldwide smash. I was absolutely bowled over.

'It was written by Bob Dylan; have you heard of him?' he said. 'He's the new American folk singer, who looks like he's going to be very big.'

I hadn't, at that time, but it didn't matter, because this was the song I'd been searching for.

I listened to it again and again. I knew that with this song, 'Mr Tambourine Man', recorded by the Pretty Things, we'd have a number one around the world. I was totally besotted by it. I took the demo immediately to the Pretty Things and told them that I had found them the song but, once more, they didn't agree with me. Try as I might, they would not countenance recording it. I continued to harass them for weeks and each time I met with a solid 'No'.

A month or so later, I got another telephone call from Dylan's English publisher telling me that the song had been recorded by an unknown band in America, and that, if we were going to do it, we should get our version out fast. Furthermore, as we were already a chart band, they would prefer the Pretty Things' version to be out first in the UK as it would have more chance of being a hit. I went back to the group for one more try and played them this superb song, but again they said 'No!'

I rang Dylan's publisher later that day to tell him regretfully that I could not persuade the band to record it. I had the terrible feeling that a huge opportunity had been lost, but that was that.

'Don't worry,' the publisher said. 'That's life.'

'By the way,' I inquired, 'what's the name of that American band?'

'The Byrds,' he replied.

The rest, of course, is rock 'n' roll history. Their single went on to sell millions around the world and the Byrds soared to huge success. The chance had been lost. We had lost the initiative and never got it back.

We were now into the era of bands performing their own material. The mantra had become 'Write your own songs', so the second of the Pretty Things' singles was the first song I ever published in partnership with one of the monoliths of the publishing industry, Southern Music. Jimmy Duncan and I set up a company by the name of Dunmo Music, and our first release was the group's next single, 'Don't Bring Me Down', which climbed to number 10 in the charts, but it was never an international hit.

The group followed that a few months later with their third single, the self-written 'Honey I Need', but that stalled at number 13. It would turn out to be their last entry in the Top 20.

However, this did not mean that the Pretty Things and I didn't have a couple of years of real fun. These were still the days when rock 'n' roll was a cottage industry and, as such, attracted numerous gentlemen of disreputable backgrounds. I remember going to see a chap who owed the Pretty Things £200 or so. I knocked on his office door, was told to enter, and said, 'Mr King. I've been trying to ring you for several days about the two hundred pounds you owe the Pretty Things, and as I couldn't get hold of you, I decided to come in person.'

'Oh,' he said, and pulled open a drawer. My spirits rose at the thought of having £200 placed into my hot hand. However, instead of pulling out the money, he pulled out a revolver, pointed it at me, and eloquently told me to 'Fuck off'. I frankly didn't see much point in dallying and so did his bidding. Needless to say, we never got paid.

Unfortunately, it was people like Mr King and several others who, through the sixties and seventies, gave the music business such a bad reputation. In today's world, though, it has gone too far the other way, becoming a totally sanitised business.

With the success of 'Don't Bring Me Down', money began to pour into the coffers of the band. One of the more memorable extravagances was the renting of a beautiful house for forty guineas a week at 13 Chester Street, in Belgravia, a stone's throw from Buckingham Palace. A song of the same name appears on the Pretty Things' first album, *The Pretty Things*.

In late 1964, 13 Chester Street became one of the hubs of what is now known as the Swinging Sixties. Most of the great writers, performers, and artists of the day partied at one time or another, or had dinner in this house. Numerous events took place in the main dining-room, often with a couple of the Beatles or the Stones, the songwriter Lionel Bart, or the glamorous actress Diana Dors, sitting round a table with their various acolytes standing in descending order behind them.

For a large part of the time the Pretties occupied Chester Street, they let the basement flat out to Brian Jones of the Stones. What with his antics and the Pretty Things, it was indeed a house of decadence, and basically covered everything that any red-blooded young man in their late teens and early twenties would love to do. If walls could talk. You name it, Chester Street had it.

During this period, Viv Prince, the Pretty Things' drummer, had met and befriended the Texan-born singer P.J. Proby. They were inseparable friends. Proby had just had his first smash hit, 'Hold Me', and he really went for it.

The excesses were such that in Proby's house during the height of the mayhem, I remember his telephone being connected to America for twenty-four hours at a time, while the various residents of his house were talking to friends across the sea. From memory, his telephone bill back then was in excess of £1,000 a month. An astronomical amount even today.

There was one particular time when Viv Prince didn't sleep in a bed for seven days or nights. In the same period, he played five gigs, some of them being two sets per day. By the eighth day, he was a walking mess.

Another of Viv's little eccentricities took place when I lent him a tape recorder. I was living in a Victorian mansion flat in Kensington. The front door of my apartment was made of mahogany and etched glass. I was sitting at home two or three days after having loaned him the machine when, all of a sudden, there was an incredible smashing sound at the front door. I rushed into the hallway to discover my tape recorder lying on the floor amidst the remains of the glass and mahogany frame, smashed to pieces. Silhouetted in what was left of the front door, was a certain scowling drummer.

I screamed, 'What the fuck do you think you're doing?'

Viv's deadpan reply was simple and concise: 'Your tape recorder doesn't fucking work and I'm returning it to you.'

With that, I took four or five paces forward, brought my arm back (like an archer drawing back his bow) and, punching through what was left of the upper part of my door, landed a heavy right hand on Viv Prince's chin. Probably more from the assorted mixture of beverages in his body and lack of sleep, rather than the power of my punch, he hit the ground like a pack of cards, pole-axed.

My anger, however, had not been requited. I opened what remained of the door, grabbed Viv by his collar, dragged him to the lift, and threw him into it, before turning to his minder and suggesting to him that he escort his charge home. Then I sought out a brush and pan to clear up the debris and mayhem.

All that because a tape recorder had failed to function.

By now I had learnt to give the media what they wanted and at this time it was sensationalism. The more bedrooms that were smashed to pieces, the more screaming, sobbing fans, the more repugnant to the older generation they were, the bigger the story, and the more interesting they were to the press. If the media wanted action, that's what they got. A television being thrown out of a hotel window today by a rock band would hardly even get a mention in a local paper, let alone national, but when the

Who first did it, it was a sensation.

When the landlord finally threw the Pretty Things out of Chester Street at the end of August 1965, with some manipulation on my part, we made the front page of three national newspapers, as well as the national TV news. Perhaps for me, the best feature I ever obtained at this time and the one I was certainly most proud of, was getting front page and inside story in the *Sunday Times* colour magazine, which was the first major feature they'd ever done on a rock 'n' roll band.

Clubs were very important then as they are today, a place where those who believe they are part of the in-crowd can go and hang out with their counterparts. One such club, the only one to belong to at the time, was the Ad Lib in Leicester Square. Whenever the opportunity presented itself, Phil May and I and a couple of the other boys would go for an evening there.

One night, I was having a long discussion with two of the Beatles about buying a sports car. At the time, I would have given almost anything for one of the new E-Type Jaguars, but they cost about £2,300 new. By the end of the evening, Ringo had decided on some other equally sporty racing machine that he was going to buy, and I'd talked myself into getting an E-Type.

What I hadn't bargained for was being twenty-four years old, and the horror with which my insurance broker greeted my decision. The next day he told me that because I managed rock 'n' roll bands, and because of my age, the annual premium fell just short of the cost of the car. As much as I desired it, it was a no-no. I settled instead for an MGB. Days later, Ringo told me he had suffered the same fate at the hands of his insurers but, nevertheless, he'd bought the car of his dreams. Then again, he could afford it.

One of the oddities of the sixties was the general perception that everybody in rock 'n' roll was a junkie. But in the early sixties, very few bands took drugs. It was principally Bacardi and Coke and other spirits that led the wrecking machine. Obviously, people smoked grass, but not in great quantities. Unfortunately, this changed with devastating effect towards the end of the sixties and in the early seventies, when drugs like acid became more and more readily available. In the meantime, vast quantities of alcohol were consumed.

The Pretty Things tied up too much of my time for me to become a casualty of either alcohol or drugs. I was constantly planning and plotting about how to promote them. For months I had been trying to figure out how to get the Pretty Things onto the international circuit. Europe had been pretty well taken care of, the boys having gigged in Scandinavia, Holland and

Germany. But since my cock-up of the year previously, I was now desperate for them to travel to further shores.

My cock-up had, in fact, happened quite early in their career. I had received a call from an American agent who had requested, as only an American could, I join him for a breakfast meeting at the Mayfair Hotel in his suite the next day.

'What'll it be? Steak and eggs, smoked salmon, coffee?' Hang on, this was breakfast, not dinner. We sat there in his huge suite and I was quite overawed, but soon got into it – the steak, that is.

He wanted the Pretty Things to tour the USA. He had, I believe, just secured the Dave Clark Five, who were huge at the time, and was keen to find a largely unknown band to take with them. The problem was that he wanted an agency commission of twenty per cent, and the going rate in those days was ten per cent. We discussed this for some time, me trying to find a compromise, but he was resolute. It was twenty per cent or nothing. Stupidly I turned him down. In hindsight, we should have swallowed the twenty per cent for a year and who knows what might have happened.

This may have been the most costly decision of my career.

I was therefore very keen to get the band into any new territories, when along came the possibility of a two-week tour in New Zealand. Very lucrative and immensely exciting.

A package was put together comprising Sandie Shaw, who had just had her first number one hit with '(There's) Always Something There to Remind Me', and Eden Kane, who'd also had a recent Top 10 hit with 'Boys Cry'.

We set off in August 1965 for the other side of the world. In those days, the flying time was in the region of thirty-two hours. On arrival in Auckland, we decided to go out for some dinner. Imagine our total surprise in finding that all restaurants closed by nine o'clock in the evening. New Zealand in the sixties was a lot like England in the thirties. The bobbies wore the same hats as the ones back home and a Sunday was really a Sunday. Nothing, absolutely nothing to do, other than to go to church.

One of the interesting phenomena was the 'six o'clock swill'. For reasons known only to the perversions of the law, pubs in New Zealand at that time opened for one hour per day, from 6 to 7 p.m. You can imagine the scene in a country town or village, forty sheep shearers lining up, waiting for the off. The doors opened and the mass of humanity poured in. The bar staff had hoses with nozzles on the end and they would literally traverse the bar pouring the beer into the pints. Bedlam ensued. One hour later, forty pissed men rolled out of the bar, fighting and swearing.

This particular tour soon became a total riot. One afternoon it was about 1.30 and we had all been up for an hour or so, as no one ever got up before noon. The whole tour party was driving in a coach through the countryside of New Zealand. In the back of the coach, all of the Pretty Things were totally out of their heads. Vodkas, rum, whiskies, the whole shooting match being poured down unquenchable throats. Regrettably, they were inducing Eden Kane to share in their fast approaching, comatose state.

In the front of the bus, sitting behind the driver, I was passing pleasantries of the day with Sandie Shaw. After a while, Sandie leant forward, tapped the driver on the shoulder and asked if by any chance he knew of a local resting place where she could avail herself of the facilities. As we were in the middle of nowhere, this didn't look very probable, but, as luck would have it, about ten minutes later the driver pulled up by the side of the road and pointed out a cottage situated about a hundred yards away.

'Try in there,' he said, 'I'm sure they'll be hospitable.' Off she hopped, and made her way towards the cottage. Within a few minutes, a stirring occurred, and a rumbling was heard approaching from the back of the coach. Two or three of the Pretty Things, obviously the worse for wear, came staggering towards me, alighted from the bus, and went about their business by the side of the coach. Another minute or so passed before an even slower, smirking, green-faced wreck, looking even worse for wear, lurched towards the door, and sanctuary.

However, in his wisdom, Eden Kane decided to dispense with the necessity of leaving the bus in order to relieve himself, and lurching from side to side with his back to me, stood on the top step, facing out. He, too, then proceeded to go about his business. Unluckily, at that precise moment, our young female singer attempted to clamber back in. Pandemonium and devastation ensued. Poor Sandie. She was inconsolable. I don't think she stopped crying for days.

On arriving at our hotel that day Eden Kane was led to his room while I was in the foyer with the tour manager, finishing off the preparations for checking in the tour party. Suddenly I heard a dreadful scream at the hotel entrance. I rushed outside with the manager and, gazing up at the first-floor balcony, we saw Eden Kane, paralytic and barely standing, totally naked. The town's inhabitants had never seen anything like it before (and probably wouldn't want to again).

Pretty Things mania was, by now, as hot in New Zealand as it was in

England. In each place we arrived, we were met by the same screaming kids. For reasons unknown to us all, Viv Prince, on arriving at a hotel would immediately camp in the foyer with a champagne bucket and a dead lobster – within a week, a pretty rancid lobster at that – and why a lobster, I never found out. He would proceed to sit in the foyer on the floor, cross-legged like a yogi and, within minutes, hundreds of kids would come through the doors and join him in his apparent meditation. This process would sometimes go on for hours.

Looking back over the years, I can't imagine why the hotel managers allowed it, as no one ever attempted to stop him. In fact, the opposite was the case. We were encouraged because we were rock 'n' roll: we were the harbingers of this new generation that was at last throwing off the shackles of conservatism.

General mayhem continued throughout the two weeks of the tour, made worse by the fact that the new game in town was playing practical jokes while their opposite number was performing. After a week, it became necessary for us to get our own back on Eden Kane, because of some of the high jinks he had pulled on us. It was his custom to walk on stage each night wearing a white suit and, of course, his customary suntan, accompanied by the orchestra playing his hit song of the day, 'Boys Cry'. He would always enter stage right, to a tumultuous ovation of screaming and clapping.

On the particular night in question, we arranged with the spotlight operator and the compere to start from stage left. On this night, the compere was as usual trying to make himself heard over the roar of the thousands of kids who were baying for Eden.

'And now, the best-looking man in the world. The one you've all been waiting for. The one and only, Eden Kane!'

Hysteria broke out. The spotlight, directed by the compere to stage left, picked out another figure in a white suit. I sauntered across the stage to the accompaniment of 'Boys Cry', before bursting into song for the first six bars, in the full glare of the spotlight. Poor old Eden was standing a yard away from me, desolate in blackness, not understanding what had gone wrong. Meanwhile, three thousand girls were all trying to rush the stage at once, to get their hands on me. The adorable man in a white suit.

'The best-looking man in the world,' I believe the compere had said.

I have two lasting memories of New Zealand. One was spending three weeks in Auckland Hospital after suffering a major internal haemorrhage. I had wanted to leave with the boys. The other was hearing on the radio that the New Zealand parliament had banned the Pretty Things and their manager Bryan Morrison from ever gracing their shores again. Whether this ban still holds firm, I don't know.

By 1966, the Pretty Things' career seemed to be on the wane (although many years later, they are still going strong). However, my partner Jimmy Duncan and I, despite being thrown together, were getting on quite well with each other. That was until a fateful Saturday morning when, for some reason, I decided to go to our offices at 142 Charing Cross Road, near the corner of Denmark Street.

They were at the top of a rank-smelling staircase. It smelled because a very famous publisher's drinking club was two floors below my office. It was known as the A&R Club, and for some strange reason that I never understood, it had an all-day, all-night drinking licence. Or indeed, it may not have had a licence at all. Maybe they just served alcohol all day. Anyway, this was the gaff where most of the old-world musos and publishers hung out, and there was always this slightly provocative smell of beer and cigarettes, with a hint of cheap perfume.

Where was I? Oh yes, I negotiated the stairs up past the A&R, then past Tony McNally's first publishing office. I opened the door to my own office, and then picked up a number of letters that had been lying inside on the office floor. I casually opened one or two, before coming to an envelope that contained a bank statement and a number of returned cheques. As I stood looking at this collection, I had this sudden, strange feeling that something was amiss.

It occurred to me that over the course of the previous seven or eight months, I hadn't come across or seen any letters or statements from the bank. I was to learn within a few minutes that running a business wasn't simply a question of having hit records and finding the right artists, but also keeping in touch with the accounting and bookkeeping of the company.

I seemed to remember being told by my partner, some weeks before, that we had eight or nine thousand pounds on deposit in the bank. He kept an eye, or so I thought, on the money. A considerable sum back in those days; the money we'd been saving for a rainy day.

I looked at the cheques and suddenly felt a sickness spreading up from the pit of my stomach. My partner had stolen everything.

Each one of my signatures on each one of the cheques was a forgery. I discovered later that he had lost the lot gambling on the horses. All I had to show for three years' hard work was a wedge of forged cheques, staring at me mockingly. My first thought, besides total anger, was that the end of the partnership was inevitable. Then for some silly reason, which I never could work out, I felt lost.

I questioned whether I had the ability to continue on my own. Maybe it was him that had created all the success in our business. Doom and despair surrounded me like a cloak. I was shattered. I sat there alone in the Charing Cross Road for hours, pondering my predicament. I finally rang my father to seek his advice. He was, as ever, precise and to the point.

'Call the fraud squad,' he said. 'Immediately.'

The die was now cast and I had to do what I had to do, even though I was scared of being alone. On the Monday morning, Jimmy and I met. My first words to him, I think, were, 'You bastard. What's this?'

In my hand, I clutched the sheaf of forged cheques. Crestfallen, he stood staring somewhere into space. The body slumped forward, seemingly disconnected with his head, his face had a look of utter dejection. Nothing was said for a full two minutes. Once again, I was feeling lost.

I finally broke the silence of that unusually quiet office.

'Give me your shares in the company. We're through, get on your bike. I don't want to see you again.'

He muttered some sort of acquiescence, and I became the sole owner of a bankrupt music company. I don't think I ever saw him again from that moment onwards.

• • •

At first glance, the story about 'Tangerine Eyes' and 'Mr Tambourine Man' appears to be impossible. How could Donovan and Dylan write almost identical songs in the summer of 1964, when they had never met and Bob Dylan only released his recording of 'Mr Tambourine Man' in March 1965?

The tale took a further twist when Dylan toured the UK in May 1965, a visit recorded by the director D.A. Pennebaker in his classic documentary, Don't Look Back. *Donovan was invited to meet Dylan in his suite at the Savoy Hotel in London. In an interview with the music critic Greil Marcus for a reissue of the film in 2010, Pennebaker recalled what happened next:*

Dylan said he liked 'Catch The Wind' [which was then Donovan's first Top 10 hit], but Donovan said, 'I've written a new song I wanna play for you.' So he played a song called 'My Darling Tangerine Eyes'. And it was to the tune of 'Mr

Tambourine Man'! And Dylan was sitting there with this funny look on his face, listening to 'Mr Tambourine Man' with these really weird words, trying to keep a straight face. Then Dylan says, 'Well, you know, that tune ... I have to admit that I haven't written all the tunes I'm credited with, but that happens to be one that I did write!' I'm sure Donovan never played the song again.

It transpired that Dylan had completed 'Mr Tambourine Man' in April 1964 and premiered the song in a concert at the Royal Festival Hall in London a month later. Donovan was in the audience and it has been suggested that he assumed Dylan had based his melody on a traditional folk tune. So Donovan thought he would write his own version.

He confessed as much when he reviewed Dylan's album Bringing It All Back Home in Record Mirror on 15 May 1965: '"Mr Tambourine Man". This is beautiful, this one. When I first heard this about a year and a half ago, I wrote my "Tangerine Eyes" from it, but I didn't ever record it, because I didn't want to steal it. I didn't know what the lyrics were. I've sung it to him, he digs it. (Sings along.) That's the best one on the LP, man ...'

So Bryan was right all along.

5

DOUBLE TROUBLE

I was now well and truly on my own and after several days of contemplation it seemed I had only one option. That was to stay in the business that I loved, find some new artists and, also, to try something new – I would become an agent as well as a manager.

I immediately applied for an agency licence from the GLC – the Greater London Council, which was then London's governing body. All I needed now were some artists and clubs to book. I also needed bookers – the guys that physically got on the phone to sell the acts to the clubs and venues. For the time being, however, I would do it myself with my personal assistant.

During my early agency days, it was not only the booking and management of bands that took up my day, but also the acquisition of new venues and clubs. There were dozens of these clubs opening every week, from jazz and blues, to rock 'n' roll. Part of my business was to acquire sole bookings, which meant that I would supply all the music that the individual club needed weekly. For this I would split the agency commission ten per cent with whomever owned the agency of the band being booked.

It all sounds pretty simple but in spite of the numerous clubs opening up, it was in the main a difficult process. There were many new agents, all jumping onto the bandwagon. So I had to isolate the manager or owner of a club, chat him up, have a lunch, and be seen in his club for perhaps weeks on end; all the time telling him what a great job I could do and how the bands or music I put in would greatly affect his customers, and therefore the success of his business. Over the course of several months, we built up a roster of perhaps forty venues, and we were soon booking hundreds of bands a week through our agency division.

It was one of these club owners, Jim Carter-Fea, who was to become a good friend and also my partner, albeit for a short time, in one of the most successful clubs in London.

Jim came to me one day and said, 'How would you like to be a club owner?'

'Sounds a good idea; where do we start?' I replied.

'Well, Bryan, I've actually found a venue on the Kings Road. Want to come and look at it?'

Twenty minutes later, we were parked outside a building about midway down the Kings Road, in Chelsea. There were no yellow lines then, only the freedom to drive and park where you liked. The entrance to the club was through a rather attractive gate, beyond a small but over-run garden. Standing magnificently and totally isolated amongst the hurly burly of the Kings Road, here was this beautiful Georgian building. It must originally have been a hunting lodge, or something as romantic as that, otherwise why would it be in this position.

The interior told another story, however – one of rack and ruin. I was told days later that the owners intended pulling it down to rebuild as offices. The ground floor and basement were a total mess – old mattresses and damp walls, with empty whisky and gin bottles strewn about like some disused distillery.

'Jim, why are we here?'

'This, Bryan, is our new club, if you want to come in with me.'

'Jim, it's a mess; what on earth could we do with this?'

'Five hundred quid to clean it up, five good-looking girls behind the bar, an opening with a couple of your bands and you will have a huge club. There is, however, one major problem.'

Jim said that the owner would only give us a six-month lease with a three-month termination clause, because they wanted to pull it down.

'Okay, let's have a go,' was my reply.

We opened the Pheasantry two weeks later, and within days it became one of the most popular clubs in London. The money kept rolling in and each night the queue to get in extended further down the Kings Road. Sadly, five months later we were given notice to quit our little gold mine and after only nine months it closed. The owners were convinced they had obtained planning permission, but this was not to be the case, and a preservation order was put on the building after months of argument. It still stands, thankfully, all these years later.

One evening, I was in another club having a drink with a lovely guy I shall call Mr X, whom I had met a couple of times before in various drinking establishments.

'Brysey,' he said. I was always called Brysey or White Morry – the white bit because they all thought I was extraordinarily lucky, and they seemed to associate white with luck. Anyway, back to Mr X.

'Brysey, a couple of my mates are really interested in the club business and they reckon they'll be booking tons of bands.' He went on to explain that they wanted to start an agency and thereby get ten per cent commission from the bands they booked. The problem his friends were having was getting a licence from the GLC. To obtain a licence, amongst other things, you needed a clean record; in other words, never having been to jail.

The problem was, Mr X said, that his boys had done a bit of 'bird', nothing serious you understand, just a mix-up really. Anyway, his suggestion was that they would book the various groups and daily or weekly give me a list that my secretary would then convert into contracts. These were printed single-sheet agreements; she would simply fill in the club name, date, timings, money and so on, and for doing this we would split the ten per cent commission fifty/fifty.

Knowing how difficult it was to get sole bookings, I doubted if they would pick up a dozen clubs in a year. I really liked Mr X, and it would hardly be any more work for my typist, so I agreed to do it.

Within weeks, I noticed an ever-increasing pile of contracts, growing rapidly by the day. On the other side of my secretary's desk was my small meandering pile that seemed to grow oh-so-slowly in comparison. I was soon in a quandary. Who were these sweet-talking guys? These upstarts, whoever they were, were becoming more successful than me at my own game.

Daily they would obtain sole bookings on a new venue. The pile rose ever higher until it began to resemble a New York skyscraper projecting forever skyward. The only good coming out of it was that I was making a lot of money. More than ever, I now wanted to meet the boys with the golden touch. I was beginning to feel an abject failure, as I just couldn't compete.

I rang Mr X. 'I want to meet your mates; they are doing a hell of a lot of business with me and I think it'd be nice if we got together.'

'Sure, I'll fix it up. I'll get back to you in a couple of days.'

True to his word, he rang me two days later.

'Brysey, the boys are going to see a new venue in Essex tomorrow and they'd love to see you.'

'Great,' I replied. 'Let me know the address and I'll meet you there!'

The place was a barn-like club, totally devoid of life, save for a bar at one end and a staircase leading up to three offices that hung on the end wall. The bar was awash with spilt beer. The beer mats sank into themselves as another full pint was squashed onto them. The whole vision was of a forgotten and forlorn building, the type you might see in the Australian outback.

'Brysey!' A hand suddenly appeared out of a quartet of giants; four heads turned towards me. 'I'm glad you could make it, this is Ron.' Another hand appeared and my little pinky disappeared inside. 'Reg, Brysey.'

By the time he had introduced the next two, something started clicking in my head. It was the combination of those two names, Ron and Reg. I had barely lifted the gin and tonic to my lips, and as a bubble or two from the tonic burst up my nose, followed by that sweet bitter smell of lime, it hit me.

They were the Kray twins.

'Bryan,' said one of them, 'we're just going to have a chat with the manager.'

With that, two or three of them set off for the rickety staircase. My head was swimming, but it wasn't the gin and tonic. All motion ceased, and I was momentarily cast in stone. The repeated words, 'They won't be long, son,' vibrated in my head.

It was a large hand slapping my shoulder that brought me back to reality. Hardly a minute had passed when, over the sound of the music crashing round the barn, came a high-pitched scream, followed by a noise that sounded like a wet sack of potatoes being dropped on the floor above the bar from a great height. Suddenly a body appeared flying down the stairs. Bouncing once, twice, it landed for a second on the half landing before continuing its headlong descent to the bottom of that unsteady flight of steps.

It ended up sitting nearly bolt upright, head hung, until from out of nowhere a pair of boots followed by a hulking brute smashed into its ribs. It fell to its side and lay prone, and silence prevailed. A silence only found at the bottom of a huge ice crevasse.

In slow motion, I saw three or four human forms converge like lions onto the fallen prey. It was all over in minutes, the ice cubes had barely melted in my drink, the bubbles in the tonic water still had enough strength to jump right out of the glass.

They walked over to where I was standing.

'Another sole booking, Brysey,' one of them announced, beaming from ear to ear.

I looked at the crazed face of the speaker; the black-and-white images that I had just witnessed starting to change into jarring movements of colour. Disbelief and anger spread through my brain.

'Well, Brysey,' he continued blithely, 'tell us about the rock 'n' roll business. We want to break into it!'

I didn't know whether they used the word 'break' as a verb, a pun, or a metaphor. I did know, however, that I wanted out, not next week, next month, but now. I've always believed that in business you can encroach the line, stare it in the face, sometimes even test it for its elasticity, but never, never cross it. Yet here I was on the borders of mob violence. I had been involved for months without an inkling as to what had been going on around me. I mumbled something inaudible and stumbled out of that hell-hole, the drive home unremembered, my nervous system shut down.

I awoke the next morning feeling like shit, with the images of the previous night slamming and then receding in my brain. I had witnessed, albeit in a microcosm, man's inhumanity to man, and it was more than enough. I was getting out now. I picked up the phone, and it rang three or four times before being answered by Mr X.

'We need to have a chat today, if possible,' I said.

'Sure, see you in an hour,' came the reply.

He arrived wearing a dark suit, a crisp white shirt and a huge smile.

'I want out right now.'

'That could be difficult, Brysey. I'll see what I can do. The boys don't take kindly to people letting them down.'

My reply was just as simple.

'Regardless of the consequences, I'm out. Go and talk to Ron and Reg.'

Two days later, he came to see me again.

'No problem, Brysey. The boys thank you for what you've done and if you are ever in trouble give them a ring.'

He handed me a card with a telephone number on it and he was gone.

The other night had been a seed from which greater barbarity grows. The pile of bookings on my secretary's desk shrank to nothing over the next couple of days and they did what they said. I never heard from them again.

Many years later, over a drink, I enquired of Mr X why the Kray twins let me go that easily.

'Well, my son, you handled some of the biggest bands in the world. They love all that game, so they said OK.'

Oddly enough they are both buried at the end of Priory Avenue, the road in which I lived in Chingford after leaving the East End.

One of the rather more infamous and remarkable men I came across in these early years was Nicholas van Hoogstraten. Recently I have read much about him in the national newspapers being described as a 'notorious millionaire slum landlord' and having had a number of visitations by the local constabulary.

When I first met him, he was a youngster, about nineteen years old. Rumour had it that by the age of sixteen, he had built up a massive stamp collection reputed to be one of the best in England, and worth a small fortune. I believe we met because he wanted to invest (as did everyone else at the time) in the rock 'n' roll business. He was always very dapper, in fact dressed more like a dandy, in a velvet coat, well-cut suit, shirt and tie, slimly built, always cocksure and whenever I saw him, always smiling.

I have to say that Hoogstraten, even at that age, always had the idea of running his own world; he would often talk about taking over a Caribbean island and, the strange thing was, I thought he meant it.

I met Hoogstraten on many occasions over the course of a few months, On one of these visits, I was listening with rapt attention to his descriptions of the histories of world stamps. By the end of this particular discussion, I had asked him how much a Penny Black was worth.

Like most non-stamp collectors, the only one I had ever really heard of was the Penny Black, the world's first and most famous stamp. Again, like most other people, my assumption was that these rarities were valued in thousands rather than tens of pounds, but here was the expert telling me that you could buy them for almost nothing, only a few pounds each. True, some Penny Blacks in mint condition – the rare ones, that were clean with good, wide edges – were worth £1,000 or more, even in those days. As for the rest, they were counted in pounds.

It occurred to me that a Penny Black on the wall would carry about as much weight with the viewer as a Picasso. As I was trying to build financial credibility, and as I knew that everyone assumed Penny Blacks were expensive, I purchased a Two Penny Blue and a Penny Black from Hoogstraten. I then inserted them in a gold frame on a square of black velvet, and hung them resplendently above my head in the office. The whole process cost me a whopping seventeen pounds!

For the next week or two, rock 'n' rollers, their managers and entourages came to view this great collection of philatelic beauty, each one gazing at them, wondering how I could possibly afford such extravagance. After week one, the community was talking up my stamps to the value of thousands of pounds. Two weeks went by and the dream was shattered.

I arrived one morning to find my secretaries in a terrible tizzy. A *Topkapi*-style operation had taken place. The thief had cut through the outer wall of the office to obtain entrance, then without a sidelong glance at the other valuables like a well-bitten biro, or a leadless pencil, and a selection of rubber bands all laying together alongside the clear plastic ruler, he grabbed and nicked those oh-so-valuable stamps.

I laughed for months afterwards at the thought of him presenting the stamps to one of those tiny little stamp shops in the Charing Cross Road, to be told by the proprietor with his half-moon glasses perching on the end of his nose, that he would give him about £9 for the job lot.

● ● ●

When Bryan had his encounter with the Kray twins in 1966, they were at the height of their notoriety as London's leading gangsters. In the 1950s, Ronnie and Reggie Kray had formed a gang in the East End of London they called 'The Firm', specialising in protection rackets, armed robbery, hijacking and arson. By the early 1960s, they had expanded their empire to include extortion and fraud, as well as several night clubs, where they became part of the swinging London scene, mixing with film stars, singers and politicians. The twins ruled their gangland empire through fear and violence, inflicting vicious punishments on anyone who crossed them.

In one of their most infamous cases, in March 1966, Ronnie Kray shot George Cornell, a member of the rival Richardson gang, in the Blind Beggar pub in Whitechapel. Cornell was said earlier to have called Ronnie a 'fat poof'. Cornell was sitting on a stool by the bar, when Ronnie casually walked in and shot him in the head. The police could not find a single witness who had seen anything.

Later that year, in December, the Krays would help Frank Mitchell, 'The Mad Axe Man', escape from Dartmoor prison, but on Christmas Eve he disappeared, never to be seen again. Later it was claimed that he had been shot and his body disposed of at sea. Then, in October 1967, the Krays lured Jack 'The Hat' McVitie to a basement flat in Stoke Newington, where Reggie tried to shoot him, but his gun jammed, so he stabbed him to death with a carving knife.

This proved to be the turning point. In May 1968, the Kray twins were arrested by

Scotland Yard Inspector Leonard 'Nipper' Read and, once they were in custody, he was able to persuade several witnesses to give evidence. The Krays were each sentenced to a minimum of thirty years in prison. Ronnie was found to be legally insane and sent to Broadmoor Hospital, where he died of a heart attack in 1995. Reggie remained in prison until August 2000, when he was released a few weeks before his death from bladder cancer, at the age of sixty-six.

Nicholas van Hoogstraten became equally notorious. He started selling stamps to collectors at the age of eleven, although it is alleged that he hired his classmates to steal the stamps from specialist shops. When Bryan met him in the early sixties, Hoogstraten was already using the proceeds to buy cheap property in Notting Hill and by the time he was twenty-two he claimed to be Britain's youngest millionaire.

He gained a reputation as a ruthless slum landlord, dismissing his tenants as 'filth', and one judge described him as a self-styled 'emissary of Beelzebub'. In 1968, he was sentenced to four years in jail for paying a gang to throw a hand grenade into the home of a Jewish cantor in Brighton, whose son owed him a debt.

By the age of thirty-five, Hoogstraten was said to own more than two thousand properties, amassing a fortune while inflicting terror on his tenants when he wanted to evict them. In 2002, he was convicted of manslaughter after a business rival, Mohammed Raja, was stabbed and then shot in the head on his front doorstep by two men who had been hired by Hoogstraten. The verdict was overturned on appeal but, in a civil case brought by Raja's family, he was ordered to pay them £6 million in compensation. Hoogstraten claimed he could not pay it, because he had handed all his assets to his children.

Following the trial, Nicholas van Hoogstraten emigrated to Zimbabwe, where he bought a substantial amount of land and rights in a diamond field, and became a close associate of the president, Robert Mugabe.

CRAZY DIAMOND

In the summer of 1966, I came across a band called Pink Floyd. I first saw the Floyd perform small gigs at the Marquee Club, in Wardour Street. Looking back through the mists of time, they were quite amateur. Their performances were quite dark, due to a poor light show and no visibility. However, theirs was the first light show I had ever seen, their music was different and they were laid back. I thought I would keep an eye on them, as they were extremely interesting. In December, they started performing at the new UFO club in Tottenham Court Road, which hosted a psychedelic evening on Friday nights. I knew then that this was a band with the potential to be great.

On 24 January 1967, having spent a hell of a lot of time trying to persuade the Floyd's managers, Peter Jenner and Andrew King of Blackhill Enterprises, to give me a sole agency agreement, they eventually agreed. This meant that I had the exclusive rights to sell every gig that the band played.

Part of my sole agency agreement was to guarantee the Floyd a minimum income, which at the time was a small fortune of £400 a week for a year, so we needed to work really hard to obtain enough money to cover such a large weekly fee. By the end of 1967, we had obtained for the Floyd over two hundred and fifty gigs; prior to my signing them, they had managed only twenty in the previous year.

These gigs took place in venues as diverse as the UFO club and the Rank ballroom circuit. They dreaded the Rank ballroom gigs, principally because the audience wanted to dance to soul acts and groups that they had seen on television. Such is the fate of a new band, and it was here that they learnt their craft, which was essential for the huge concerts of the future.

My first meeting face to face with Pink Floyd had taken place at a recording studio, where they were recording their first single, 'Arnold Layne'.

I arrived with two of my bookers, Tony Howard and Steve O'Rourke, who would later become their manager. We were all smartly suited and booted, and I think the boys thought it was a raid by the Krays. The song was magical and, as the session wore on, I suggested that I could probably get them a really good record deal with EMI, as I had a number of great contacts there.

Sometime before, I'd met a producer called Norman Smith who worked for EMI, and through him I had met Sidney Beecher-Stevens, the head of EMI's A&R Department. Beecher-Stevens was probably about fifty, although he seemed ancient, and it was to him that I went to try to persuade EMI to sign this amazing new band.

He got it immediately. Sadly, this man, who made one of the major contributions to the British record industry by signing the Floyd, is now long forgotten.

On 28 February 1967, Pink Floyd signed a recording agreement with EMI that I had negotiated. They received the then astronomical figure from a record company for a new signing of £5,000. Advances were rarely, if ever, paid in the sixties. I remember all of us running out of the EMI building in Manchester Square shouting and hollering with sheer delight.

The lead singer and guitarist, the front man of the band, was Syd Barrett. He was a truly remarkable individual. As a young man, Syd was one of those people who seemed to have it all: the looks, the intelligence and, more importantly, the ability to write great songs.

He had the potential to be a great leader of youth. An artist who set out on a trip of discovery that, through his own genius and finally with the mind-boggling drug, LSD, sailed a deep, new channel that inspired, confused, and changed a generation of people. This was referred to as 'acid' music, after the hallucinogenic drug that brought colour, self-liberation and a feeling of being able to achieve the impossible. But Syd's raw and exquisite genius would be destroyed by his overuse of acid and nervous breakdowns.

'Arnold Layne' was released as Pink Floyd's first single in March 1967, reaching number 20 in the charts. Written by Syd, it was, in fact, published by my first music publishing company, Dunmo Music. It was followed in June with 'See Emily Play', which hit number 6.

It was after the release of 'See Emily Play' that Syd's deterioration became more apparent. During a recording for *Top of The Pops*, he found it impossible to stand up, let alone sing, because he was out of his head. After a couple of attempted takes, and much to the dismay of the producer, we had to drag Syd back to the dressing room to try to put some normality back into his life.

Almost an impossible task. Eventually, they managed to get a complete run through on the next take, but as far as the band was concerned, the situation could not continue. Syd would have to go.

The band's first album, *The Piper at the Gates of Dawn*, was released in August, but the pressure of Syd being unable to perform gigs or do interviews was beginning to take its toll on the other members of the band. Finally, their bass player, Roger Waters, who had now become the main spokesman for the Floyd, told me that they had taken the precaution of finding another guitarist for the band, that man being David Gilmour.

Slowly Syd stopped functioning as a member of the band and in early 1968 they started gigging without him, with David taking his place. At this time, Jenner and King decided that they wanted to stay with Syd, which left Pink Floyd without a manager. The band then approached me about filling this function, and it was agreed that I would become their manager. Shortly afterwards, principally because of the enormous workload that I was under, managing four bands plus running the agency, I asked Steve O'Rourke to take over the day-to-day organising of the Floyd. Steve went on to become their full time manager sometime towards the end of 1969.

One of the first problems that confronted me as manager of the Floyd was to find money for them to tour abroad and, in particular, the honey pot of world rock 'n' roll – America. Raising the money proved to be impossible, until one day I had this wonderful, stupendously marvellous idea. Later I was to realise that only an idiot like me could have dreamt it up. At this time, I was also Pink Floyd's worldwide music publisher and, with the incredible naivety that has followed me through life, I offered to sell the American rights to the Floyd's publishing, and to put all the proceeds towards the band and their touring schedule.

A brief explanation is probably prudent at this point. Normally when an artist is signed to a music publishing agreement, the contract covers the world. The publisher will then sub-license the song or songs through other publishers around the world. These sub-publishers duly collect royalties within their territories, which are then repatriated to the original copyright owner, who then pays the writer their share of the income.

So, in Pink Floyd's case, I effectively split the world in two, making myself owner and sub-publisher for the world bar America. The American publishers accounted to the Floyd direct and, for this extravagant action, I was paid some £20,000, which was then immediately reinvested into major tours of the States.

Strangely, I never received any thanks for this extravagant gesture.

The first tour we did took us all across America, with a number of the gigs being promoted by Bill Graham, who was then the promoter of such names as Jefferson Airplane, the Mamas and the Papas, and the Doors. He promoted Pink Floyd in his two legendary music venues, the Fillmore East and West.

Money was always a problem in these heady days, and travel and accommodation were the two commodities that swallowed most of the cash. On one occasion, we all sat in the car for about thirty minutes, trying to persuade the Floyd's keyboardist, Rick Wright, that the two or three dollars he had in his pocket were more important to us so that we could pay a road toll, rather than the hamburger he was contemplating buying for lunch.

The tour was a resounding success, but for me, strangely enough, the most important visions that I have retained were not of late nights and rock 'n' roll, but the beauty and unspoiled tranquillity of Carmel, Yosemite Park, the great Nevada desert, and the Pacific Ocean. Of course, there were many other things that one may care not to remember – the Plaster Casters, for instance.

This was a group of young ladies led by Cynthia Plaster Caster, who used to spend the best part of their time getting into the rooms and beds of unsuspecting rock stars, where they would then perform an operation that involved the mixing of plaster and water, then finding a suitable appendage of which to make a plaster cast. I can only assume that somewhere in California today there are a number of fireplaces bearing these mementos of a bygone era. They actually tried to capture me one night but, being forewarned, I moved rooms and was able to escape being plastered.

Another incident I remember with total recall happened at a gig the Floyd did at the Whisky a Go Go club in LA. During one of my frequent sojourns on the dance floor, some idiot spiked my drink with acid. I spent the next five hours or so believing that I was a giant and taking great care not to tread on people as I left the club and walked down the street.

At about three that morning, absolutely out of my brain, I found myself in one of the A&M studios, singing on the chorus of Joe Cocker's recording of 'With a Little Help from My Friends'. Over the years, I've listened to this wonderful song, but I never did ascertain if my vocal refrain had been captured for posterity.

For me, the most devastating decision I made on this particular tour was when I was invited by Ike Turner to have dinner with Elvis Presley at his home in Memphis. I had first brought Ike and Tina Turner to England on a tour a year or so earlier and I published some of their earlier songs. Presley had been watching and listening to Pink Floyd and when Ike mentioned that he knew their manager, he asked Ike to invite me along. In my total stupidity, I turned him down, the reason being a beautiful, long-haired blonde with powerful blue eyes, who had already invited me to dinner on the same night. This was without doubt the worst decision that I ever made and regretted most in my musical career.

In June 1968, Pink Floyd's second album, *A Saucerful of Secrets*, was released, and though this was not one of their biggest sellers, for me it was the first true Pink Floyd classic. This was followed in December by the release of their third single, 'Point Me at the Sky'. I still think that *Saucerful* is one of the Floyd albums that they will be long remembered for. It was a unique first, even though *Dark Side of the Moon* was a much bigger record in terms of sales and exposure.

In late 1968, I was approached by the French film producer Barbet Schroeder, from a French company called Les Films du Losange, who wanted to commission the Floyd to record the soundtrack to his new film, *More*. The film wasn't particularly successful in England but in France it played to ecstatic audiences, who almost broke down the cinema doors to get in to watch it, and it has remained a cult movie there ever since. By now, the Floyd were becoming a major talent, and were moving from 'underground' to 'overground'.

My management of the Floyd was to cease, or rather was to come to an abrupt stop, on the night of 26 June 1969. It had become obvious that the band, who were now working continuously building an ever-bigger fan base, needed the next step up. They had to do a major concert, as opposed to the club circuit, but it was a gamble, because the kind of place they needed to play had to be a big capacity venue.

Undoubtedly the most prestigious London venue then and now is the Royal Albert Hall. This beautiful building, inspired I am sure by the Colosseum in Rome, was to be the springboard for the band to put them well and truly on the map. However, there were no promoters around who believed the Floyd could sell out such a large venue, the capacity being in the region of five thousand, so it fell to yours truly to take the plunge. The booking fee was the staggering amount of £350. It sounds such a paltry sum today – but back then it was a fair amount of money.

What happened next was quite incredible. Within hours of the tickets going on sale, the 'house full' sign was put up; we literally sold out in a little over two hours. It was to be my first and last concert promoting the Floyd. The concert was a tremendous success; the press and the audience all went potty for this new phenomenon.

Having talked to a few of the press and media boys at the end of the gig, I walked into the dressing room, and everybody was euphoric; we all knew what huge strides had been made that night. After ten minutes of conversation with the boys, Roger Waters asked me to step outside for a minute, as he wanted to talk to me about something urgent. Roger's first words were those spoken so many times in the world of rock 'n' roll: 'Bryan, you're fired. You are not our manager anymore.'

I would like to say I was gobsmacked; however, with Roger Waters, nothing really surprised me. Having just promoted their most important gig ever, I would have hoped that he could have gone to bed, had some bacon and eggs in the morning, come to see me in the afternoon, thanked me for the last couple of years, then doubly thanked me for putting on the gig that was the precursor for ever more extravagant events in the years ahead.

But no, he just spat out, 'You're fired.'

I was hardly surprised, therefore, when many years later the same Roger Waters decided that Pink Floyd should be no more, much to the chagrin of Rick, Dave and Nick, but fortunately for all of us they won their court case to keep the band's name, and he lost.

The pity of it is that I was within months of passing my management of the band to Steve O'Rourke anyway, as I will explain in a later chapter.

In late 1972, I received a call from Steve O'Rourke, who was now the manager of Pink Floyd. He wanted to see me about my ongoing publishing agreement with Dave Gilmour, who at this point was still under contract to me. Under the terms of this agreement, he owed me only one more song. Steve's request was quite simple. Would I sell Pink Floyd the rights to this song, as they shortly had a new album coming out and they wanted to put all of the publishing into their new company, Pink Floyd Music Publishing.

My reply was equally simple. 'No', or should I say, 'No thanks.' I had been brought up as a publisher never to sell a copyright.

'Come on, Brysey, name your price,' retorted Steve. I was adamant, however, that the copyright was not for sale.

Over the course of the next few weeks Steve must have phoned four or five times, each time suggesting that I name my price. Eventually I thought, why not, if the deal was right, let's do it, so I sat down to work out some figures. The previous Floyd album had sold a few hundred thousand copies. The Beatles at this point had barely sold a couple of million of a single album, so I came up with what I thought was an unimaginable figure.

I would sell the song based on an album sale of three million copies. Tongue in cheek, I let Steve know what I wanted, confident in the fact that he would not agree to my price, but if he did, it would be a nice little earner, or should I say, a large earner. I couldn't imagine any album at that time selling in such vast quantities.

My next questions were to ask when the album was coming out, and what its title would be. 'February or March 1973 and it's called *The Dark Side of The Moon*,' was his reply.

'Great. I hope it's successful.'

The paperwork done, I sat down and laughed all the way to the bank, figuratively speaking. The rest, as they say, is history. Over the years, *Dark Side* has been on the American charts for more than seven hundred weeks, longer than any other album, and at the last count had sold over thirty million copies.

In retrospect, Steve did a fantastic deal, and old clever clogs here missed out on one of the biggest albums ever. I look back on this today and it still brings a smile to my face. I may not have seen the money, but relating the story still makes me laugh.

● ● ●

The worldwide sales of The Dark Side of the Moon *have now reached more than 45 million copies and by January 2019 the album had amassed a total of 940 weeks on the* Billboard 200 *album chart.*

The album made millionaires of the four band members, but not everyone involved in the recording was so lucky. Abbey Road staff engineer Alan Parsons received a Grammy Award nomination for his innovative recording techniques on The Dark Side of the Moon, *but he was paid only a wage of £35 a week while he worked on the album. Fortunately, he went on to have a successful career as a recording artist with The Alan Parsons Project.*

The singer and songwriter Clare Torry, who sang the extraordinary improvised vocal on 'The Great Gig in the Sky', was paid a session fee of just £30 for her contribution. In 2004, however, she sued EMI and Pink Floyd for fifty per cent of the songwriting royalties from the track, claiming co-authorship of the composition with Rick Wright. In her book, Music: The Business, *the media lawyer Ann Harrison discloses how the case was finally settled out of court for what is rumoured to be a substantial cash payment and the song is now credited on all post-2005 pressings to both Wright and Torry.*

The Pretty Things: (l-r) Dick Taylor, Brian Pendleton, Viv Prince, Phil May and John Stax, in London, 1965. 'I'm not working with that bunch of animals!'

Folk singer Donovan in 1965. His song 'Tangerine Eyes' was rejected by the Pretty Things.

Eden Kane, who toured New Zealand with Sandie Shaw and the Pretty Things in 1965. 'The best-looking man in the world!'

◀ *Swinging London's most notorious gangsters, Reggie and Ronnie Kray, about 1965.*

◆ *Property baron and self-proclaimed 'Britain's youngest millionaire' Nicholas van Hoogstraten in 1968.*

Alamy

Shutterstock

◆ *Pink Floyd: (l-r) Nick Mason, Rick Wright, Syd Barrett and Roger Waters, at the Saville Theatre, London, October 1967.*

Alamy

🔺 Pink Floyd: (l-r) Rick Wright, David Gilmour, Roger Waters and Nick Mason, in Stockholm on a European tour September 1968.

🔺 Victor Brox with Aynsley Dunbar's Retaliation, at Bristol University, October 1968. He sang the role of Caiaphas on the original album of Jesus Christ Superstar.

◀ Keith West, whose 'Excerpt from a Teenage Opera' reached only number 2 in the charts, July 1967. 'I'm sacking you. You're useless.'

◀ Marc Bolan with T. Rex in 1971. 'He was like a beautiful lost animal, singing in the forest on the night of a full moon.'

⬤ The eccentric Armenian oil millionaire Nubar Gulbenkian in London, July 1962. 'I believe in comfort. I enjoy life. I enjoy everything I do.'

Alamy

Alamy

▶ Free: (l-r) Paul Rodgers, Simon Kirke, Andy Fraser and Paul Kossoff, in 1969. Bryan sold their recording and publishing to Island Records to pay his mortgage.

Alamy

Elton John in 1971. 'Whatever you offer him, I'll offer him ten thousand pounds more.'

Robin Gibb begins his first British solo tour after leaving the Bee Gees, June 1970.

The Bee Gees together again and No.1 in the USA with 'How Can You Mend a Broken Heart'. Maurice, Barry and Robin Gibb in 1971.

◗ *Syd Barrett in one of his final appearances with Pink Floyd at Kensington Olympia, London, 22 December 1967.*

◗ *Bryan and Greta Morrison's wedding at Kensington and Chelsea Register Office in London, with Greta's mother, Florence van Rantwyk, 12 December 1972.*

Shutterstock

◀ *John Otway, feeling 'Really Free' in 1978. 'I spent it. But it was sure fun.'*

Alamy

▶ *Bryan with Rodney Kinsman at their modern furniture design company, OMK Design.*

⬇ *The Jam: (l-r) Paul Weller, Bruce Foxton and Rick Buckler, in 1979. 'I think I've found the new Beatles.'*

Alamy

◑ *Fashion designer Bill Gibb with one of his models, January 1981. 'He's the only innovative designer in England today.'*

▶ *Haircut One Hundred with Nick Heyward (right), on the cover of their third Top 10 single 'Fantastic Day', April 1982.*

7

KING OF THE RUMBLING SPIRES

In 1967 the Bryan Morrison Agency Ltd, as it was then called, was reaching its zenith. Not only were we the agent and managers of Pink Floyd, the Pretty Things, and several more bands, we were now booking international stars such as the Byrds, Ike and Tina Turner, and Ravi Shankar, while our English agency acts included Soft Machine, the Incredible String Band, plus a host of others.

We also had the sole booking agreements for most of the major London clubs, such as Blaises, the Speakeasy, and the Revolution. So unbelievable were these times, that when one of my partners got married in 1967, I gave him Blaises as a wedding present, and the band who rocked the night away was Ike and Tina Turner.

They were only two of the great artists that we acted for in one capacity or another. When Jimi Hendrix toured England for the first time that year, I took half of the tour at the then ludicrous price of £30 a night, and by the end of the first week, his single 'Purple Haze' was a Top 10 hit.

Keith West, whose one big song was 'Excerpt from a Teenage Opera', was being managed by me when his record became an unprecedented success. It went to number 2 in the charts that summer, only to be stopped from reaching the coveted number one spot by Engelbert Humperdinck's massive hit 'The Last Waltz'. The phones burnt hot with promoters trying to book this new act. However, the failure of his record to make it to the top led Keith to invite me out to lunch in a nearby restaurant off Soho Square, which was charmingly known as the Romeo and Juliet café. During this pleasant lunch, he dropped one of those intermittent rock 'n' roll bombshells. I don't recall the exact words, but it went something like, 'I'm sacking you. You're useless.'

'Why?' I enquired.

'Because my record never made number one!'

To say I was hurt would be an understatement. I'd been managing Keith West in his band Tomorrow for a year or so. Indeed, out of this band rose a great guitarist by the name of Steve Howe, who went on to become lead guitarist of Yes. You can imagine that having finally achieved such success, I was not pleased to be so summarily dismissed.

Anyway, as I was booking all the top venues up and down the country, it was hardly surprising that within days of Keith's decision, promoters began cancelling all the dates they had booked through me. Sadly, within days, he found himself with a hit record but no work. I hasten to add that I was not torn apart with remorse. His next record was a flop and he never had another hit.

I seemed to be in demand a lot in those days. One morning, I received a telephone call from another artist who was to become a superstar over the next two decades.

'Bryan, it's Rod here, Rod Stewart. Do you think we could maybe have a cup of tea and a chat?'

'Sure,' I replied.

'OK, how about the Giaconda?'

Over a cup of tea, Rod asked me if I would consider becoming his manager. I had been watching him for many years singing in bands at all the top London venues. Many a great night had been spent watching him and Long John Baldry singing their versions of the blues. Long before he became an international star, Rod Stewart had been regarded by most of the aficionados of rock 'n' roll music as being the finest singer around.

At the time I was managing four rock bands, plus running a huge agency business, so I knew that I would not have the time to spend on managing Rod. It was with regret that I had to say no. We finished our tea, he left and found other management, and the rest of the story we all know. He became a megastar and justly deserves it. As for me, I simply missed out.

It was clear that we could no longer manage the business in Charing Cross Road. We were now five bookers, a secretary and receptionist and me, in two little offices. I was planning a major expansion.

After a great deal of searching, we found an excellent office located in Bruton Place, just off Berkeley Square. For the next two years, our office at 14-16 Bruton Place, above the trendy Revolution Club, became one of the major agencies and management businesses of its time. Within two or three months of moving in, there were more than a dozen people in the office, working the phones and booking bands. If a band had a couple of hundred watts of PA, a transit van, some guitars and a drum kit, we were the boys. We brought virtually all the major American artists to the UK.

After a tough day, we all used to go a few doors down the road to a pub in Bruton Place called the Guinea. At that time the Guinea cooked the best steaks in London in the back of the pub; the best steak pies in the world were served in the front. An old boy with a broad Scots accent, called Jock funnily enough, used to clear the glasses and generally tidy up.

He lived in the council flats behind Bruton Place and he could get you anything. Tickets for a first night, tables in a restaurant, ask Jock, give him a ten pence tip, and the world was your oyster. I once mentioned in passing that I would kill for a couple of seats for the Bolshoi Ballet that was due in town in a couple of weeks, and to which it was impossible to get seats.

'Let me have a little look at it, laddy; I'll see what I can do.' Days later, Jock came up with the seats, not merely seats, but three rows from the front and bang in the centre.

One evening I went to the pub accompanied by my white Alsatian, Lupus. I ordered a drink and the dog settled at my feet. Imagine my surprise when Jock came shuffling out of the kitchen, clutching a plate of delicious looking steak. He yelled, 'Lupus, here boy!' and then threw a piece of this succulent meat towards the dog. It was about seven o'clock and I was getting rather hungry, so seeing this steak nearly drove me crazy.

'Jock, stop! What are you doing? You can't feed a dog in a pub like that. It's not hygienic, give me that plate.'

I swiftly disarmed poor old Jock and, putting on my most indignant face, I walked outside, calling Lupus to heel. Once in the street, I pulled the door to the pub shut, took a long look at those delicious pieces of steak, and popped a nice juicy lump into my salivating mouth. As I swallowed the first sizeable chunk, the pub door swung open.

'Whatever are you doing!' exclaimed Jock, his red face turning blue. 'Bryan, I just got that meat out of the dustbin – I got it for the wee dog!'

The second piece that I had just slipped into my mouth shot back out again and hit the pavement near Berkeley Square. They didn't stop laughing at me for days.

Jock, this wretched but lovely little Scotsman, would always tell me about his best friend, the great American comedian Bob Hope. Now if you believed for one moment that Bob was Jock's mate, then pigs can fly.

That was until one sunny morning when I was walking around Berkeley

Square, and this huge limousine, like the cars used by the Queen, drew up. With a toot of its horn, the blacked-out window slowly descended to reveal – you guessed it, Jock. He waved me closer to the window.

'Bryan, say hello to me mate!'

There sitting next to him, with a big smile on his face, was Bob Hope.

'We're just going to lunch,' Bob drawled, and with that, the limo slipped away.

This next story is about one of the nicest musicians I have had the good fortune to meet. His name is Victor Brox. Victor was in a blues band called the Aynsley Dunbar Retaliation. I had signed them in 1967 and, although they didn't have any single success, they had two Top 40 albums and earned pretty good money on the road. Aynsley Dunbar was a brilliant drummer and later went to America, where he teamed up with the hugely successful rock band Journey.

One evening I went to see the Retaliation in the Marquee Club. There were two groups playing on this particular night in question, Aynsley's being the main band. I happened to arrive early at the gig, halfway through the support band's performance.

I stood watching this support band and, the more I watched, the more I realised that they were a major act in the making. In fact, they were potentially much bigger than the group I had come to see. At the end of their act, I rushed backstage to talk to the band, who went under the title of Jethro Tull. This was a sensational group, and I knew I had to move fast.

Within minutes of my arrival in the dressing room, another person appeared, whom I knew fairly well; I had dealt with him many times on the telephone when he had been social secretary at his university. Terry Ellis was one half of what was later to become Chrysalis Records. Unbeknown to me, on leaving university, Chris Wright and Terry Ellis had decided to go into the music business. They had been negotiating with Jethro Tull for some weeks and were at the point of signing the band for recording and management. Now this larger predatory shark was about to move in before their very eyes.

Terry, looking a bit dazed, asked me if I could step outside.

'Bryan,' he said, 'we want to manage this band. We've done an awful lot of work with you in the past through the university. Do us a favour; your intervention will only make matters more difficult for us. Would you mind passing on this for old time's sake? We really want this band.'

I don't remember the exact conversation, but it boiled down to Terry Ellis appealing to my better nature (assuming I have one), not to get involved with this band. Because of our past business relationship, I agreed and bowed out. In addition, I also gave Chris and Terry some excellent advice later, when I met them in a bar in Rome after a Pink Floyd concert in May 1968.

They asked my thoughts on whether they should start an independent record company, or start a label as an affiliate of one of the majors. I advised them on the former. Whether they had already made a decision, I don't know, but they certainly built one of the most successful independent record companies in the world. They brought a bit of class to the music business through their acts, and Jethro Tull would become the foundation upon which Chrysalis Records was built.

What does all this have to do with Victor Brox, you may ask. Well, one day in 1969, Victor arrived in my office and posed me a fairly simple question. He'd been asked to sing the part of a high priest on the recording of a new musical about to come out, called *Jesus Christ Superstar*. He'd been offered either a session fee of a few hundred pounds (quite a decent sum at this time), or a royalty of between some three-quarters and one per cent. The question was which one should he take. My answer, without hesitation, was to go for the royalty. Victor explained that he had many pressing financial problems, and that his preference was to go for the session fee.

'Victor,' I insisted, 'you must go for the percentage.'

At the same time, I was asked if I would release Victor from his contractual obligations for this one album, to which I agreed. I mentioned that I wanted my company to have a credit on the album sleeve, to which they also agreed. Victor finally left my office that day more or less convinced to take the percentage.

A week or two later, he was back in my office recounting to me the making of this album. It took him about forty-five minutes to get to the point, when he told me rather shamefacedly that he had taken the money. That one decision over the next twenty years was to cost him tens of thousands of pounds. *Jesus Christ Superstar* is not only a phenomenal stage show, but the album keeps on selling many years later. Victor was the one artist that I would have liked to see make a killing. Sadly, it was not to be.

In the autumn of 1968, I was talking to a very pretty young girl by the name of June Child, who was the general factotum of Peter Jenner and Andrew King at Blackhill Enterprises. She was soon to introduce me to another supernova, whom I was to sign within a few weeks.

'Bryan,' she said, 'my boyfriend's really talented; you would just love his songs and ideas. You must see him.'

'Yes,' I said, but did nothing about it. I had these kinds of recommendations ten times a day.

A week or two later, I bumped into June Child again and I was reminded of our conversation. I liked June a lot, so I agreed to meet her boyfriend at the next opportunity.

'Why don't you get him to come over to my house tomorrow night?' I said. 'Tell him to bring his guitar, so he can play me some songs.'

It was quite unusual at this time to find a solo singer-songwriter unencumbered by a band. I was intrigued, and so the meeting was fixed. The following night, there was a ring of the doorbell at my house in Eastbourne Mews, near Paddington Station, and there in the doorway stood this elfin-like figure. The light of a streetlamp haloed a little impish face, dark brown eyes, long curling hair and a dazzling smile.

I invited him upstairs, and we both clanked up the metal staircase to my first floor sitting-room. Without invitation, Marc sat cross-legged on the floor, with an expression and an attitude that was to be his trademark for years to come. We talked for five to ten minutes, principally about his dreams and aspirations. It soon became evident that the man with the impish grin knew what he wanted and where he was going. As with all the great artists I've come across, it was never a question of 'if I make it', rather than 'when I make it'.

After a few more minutes, he leant over to his guitar case, hit the catches on it and pulled out a six-string acoustic guitar, giving me one of those whimsical looks that I was to see many times over the ensuing years. Then he threw me a cheeky smile and said, 'Do you want to hear some songs, then?'

Thirty years later, I still remember with total clarity the minutes that passed as he played to me. The room filled with magic. Sitting there on the floor, hunched over his guitar, he sang his first song 'Debora', while his fingers flicked up and down the frets. His voice was unique, and so too were his songs.

He was like a beautiful lost animal, singing in the forest on the night of a full moon. I was mesmerised, elated, transfixed. The room took on a glow, and the little elf burst forth with one great song after another, always this uncanny voice adding a resonance to the guitar and the lyrics. He finished with a song called 'King of the Rumbling Spires' and, to me, that's what he was.

Each song had been as brilliant as the last. I was breathless and knew without hesitation, then and there, that I was witnessing the most magical moment that occurs in any galaxy – the birth of a new star.

Marc had formed an acoustic duo with percussionist Steve Peregrin Took and they called themselves Tyrannosaurus Rex. A couple of months earlier, they had released their first album, *My People Were Fair and Had Sky in Their Hair ... But Now They're Content to Wear Stars on Their Brows*, but Marc had fallen out with his management at Blackhill Enterprises.

A week later, I had become Marc Bolan's new agent and manager.

Breaking bands like Tyrannosaurus Rex and Pink Floyd was extremely difficult, to say the least, as the mainstream media were not into what became known as 'underground' bands. Over the next two years, I tried on literally dozens of occasions to get the disc jockeys at BBC Radio 1 to play Bolan's songs, but met with total refusal, mainly because they didn't think he was much good anyway.

The one exception to this, the only gem in an otherwise barren desert, was John Peel on his weekly radio programme, *Top Gear*. To him goes total credit as far as the broadcast media goes. In spite of powerful resistance, he pursued and played the songs of artists that he liked, and especially, Tyrannosaurus Rex. Many, many artists of this period owe their ultimate success to John Peel.

One day Marc came to me and showed me a whole file of poems that he had written, and asked if I thought I could get them published in book form. With due diligence, I went to see publishers and sent out copies of the manuscript, but to no avail. Throughout this whole period, Marc constantly nagged me as to what was happening with the poetry book. My reply was always the same, 'There's no interest.'

Finally, I decided to do what I've often done in circumstances such as these, and that was to publish it myself, through my company Lupus Music. I set about getting quotes from printers and putting advertisements in *The Bookseller* magazine, looking for salesmen. A couple of months later, in March 1969, I took delivery of 5,000 copies of *The Warlock of Love*. We reprinted it twice and sold in excess of 20,000 books, which was probably one of the biggest sales of modern poetry for decades. Although over the years I've had many people approach me about reprinting it, I have not yet done so, but with a huge surge of interest in all things 'Bolan', maybe the time is right.

Marc wanted to be a rock star. In late 1969, he dumped Steve Took and replaced him with Mickey Finn. He also started playing electric guitar. The breakthrough came in October 1970, when turning on the radio, I heard one of those ever-so-friendly deejays proclaiming the existence of a new band called T. Rex, and a smash single called 'Ride a White Swan'. It soared all the way to number 2, but sadly it was to sever the relationship between Bolan and me.

Unfortunately, sycophantic mania took over, the acolytes crawled out of the woodwork, and the court of King Bolan was created. From here on in, Marc engulfed himself in the Presley style of omnipotence. It was this that pushed Marc towards the brink of failure, not because of his music, but because of the financial and business advice he was given.

In one example, he was encouraged to start an art collection, and spent hundreds of thousands of pounds doing so. I advised against nearly all the paintings that he bought, but he took no notice. On his death, the estate found that most of the paintings were virtually worthless. There were a lot of unscrupulous people around at the time, all of whom preyed on rich pop stars such as him.

Marc also asked me to advise on overseas companies that he wished to set up, principally to escape paying the crippling tax that existed at the time. I was never into blind trusts and tried to warn him against them, but sadly he went ahead. Today his family, son and mother receive absolutely nothing from his songs and recordings. Totally immoral, and all the result of punitive taxes in the sixties.

I could not and would not tolerate being what Marc wanted me to be. He required me to show him the same obsequious loyalty that the rest of his hangers-on gave him, so we parted company. From this point onwards, I never saw Marc again for about six years. Until one evening, I was in a club at the end of the Kings Road. It is now very up-market and fashionable, but I can remember when this self-same club was a fish and chip shop.

Anyway, there I was, having a good time on one of my rare incursions at a rock 'n' roll party, when who should tap me on the shoulder but the little imp. He sat down at my table and we started reminiscing about the good old days. Suddenly, without warning, he got up, came over to me and sat on my lap, throwing his arms around me in a flood of tears. It seems that many years of emotion suddenly welled up inside of him, because he asked me to forgive him for his stupidity and arrogance towards me in those earlier days.

Tragically, Marc was to die in a car accident five days after our last meeting. A piece of timing that to this day I can't come to terms with.

For me there was nothing to forgive – I had been Marc's sole manager, agent and part publisher from 1968 to 1971. Time is a great healer; I had derived so much from Marc's success over the years and felt that I had been one of the small catalysts in his life. Someone who helped to bring his songs and music into the world. Songs that were to give so much joy and pleasure, because Bolan was and indeed still is, one of the great singer-songwriters.

The terrible sadness was that Marc was dead. The life crushed out of him when his car crashed into a tree on Barnes Common in September 1977. Yet another one of those great rock 'n' roll tragedies.

Before I signed Marc Bolan, another of my artists, the fabulous blues singer Alexis Korner, mentioned that he had seen a fantastic young band playing at a rehearsal room in Battersea. His suggestion was that we should go and see them immediately. Alexis was probably the greatest exponent of the blues that this country has seen; he was a wonderfully craggy-faced guy with an even more craggy voice. In those early days, every musician and singer wanted to play with Alexis. I actually recorded two albums with him, and also designed the covers for both of them; one of these designs I am proud to say is in a book of the best album covers of all time – four years at art school obviously paid off.

The two of us set off to have a look at this young new band and, boy, were they good. They were raw, powerful, exciting and they could write great songs. When we first saw the band, they were unnamed, but within days Alexis came up with the name Free. I signed them to management, agency and publishing. I knew I had a huge band on my hands, so we set about getting them gigs and preparing songs for recording.

Weeks later, for some forgotten reason, I was having a serious financial problem paying the mortgage on my house in Eastbourne Mews; the very same house that Marc Bolan had sat in, and which I was to sell later to a great friend of mine, David Essex.

In desperation with the bank threatening foreclosure on my home and unable to find any other finance, I went down to Island Records to have a meeting with Chris Blackwell. Chris was then the owner of the most unique record company of the time, in as much as the public bought artists released on Island Records virtually sight and sound unseen, such was its credibility.

How or why I descended on Island Records to see Chris on that particular day I don't remember; however, I found myself at the record company in Oxford Street at the appointed hour. After the usual preamble, I came to the point. 'Chris, I need £3,000 desperately.' (First mistake, never appear desperate when begging.) 'I owe the bank £3,000 and they have a guarantee against my house; they are threatening to foreclose on the loan. I've only got days and I'm pretty desperate.'

Chris's reply was brutal and to the point. 'Sell me one of your artist's publishing or recording or both. Let's see, you've got Tyrannosaurus Rex, the Floyd and that new band Free.'

'Not on your life, not one of my bands.'

'Sorry, Bryan, I can't help you. Look, you've got to do a deal on Free anyway.' I hadn't as yet tried to get a recording deal for them. 'Sign them to me, plus the publishing and I'll give you the money.'

It was true that I would have loved to place Free with Island anyway, but the publishing was a no-no.

'Chris, they are going to be huge; not the publishing as well.'

He shrugged, 'That's the deal.' I left. Four days later, my problems with the bank became even more acute. In desperation, I called Chris and gave in. Island Records became Free's record label and publisher. I was sick as a dog, but I did retain my house.

● ● ●

The Bryan Morrison Agency had become one of the biggest booking agents and managers in the business but, with the offices in Mayfair and more than a dozen staff, the overheads were enormous. The money was pouring in, but it was going out even faster. The situation was not helped by the fact that Bryan enjoyed an extravagant lifestyle, from champagne and handmade cigars, to driving luxury sports cars and collecting works of art, but he often spent money that he could not really afford.

So it is perhaps no surprise that he suddenly found he had run out of cash and was unable to pay the mortgage on his house at 109 Eastbourne Mews. The band Free signed with Island Records in late 1968 and Bryan continued living in his mews house until he got married in 1972.

8

A SAFE HAVEN

By the summer of 1969, the strain of being a manager, a publisher, and running the Bryan Morrison Agency was beginning to tell. One day I visited my GP, who in his absolute wisdom assured me that if I kept up this crazy lifestyle for a few more years, I might not be around for much longer. His suggestion was that I should totally give up managing rock 'n' roll bands, as I patently couldn't take the stress. Reluctantly, I decided to sell the agency.

The purchaser of my agency was NEMS, the company set up by Brian Epstein to manage the Beatles, Cilla Black, Gerry and the Pacemakers, and others. A name that in the sixties signified one thing only: the Beatles.

I was in a car going from Paris to Charles de Gaulle airport. It was about 7.30 in the morning, as we sped down the flat, boring motorway surrounded on all sides by modern factories, designed in that most dreadful way that only the French seem to achieve with most of their modern buildings – an exception, of course, being the Pompidou Centre in Paris.

Back in the taxi, a Beatles song was playing on the radio, 'Eleanor Rigby', and amongst the swirling mist and bleakness of the run into Charles de Gaulle, my mind became totally honed into the most marvellous lyrics of this song. It is incredible to me that two twenty-year-olds had the depth of perception to write a lyric like that – quite staggering.

So NEMS it was. Brian Epstein had died two years earlier, and he had run his Merseyside operations and management of the Beatles from 3 Hill Street, in Mayfair. The new master of the empire housed in that spectacular building off Berkeley Square was Vic Lewis, an ex-bandleader, now managing director of NEMS Enterprises.

NEMS at this time were agents for such American stars as Andy Williams, Tony Bennett and Frank Sinatra. However, they were very weak in their rock division, so the amalgamation of my company and theirs was consummated. I became a director of NEMS Enterprises and set about trying to build up the division.

Interestingly enough, the manager of Pink Floyd, Steve O'Rourke, who had taken over their management some months earlier, was negotiating with NEMS for some kind of joint management agreement. I believe Steve took this course of action for two reasons. Firstly, the large advance which had been offered and, secondly, for security. He would then have an office to work from, a secretary and so on.

What neither he nor the Floyd knew was that I was about to become a director of NEMS, the result being that a week after they moved into 3 Hill Street I appeared on their radar again. It must have been a bitter pill for the band, as they once again found themselves having to deal with Bryan Morrison. I laughed for days at this wonderful checkmate. It must have driven them crazy.

Recently I had the opportunity to read Nick Mason's excellent book, *Inside Out*, and happened to notice one or two errors. Firstly, Nick suggests that I sold my agency in August 1968, when in fact it was August 1969. Secondly, the suggestion is that I asked Pink Floyd to sign another agency agreement, and I quote, 'Roger smelt a rat', and therefore they signed only a six-week contract. I hardly think that NEMS would have given me £40,000 if they only had my biggest artist for a further six weeks.

Thirdly, Nick, and I quote again, suggested that 'Bryan had overlooked the management aspect and neglected to get us to sign the relevant contract. This gave us enough leverage to extract some cash from NEMS - a great assuage of artistic pain, I find - and to insist that Steve, who was due to join NEMS, be released to become our personal manager.'

As mentioned previously, my management had ceased on 26 June 1969, when Roger, who could always 'smell a rat', sacked me. Steve took over as full-time manager the next day.

Nick also mentions how I understood the 'importance of getting them back to the US for a second tour' and was instrumental in making this happen. However, he doesn't mention what a great act of charity this was, which required the sacrificing of my North American publishing to raise money for their second US tour.

Lastly, Nick is incorrect in suggesting that when I signed the Floyd to management, I gave them Steve as their manager while I got on with my publishing. Steve was always my booker and I was their manager; what I did do was to give my three principal bookers a main artist each to work on specifically, on getting gigs and so on. I was the sole manager of Pink Floyd until my demise in June 1969.

A couple of months after selling to NEMS, I was playing happily on the Côte d'Azur. St Tropez was a wonderful place then. It had still managed to retain most of its charm, which it was to lose in the oncoming decade. One evening, for the third time in my life, I was at death's door, struck down by an internal haemorrhage, and with the life blood flowing rapidly out of me.

I was rushed to the Anglo-American Hospital in Nice. Within minutes of my arrival, a French surgeon explained, in rapid detail, the life-saving operation I would require. My personal thoughts were that I didn't want any French butcher cleaving me at the seams and so I asked him if I could make my decision the following morning. His answer was blunt and to the point.

'I don't think you will be able to make this decision in the morning because if I don't operate on you within about ten minutes, you will be dead!'

There's nothing like a *fait accompli* to focus the mind, so common sense prevailed. I was still conscious on the operating table, staring up at that bright arc light, while the surgeons, nurses and anaesthetists formed a masked dome above me. Then it all went black.

I woke up in a small, white, clean room. As I stirred back into sensibility, I could hear the distant cry of small children playing. I could imagine them in a bright sunny garden. To this day, whenever I hear children at play, the memory is immediately evoked of that awakening, and then the heartwarming thought that comes with it that you have survived, and are once again free to live in this beautiful world.

I was suddenly aware of the presence of another person in the room, at the same moment as I felt a large, firm hand clasp my shoulder. My eyes blinked again and sitting beside the bed was a large man with a huge reddish face that peered at me intently.

'Welcome, my boy, we'll be spending a lot of time together, so you had better read this.'

With that, he tucked a hardback book gently down into the side of my cot. Odd, I thought, and remembered no more as once again I slid back into unconsciousness. Many hours later, I resurfaced to see the smiling faces of two nurses, who turned out to be the personification of angels. They looked after me with a devotion that I have never witnessed before or since.

'We see you've met Mr Gulbenkian,' one of them said.

'Who? Gul ... Gulbenkian?'

'Yes, that's his book lying on the bed.'

One of the nurses rummaged down the side of the cot and produced the autobiography of one of the great eccentrics of this period. So this was Nubar Gulbenkian, son of the great Calouste Gulbenkian, an Armenian businessman and philanthropist who, in the late twenties had managed to persuade most of the Arab Emirates and States that he would be the middle man and go-between to represent the Arab cause against the mighty Western nations in the sale of their oil.

For this service he had been awarded five per cent of the generated income. The other ninety-five per cent was shared equally between the British (BP), the Dutch (Shell), the French (CFP, the Compagnie Française des Pétrole), and a Rockefeller-controlled American group (Exxon + Mobil). Even with the relatively low price of oil up until the cartel of the seventies, this was not an inconsequential sum. He became one of the wealthiest men in the world.

His son, Nubar Gulbenkian, was one of the great characters of the thirties, forties and fifties. He was probably best known for driving around London in his very own chauffeured London taxi, which had been rebuilt on the original chassis by Rolls-Royce. He always wore a monocle over his right eye and had a long, bushy beard. His autobiography, which I started to read within days, contained even more of his eccentricities and thoughts, but I had something much better than the book. I had the man. Real, alive and breathing.

For over two months, the two of us lived together in this small hospital. Its wide, pretty lawns, and the high, stuccoed, white brick wall, made it a veritable oasis of tranquillity. In fact, all the time I was there, our little world was punctured only once, by a pregnant woman who remained with us for three or four days.

Other than that, there was the odd coming and going of Nubar's men – always at least a dozen of them, in suits – all huddling and clucking on the lawn like pigeons pecking at the newly sown seed. Nubar had three nurses, who constantly attended upon him. Where he found them, I don't know, but each one was prettier than the next. Even his physiotherapist, who came at regular intervals, was an absolute stunner.

One morning, after breakfast, I was aware of more than the usual toing and froing among Mr G's nursing staff. A large machine was being trundled up the corridor. It made not a dissimilar sound to a slow goods train, as it clicks over each section of a sixty-foot track. The corridor tiles were pockmarked and cracked after decades of use. They had been lovingly cleaned and polished over the same period of time, however, and now had a lustre and smell only found in the cared-for homes of the gentry.

Pulling myself slightly higher than the prone position, I enquired of one of his beautiful nurses as to the cause of this pandemonium. She smiled slightly, clasped her hands in front of her, and shrugged her shoulders.

'What's the problem?' I repeated.

She looked first left, then right, stepped forward a pace, and gently clutched the rail at the foot of my bed.

'It's a bit of a secret,' she said, 'but actually Mr Gulbenkian is having a cardiograph done.'

'Oh no!' I cried. 'He's not in trouble, is he?'

She smiled again and said, 'Oh no, he's just got a lady-friend coming to visit him and he wants to make sure the old body can take it!'

It took at least two seconds before I realised what I'd just heard, and when it finally sank in, I exploded with more laughter, mirth and hysteria than I had experienced for ages, for here was one of the greatest acts of heroism I'd ever encountered. Nelson put his telescope to his blind eye before turning his ships on the French fleet at Trafalgar, the Greeks used a huge wooden horse to enter the city of Troy and, of course, Neil Armstrong needed a rocket before he could land on the moon.

All Mr G needed before making his conquest was an electrocardiograph machine. A few words can indeed speak volumes. This was one of the funniest things I'd ever heard, and I live in anticipation of the day when I am seventy-five years old and have my cardiograph done before embarking on a night of passion and debauchery with a young lady.

Lunch and dinner times were nearly always conducted with the same ritual. My food came from the hospital kitchen – not so 'his lordship'. Virtually every day, a large stretch Mercedes limo would purr its way down La Croisette to the Carlton Hotel to fetch Mr Gulbenkian's food. On his return, the chauffeur would step out in his full regalia; britches tucked into knee-length boots, over-flap buttoned jacket fastened to the neck, gloves and a peaked cap, on which was a small crescent of filigree, denoting a crest of sorts. And, oh yes, don't let us forget the black Ray-Ban shades.

As he leapt from the car and opened the rear door, from somewhere within the tinted glass interior he would pluck a silver tray on which stood several silver serving domes, standing erect like igloos in an Eskimo village. With the tray carried forth at waist level, he would then place it with due solemnity in front of our hero.

Some time passed before I was eventually allowed to get out of bed and be taken by wheelchair to the garden. Once positioned on the front of the small terrace, I would spend precious hours alone, while Mr G would sit with a straw hat perched on his head some ten to fifteen metres away. Every time the 'pigeons' alighted on our patch, I would be approached by one of Mr Gulbenkian's nurses who would ask if I minded moving to some far-flung corner of the garden as the great man had some important business meetings.

I thought this was all rather odd as, even on the days when we would talk together in the garden, I could barely hear what he was saying. What he thought a mere mortal such as I could do with any of the precious droppings of information that he might have divulged about the Middle East or its environs, I have no idea.

Finally, the time came to depart from my sanctuary. I was in tears, the nurses were in tears, and it was a very, very sad day. However, I'd learnt one salient fact – one part of life's jigsaw that was to dominate the rest of my life. When you have stared death in the face, with the flame of life about to be extinguished, and then risen up like a phoenix through the canyons of darkness to once again hear the distant babble of children's voices, then, and only then, are you aware that each and every day is a bonus.

I returned to England from my hospital in the South of France where, for the second time in five years, I had been literally minutes from death having suffered a major internal haemorrhage. After spending a month or two recuperating, I returned to work.

Part of my deal in selling to NEMS had been to have my own suite of offices, plus staff of my choice. It did not take me long to find a very pretty young girl with a tweed skirt cut above the knees, plus the then obligatory pink, grey, or blue twin set and, of course, the ever-present white pearl necklace, to become my secretary. Her name was Cora Jackman and she had been working at NEMS as a junior secretary for about eighteen months. Over thirty years later, this young lady is still one of my great friends and confidantes and still works with me.

Within days of her starting as my secretary, I had cause to remonstrate with Cora about someone who had annoyed me and, in a long tirade of verbal abuse, I ordered her to tell this particular person to 'Fuck off'. Cora went white and visibly stuck to her chair at this terrible onslaught. It turned out that in all her twenty-one years, I was the very first foul-mouthed man who had ever sworn in her presence.

Without the pressures of management, life became much easier, and it was during some of these more refined days that I decided my future in the music business was in publishing. I took on two young men, the first named Peter Barnes, who had no previous knowledge of the music business and had been an engineer with British Airways. Many years later, Peter was to publish Pink Floyd, Elvis Costello, and many others, and he also married the lovely Cora. He was followed shortly afterwards by a young rake named Ray Williams.

One day while talking to him, I asked Ray if there were any other artists besides the ones that we were currently looking at that he thought might have talent.

'Well,' he replied, 'there was someone a year or so ago who was very interesting. Maybe we should look at him.'

Ray explained that a year or two earlier, he'd arranged an audition. Ray had stuck an advertisement in one of the music papers seeking musicians for a new band he was putting together and well over fifty people turned up. Ray particularly liked the piano playing and singing of one young man by the name of Reg Dwight. He had suggested that Reg should get together with a young poet called Bernie Taupin and write some songs. It was the self-same Reg Dwight who came to see me in my offices a few days later to play some of their music.

The songs and the voice were stunning, and I immediately asked Reg, whose stage name was Elton John, if I could be his publisher. There was a problem with his publishing, however, but one that wouldn't be too difficult to overcome. The problem was that he was signed to Dick James Music. Nevertheless, he assured me that in about four months' time, the contract was due to terminate and he would then sign with me.

Although reluctant to go back into managing an artist, it looked as if I would have no choice, as Reg wanted me to be his manager. In return, when his contract was up with Dick James, he would sign his music publishing to me. His songs were beautiful, and I was desperate to publish them in my fledgling company. When you want something that badly, well, a man's got to do what a man's got to do.

I agreed that I would manage him, as long as the publishing fell into place. Reg felt very confident that the James empire was not particularly interested in him or his career. They would surely let his contract lapse, so signing to me would be a mere formality.

Three to four months later, I was to dance to a different tune. Out of the blue, the great man who published the Beatles rang me up and asked if we could have a chat. A time and date were duly set and I arrived for the meeting at Dick James's office, off Oxford Street. He came straight to the point with a very potent message.

'Bryan, I know it is your intention to try to sign Reg on termination of his contract with me, but I'll tell you this, my boy, whatever you offer him, I'll offer him ten thousand pounds more.'

Ten thousand more? A king's ransom.

I could barely afford to pay Reg the first ten thousand, let alone the next; it was far too rich for me. (I'd heard people say that Dick James was lucky when he signed the Beatles and Elton John. Let me tell you now that this man wasn't lucky, he knew exactly what he was doing. He was a great music publisher.) I knew in that instance that I was about to lose Elton John. Later that day, I repeated to Elton the offer that he was about to receive, knowing full well what his intention would be. His first reply was no, he wouldn't accept it, as he wanted to stay with me.

Elton's response was a great surprise; I mean, you could buy a nice house for that.

'You've got to take it,' I said wistfully. 'It's a bloody fortune.'

It was a *fait accompli*, and I knew it. Elton signed with Dick. I suggested to Ray that he took over the management, as I was not interested in being a manager without the publishing. However, NEMS kept the agency for a year or two, so I missed out on arguably the greatest singer-songwriter the world has produced in the last thirty years. The good news is that, along with the rest of the world, I do get to listen to his wonderful music.

● ● ●

Nubar Gulbenkian died at the English Hospital of Cannes on 10 January 1972 at the age of seventy-five. He had been confined to a wheelchair after suffering the first of several heart seizures in 1968, the year before Bryan Morrison met him in the hospital in Nice.

Gulbenkian relished his reputation as an eccentric multi-millionaire, and a bon viveur with a taste for the good things in life. He loved fine food and wine and once said that the perfect number for dinner was two - himself and a head waiter. When he was asked whether he preferred city life or country life, horses or Rolls-Royces, old brandy or young women, he is reported to have stroked his luxuriant beard and puffed deeply on his cigar before declaring: 'I prefer everything.'

At Cambridge, a friend said, 'Nubar is so tough that every day he tires out three stockbrokers, three horses, and three women.' According to Life magazine, he spent much of his youth in London chasing chorus girls, before getting married - three times. He was divorced twice and commented wryly, 'I've had good wives, as wives go, and as wives go, two of them went.'

In later life, Gulbenkian enjoyed driving around London in his custom-made, gold-plated taxi and used to claim proudly, 'It can turn on a sixpence - whatever that is.' A flamboyant, larger-than-life character, he was one of the richest men in the world and that rarity, perhaps, the happy multi-millionaire.

His credo was: 'I believe in comfort. I enjoy life. I enjoy everything I do.'

9

SAVED BY THE BELL

Shortly after joining NEMS, I found myself embroiled with another great artist; he and his brothers must certainly rank in the top five pop writers and artists of the sixties and seventies. The man I am talking about was Robin Gibb, of the Bee Gees.

I received a call from Vic Lewis, asking me to pop up to see him in his luxuriously appointed office on the first floor of Hill Street. I sat down and was poured the ever-ready cup of tea in a fine bone china teacup. Vic was always pedantic about being surrounded by and using the best. Not I may say in a flash way, but as a point, of course. He asked me if I was interested in managing Robin Gibb of the Bee Gees. He had left the group acrimoniously a few months earlier, and wanted to pursue a solo career.

The Bee Gees had ranked as one of the three great bands of the late sixties, along with the Beatles and the Rolling Stones, with hits such as 'Massachusetts' and 'I've Gotta Get a Message to You'. There had been a period of about a year when the Bee Gees nearly eclipsed the Beatles in popularity, but now they had split up. The reasons for Robin's departure from the band were legendary. Only the laws of libel forbid me from recounting the conversations I had with Robin Gibb and his portrayal of the internal machinations, which involved sex, drugs, and rock 'n' roll.

It transpired after further conversation that Vic Lewis had taken on Robin's management and had been attempting, without very much luck, to gain a publishing deal for him. His question was simply, could I take over and try to obtain one for him? By his own word, Vic was not a publisher, and knew nothing about it.

'What's been the problem?' I asked Vic.

'Well, simply, I've been to two or three of the major publishing houses and asked them for a deal on Robin. Each one, without a second's hesitation, has turned the project down, saying that the Bee Gees are finished and therefore so is Robin Gibb.'

'Crap, absolute crap,' I replied, leaning forward and banging my fist heavily on Vic's etched-leather, Georgian desktop. (It wasn't quite like that, but it reads well, and a little bit of drama never goes amiss.) 'You're talking about one of the greatest writers in the world today. You're talking about the man who wrote "Massachusetts", "I Started a Joke" and "New York Mining Disaster".'

I was definitely interested in taking on Robin Gibb and I couldn't understand why no one else was. At this juncture, I think I should explain the categories of songwriters.

The first category of songwriter is a journeyman of some talent who, in the course of his career, if he's lucky, will have a sudden flash of inspiration and write one or two good songs. Rarely do these writers ever achieve a song that attains 'Evergreen' standard. The Evergreen being a tune to stand the test of time, the song of songs. One that will crawl over the backs of generations. This is the genius of such greats as the Beatles, George Michael, Elton John, and their ilk.

Freddy Bienstock, one of the world's great music publishers, told me many years ago that if you ever got to own three Evergreens, you were a) very lucky, and b) made for life. Freddy has published many Elvis Presley songs, as well as countless others, so he knows what he's talking about.

The second category of songwriter is a man or woman of exceptional talent who over the course of years will write several very good songs. I suppose they could be labelled as Premier Division. Names like Geoff Stevens, Don Black, and Les Reed, whose songs include 'Winchester Cathedral', 'Born Free' and 'It's Not Unusual', which exemplify their status.

Finally, we have the true genius, a songwriter who over a period of years will continually produce magical songs. For me the mantles of excellence would go to Lennon and McCartney, Elton John, Sammy Cahn, Henry Mancini, Lerner and Lowe, Rodgers and Hammerstein, Bacharach and David. I would also like to include in my list Andrew Lloyd-Webber. These are some of the all-time greats.

These men have written the truly great songs of each generation, songs such as 'Yesterday', 'Three Coins in the Fountain', 'On the Street Where You Live', 'Moon River', 'Imagine', 'Candle in the Wind', 'The Look of Love', and 'Memory'. These gems, hacked from the human mind, express a quintessential composite of life in one exquisite message. It is this that has fuelled my ongoing desire to find that one pearl in that one elusive oyster.

And here I was being presented with one of the geniuses. It was inconceivable to me that others in the music industry were not aware, as I was, that the very fibre of Robin's soul was the creation of music and songs.

'No problem, Vic,' I said. 'I'll get you a deal in a couple of weeks.'

It turned out that my belief was not shared by others. Over the next two months, I traversed the steps of nearly all the major publishing houses in the USA and England, and they were universally of one opinion. Robin Gibb and the Bee Gees were finished.

'Bryan,' they would say, 'their last two records have bombed out. There's no future.'

I was incredulous, and began to realise what a totally useless bunch the music industry were in those days. It was no wonder that by the time we got to the end of the seventies, music publishers had seen their share of the cake cut down to a few crumbs. They were to get only what they deserved. Nothing more in most cases than mere collection deals, non-creative; simply accountancy and banking.

I would hasten to add that I have specifically mentioned music publishers here, as I don't believe that record companies had fallen into this category. Indeed, the opposite is true. In the past, the publisher of a song was the instigator, the creator of the written song. During the thirties, forties and fifties, the publisher was the hub of the music industry.

A writer would compose a song, and the publisher would contact singers in an attempt to get them to perform the composition at their shows; then he would go to the record companies and persuade them to release the track. His next action was to print the sheet music for the song. This was one of his most important functions, there being a lack of national and virtually no local radio stations, as the big bands were the means of getting new music into the public domain.

The record companies were more of a distributor of the product. But by the seventies, most publishers had become virtually moribund, and the record companies were now not only the distributors, but the creators of music.

After my soul-destroying trawl of the world's music publishers, I finally called Robin into the office and, without wanting to bruise his ego too much, explained that times were hard and that deals weren't growing out of barren ground. It was a week or two after I'd given him this bad news that I had the idea of offering Robin my own deal.

We would set up a new company called Robin Gibb Music. He would own fifty per cent, I would put £20,000 into the company, which I would pay him as an advance, and Vic Lewis and I would share the other half, twenty-five per cent each. This idea was jumped upon by Robin, and the various contracts and obligations were put in place. I then suggested to Robin that he set about writing some new songs.

His first solo single was a song that I never particularly liked, but had a certain mundane commercialism about it. It was called 'Saved by the Bell', which proceeded on its release in July 1969 to climb all the way to number 2 in the UK. He had also finished recording a solo album but, again, they were the songs of a man under pressure and not in free flow. But now his life was becoming more stable. A year earlier he had got married to Molly Hullis, the receptionist at 3 Hill Street, whom I assume he had fallen madly in love with. The songs he was writing now were getting back into the groove of the great old days.

Through all of his success, Robin had earned and spent an absolute fortune and I found it quite remarkable that he had nothing to show for it other than his stretch Mercedes. I spent a not inconsiderable amount of time persuading him to buy a house, at least to have some bricks and mortar. This he did shortly in Virginia Water.

But further success proved elusive for Robin and his brothers. Robin's next two singles failed to crack the Top 40. Meanwhile, Barry and Maurice had continued to record as the Bee Gees but, after a year without a hit, the group was about as dead as the proverbial dodo. By the summer of 1970, Robin was under increasing pressure to reunite with his brothers, and he took on the mantle of gentle persuader. Many meetings took place and after a particularly successful one at the end of the summer, in a sauna bath in Dover Street, it was finally agreed that they would write and record together again.

I soon became very involved with Barry and Robin and it wasn't long before they came up with *the* song – an Evergreen if ever I'd heard one. The title was 'How Can You Mend a Broken Heart'.

First the Bee Gees released a comeback single, 'Lonely Days', which became a major hit for them in the States. Then in June 1971, they put out 'How Can You Mend a Broken Heart'. Within weeks of its release in America, it had shot to number one. In a relatively short space of time, it would become an American classic, clocking up over one million airplays on American radio.

I was taken by surprise at the speed of the record's climb to the top of the charts in the US, as I was holidaying in Australia at the time. On being telephoned and given the news, I immediately caught a flight for the West Coast of America to repay a few debts. More poignantly, to rub salt in a few wounds.

A black-on-black limo had pulled up outside the arrivals door at LA airport and after a twenty-hour flight it was a very necessary accoutrement. Along with the stretch limo was an immaculately turned-out chauffeur who, with a deft hand, pointed out what was a fairly new custom at the time. One that has now grown out of all proportion. Lying in a champagne bucket was a bottle of Dom Perignon surrounded by steadily melting chunks of ice, a small pot of caviar and some toast. The ultimate. It was star time.

More recently, while going to a Wham! concert in Los Angeles in the mid-eighties, we had to squeeze our way round a fairly large table that took up the majority of the space in the limo, but there it was – a full-blown Chinese meal. I couldn't eat for laughing. I suppose the next step will be not only food, but a couple of waiters sitting in the back with you.

The driver put his foot down and we glided from the airport towards the Sunset Strip and the Beverly Hills Hotel. A touch on the electric window brought a wave of warm air into the car, and the stereo blared out with a choice of 120 rock stations, which all confirmed that you were in LA, the City of Angels, if you didn't already know.

After we arrived, I told the receptionist at the Beverly Hills Hotel to page Mr Bryan Morrison at the pool ten times in the next hour, the purpose being to announce that I was in situ should the odd film producer wish to meet me; a very necessary process while staying at the hotel. One hour later, I retired to my suite to take a shower before sallying forth to the various publishers and record companies, whom I knew would be as sick as dogs for not having signed Robin.

One by one I visited their offices, the air-con pumping out a cooling eighteen degrees.

Always the same chat. Refraining from mentioning the Bee Gees, until came the moment when, sheepishly, they had to congratulate me on having a hit, while kicking themselves for not doing a deal months before. I thoroughly enjoyed my four days on that particular trip.

Prior to the release of the record, Vic Lewis had asked me if I wanted to buy his twenty-five per cent of Robin Gibb Music. Vic was a promoter and agent and had little interest in being a music publisher, so this I did, and now became equal partners with Robin.

In January 1971, after only eighteen months at NEMS, I was bored and decided to leave the company. I resigned as a director and returned to my old offices at 14–16 Bruton Place, where I still ran my publishing companies Lupus Music and Robin Gibb Music, and my furniture design business, OMK Design (of which more later), and Cora Jackman came with me as my personal assistant.

Even though Robin Gibb was now married, he soon resumed his old ways, and one morning a young lady turned up at our office. Cora came in to inform me that she was waiting outside and needed to speak to me about Robin Gibb business. Having a million things to do, and as the girl had no appointment, I asked Cora to tell her to come back the next day.

I thought nothing more about it until two or three o'clock that afternoon, when Cora came in, ashen-faced, telling me that there were now two young ladies, who were hurling all sorts of verbal abuse at her, including what they might do to Robin and me if they didn't see me post-haste.

'Tell them to go away, Cora. I'll see them tomorrow.'

Another hour or so went by, when Cora knocked again and walked into my office. This time, however, her face was as white as the pearls hanging around her neck, and she was visibly shaking.

'There's two giant men with them, Bryan, and if you don't see them now, they said they're going to come in anyway.'

'Who? Which giant men?'

'You know, the two girls who have been trying to see you since this morning.'

As the whole episode was by now getting quite exciting and out of control, I told Cora to usher them in. The chaps were indeed very big. Their story was simple and plaintive, although I had no idea if it was true or not. A week earlier, the young ladies had been requested by Robin to organise a gathering of about fifteen people, who then partook in some school-time fantasies, complete with uniforms.

Apparently, it was a lot of fun, or so they told me, the only problem being that they hadn't been paid, and this was what they wanted, the readies. It could have been a complete scam and Robin may well have done nothing of the sort, but, discretion being the better part of valour, I decided not to kick up a fuss and handed over the cash. Another major crisis was averted.

But that was nothing compared to what happened next.

• • •

The story of Robin Gibb and his split from the Bee Gees had started in February 1969 with the release of their single 'The First of May'. Robin had wanted his song 'Lamplight' to be the A side. He had written the group's three biggest hits, 'Massachusetts', 'I've Gotta Get a Message to You' and 'I Started a Joke' but, according to his wife, Molly, Robin felt he was not getting enough credit for their success. This was because their songs were always attributed to the three brothers – B.R.&M. Gibb – which also meant that he was missing out on two-thirds of his songwriting royalties.

Barry Gibb was talking about going into films in Hollywood and Maurice was beginning to produce other artists, so Robin felt ignored, and, in his words, 'something snapped and I went off'. For several weeks, his brothers insisted he was suffering from 'nervous exhaustion'. But then their manager, Robert Stigwood, announced that Robin was still under contract to the Bee Gees, and he was issuing an injunction to prevent him making any solo records.

Eventually, an agreement was reached and, in June 1969, Robin released his first solo single, 'Saved by the Bell', which peaked at number 2 in the UK charts.

A few weeks later, he signed a new management deal with Vic Lewis at NEMS Enterprises and set up his own publishing company, Robin Gibb Music, with Lewis and Bryan Morrison. Finally, he agreed to give up his share in the Bee Gees publishing company in exchange for his full release from the Robert Stigwood Organisation.

But solo success proved hard to achieve. In January 1970, he released his first album, Robin's Reign, but it failed to sell, as did the subsequent two singles, 'One Million Years' and 'August October'. That summer, the Robin Gibb Fan Club was closed down, citing a lack of new members. The Bee Gees' latest single, 'I.O.I.O', had bombed on both sides of the Atlantic. The writing was on the wall. Record Mirror *revealed that the brothers were talking once again.*

In August, the three brothers met at Robert Stigwood's office to finalise plans for an official reunion. It was reported that Stigwood had to pay £50,000 to NEMS to release Robin from his management contract. However, he would retain his publishing company with Bryan Morrison, for the time being.

Soon afterwards, Barry and Robin reunited for their first writing session in nearly two years, which resulted in two songs, 'Lonely Days' and 'How Do You Mend a Broken Heart', that would go on to be million sellers in the USA. The Bee Gees were back together, but the legal battle was far from over.

10

HELPING POLICE WITH ENQUIRIES

The Bee Gees' saga continued apace. The greater their success, the greater the pressure from the other Bee Gees and their management to get Robin Gibb back into the fold.

It started nicely enough, and the request was simple – would I release Robin from his publishing obligations. My answer, of course, was no. Until one day, the whole episode took a nasty turn. I returned home to my mews in Paddington one evening and within a minute or two of my arrival the telephone rang. I put the receiver to my ear and mumbled the customary, 'Hello.' In those few seconds, life was to change inconceivably. The voice at the other end snapped like the crack of an ice-flow parting with the mass.

'Watch it when you cross the road tomorrow, because you're going to have an accident.'

The line went dead and I was left listening to the mesmerising purr of the dialling tone. The process was repeated daily over the next week, the threats becoming more and more aggressive. Although I wasn't letting it worry me particularly, the constant harassment was finally getting to me. By coincidence, at the end of that first week, one of my old road managers arrived back from Italy for a short holiday. Phil was tall and very good-looking, with gold chains hanging round his neck and wrists, but, oddly enough, it was all in the best possible taste. He was tough, although he didn't look it.

We had some dinner that Saturday evening and during our conversation I recounted to him that I had been receiving many threats to my life over the telephone in the last week or so, and I was unsure about what to do – whether to go to the police or ignore it.

'No problem, Bryan,' he said, looking at his watch. 'Let's go down the East End. I know a couple of ol' mates down there who'll sort out yer problem for you.'

Looking back with twenty years' perspective, it is hard for me to even consider why I went to the East End that night, why I didn't just go to the police. The immorality and stupidity of the next two or three hours corrodes my soul, but it is irreversible. I was twenty-eight years old, happy but soft. Soft because of my upbringing, in spite of being brought up in the East End for the first eight years of my life. Soft even despite spending my formative years in tough secondary schools. Nothing had prepared me for the ritual abuse of the thug.

I was brought up after the Second World War and lived in one of the most civilised countries on earth. Yet, even within this law-abiding country, I was being threatened. I think that was the reason for me taking fate into my own hands.

I had seen enough evidence in those black-and-white newsreels of man's inhumanity to man, enough of the wretched, starving masses standing gaunt behind the wire simply because they did not resist. The success of the dictator is by the acquiescence of the people. I needed to stand up and be counted. I did not want the forces of the law to do my bidding. Unfortunately, every general needs an army, and the only recruits awaiting me – although I didn't know it at that particular moment – were the Dixon brothers, sitting in a pub in the East End.

We cruised through the city on that fateful evening, through Whitechapel and down the Mile End Road. The pub was packed to the gills, and peroxide blondes in white, high-heeled shoes were everywhere. I ordered a gin and tonic, and an orange juice for Phil, while he elbowed his way through the crowd to find the boys. They materialised like two battleships in the night, menacing and powerful.

'What's yer problem?' they asked.

The expressions on their faces never revealed whether they thought I was a friend or foe.

'Gotta problem then, have you?'

'Er ... yes,' I stumbled.

'Who izit, then? We'll sort it out for you.'

It was at that precise moment I knew that as much as I needed an army, these were not the troops I was looking for. These guys wanted revenge – I only dreamed of it. I paid my respects and left. This was all too much for me to handle. We drove back through the hurly burly of the West End, my only pleasure being that I'd managed to extricate myself from my stupidity. Fortunately, I had not mentioned who I thought was threatening me, so there was no question of the Dixons going off and doing anything on my behalf.

For reasons that I have never ascertained, the threats grew less over the next few days, and finally, within a week, they stopped. One of the reasons may have been that whoever was on the other end of the telephone was now getting more verbal abuse from me each time he rang.

The whole episode was about to be dispatched onto the pyre of rock 'n' roll history, when about a month later my phone rang in the office and Cora explained guardedly that some friends of mine from the East End wanted to speak to me.

'Bryan, how are ya, my son? It's the Dixon bruvvers 'ere.'

'I'm all right, but why are you ringing me?' I enquired nervously.

Well, the truth was (so they said) that they'd just 'come up West' to get some business done and had decided to give me a ring to see how I was. I immediately grabbed the opportunity to assure them that the problem I'd mentioned to them had long since ceased to exist.

'Everything's sorted out, but thanks for calling. Good luck, and I'll see you one day.'

'Hang on, hang on, Bryan. Hold up son, we wanna come and see you,' commanded the voice defiantly at the other end of the telephone. 'We only wanna come up and say 'ello, Brysey. No big deal.'

With no room to manoeuvre, I gave in and told them the address.

'We'll be round in two minutes.'

And never was a truer word spoken. The sound of giants echoed up the stairs of my office as the brothers and their henchmen lurched towards me.

The first one who entered slid sideways through the door of my office, his massive frame unable to pass through on a full-frontal. He didn't so much stoop as bend his head forward to avoid the upright of the door. If this man had passed you in a park on a sunny day, he would have caused a total eclipse of the sun. He was followed in by the brothers, one smiling from ear to ear and the other looking as mean as ever. The non-smiling one I'd guess was about five-foot-six square.

The three of them arranged themselves on the various sofas and chairs in my office. One of the brothers soon made it apparent that what he really wanted to be was a singer and even asked me if he had any chance of making a record one day.

I have to say that in spite of their physical menace, the two brothers had a certain boyish charm about them. Their associate, the blond one, however, was pure evil. After three or four minutes, he suddenly placed his arm on the side of the chair and began tearing at the soft leather in the way that a vulture might tear at his fallen prey. Within minutes, his fingernails had gouged a six-inch-long streak. All I felt was a sickening emotion that was welling up inside me.

'There's only one way to deal with geezers that threaten you. You gotta take an arm or a leg off,' he sneered. 'That way, they won't forget about you.'

I snapped back into the present, and the words, 'Look, that's all over now,' fell from my lips. 'Please will you go now?'

'Listen, Brysey,' five-foot-square said, 'it cost us a few bob to come up here today. How about a hundred 'n' fifty quid in exes and we'll be gone.'

I knew it was pointless to say no but, nevertheless, that's what I said.

'Come on,' he replied. 'How about fifty quid then and we promise you it'll be the last you see of us. That's unless you get us a record contract and want us to record for you.'

I have to say, I still have a soft spot for the brothers who, in their own way, were East End gents. Reluctantly I handed over £50 and they left. To give them their due, they were as good as their word and nothing more was heard from them until some six months later.

It was about 1.30 in the afternoon and we were all about our business when two squad cars with a number of plainclothes policemen arrived in their vehicles outside of our office in Bruton Place. They poured into the next-door office, where they tried to arrest the managing director who, fortunately for him, was not in that day.

They left empty-handed, but promised to return the next day to interview him. It turned out, after Cora had gone next door to see what the fracas was all about, that the police were looking to interview someone by the name of Peter, who they had reason to believe had a meeting some months previous with some rather large gentlemen.

Now, as I explained earlier, I had once employed Peter Barnes, but I had also had a meeting with some men fitting that description many months before. So when the police arrived the next day, I boldly stepped forward and suggested that I was possibly the person they were seeking.

It took only a few minutes for the CID officers present to ascertain that I was indeed the one they were looking for, or in police jargon, 'the one they wished to interview'.

'Can you come with us, please, sir?'

'Well, can't you do whatever it is here?' was my hapless reply.

'Sir, please.'

With that, he pointed towards the door and we headed down to the street. It just so happened that my Aston Martin was parked outside of the office. I walked towards it, assuming that I would follow them in my car to wherever we were going.

'Leave your car.'

'But I thought I'd follow you.'

'No, just leave your car, sir, and come with us.'

I didn't like the way he said 'sir' and had an uneasy feeling that events were beginning to take a turn for the worse. This thought was immediately clarified when I found myself in the back of the car, squeezed between two plainclothes CID officers. A cop at each shoulder, the car suddenly accelerated with the urgency of a Formula 1 driver at the start of a Grand Prix.

We screeched down Bruton Place, barely missing the two bollards at the end of the mews by inches. This fast right-hander took us to the junction with Bruton Street. Normally cars pause or come to a complete stop here, principally to give the driver a view of oncoming traffic. This formality, however, was not deemed necessary, and set the scene for the rest of the journey across London.

These guys were not simply late for tea – they were on a mission. They also operated under a completely different set of motoring laws than the rest of us mere mortals: overtaking into oncoming traffic, and ignoring all road signs, particularly those annoying little stop lights that tend to proliferate around major junctions.

We finally reached the relative tranquillity of Westminster Bridge and another few hundred yards later we screeched to a halt in front of a nondescript building that went by the name of Tintagel House. For the uninitiated, let me explain. In the late sixties, this anonymous edifice, on the opposite side of the Thames from the Houses of Parliament, was home to the Metropolitan Police and its serious, nay, very serious, crime squad.

I was hustled out of the car and up to the second or third floor, my state of mind at the time being extremely confused – I really didn't know if I was coming or going. A door was thrown open and I was shown into a room, long and fairly narrow with one solitary window at the end showing a glimpse of the Thames.

The room held a dozen or so men and there was a faint smell of sweat and cigarettes. They all either sat or lounged around against walls, some hands in pockets, but each one's eyes locking in on me as I entered their realm. Suddenly the tension disappeared, and I was addressed in an almost polite manner by one of them, who turned out to be Chief Superintendent Wickstead of Scotland Yard, known as 'The Old Grey Fox'. He introduced the men in rapid succession – all manner of supers, chiefs, and commanders. The list was reeled off and, each time, one of the faces nodded to me in some form of acknowledgement.

'Sit down, please.'

'Watcha been up to, then?' one of them asked.

I looked from side to side, wondering whether this question had been directed at me, or was merely the tail end of some discussion that had taken place before my entry. The question was asked again. This time I realised that it was me they were addressing. I remember having a momentary but hilarious thought: maybe they wanted to know what I'd had for breakfast, or who'd been the object of my desire the previous night.

'Bryan,' the voice came again, fired like an arrow from a crossbow. 'Why were the Dixon brothers in your office?'

'Who? Who?' I spluttered.

Petulantly now, he repeated the question.

'The Dixons. The little team that came to see you a few months ago.'

'Oh yes, them. You mean, you've brought me here because of them?'

My demeanour suddenly changed from obsequiousness to indignation.

'Are you telling me that you've brought me here, wasted my time, gone through all this charade, just because a couple of East End boys came to my office for a chat? This whole thing is bloody ridiculous.'

They carried on questioning me for another twenty minutes before it became apparent that, in spite of my protestations, the gentlemen on the other side of the table were not particularly impressed. My ramblings were cut short by a senior detective, who signalled to the rest of the men in the room to go out and take tea.

They departed and I was left in this friendless room with nothing but a few chairs, a table, and old Father Thames flowing by outside. Oh, and one policeman. I shuffled over to the solitary window and peered at the flowing river. On the other side was the Tate Gallery, a place of such joy to me over the years.

'What kind of business are you in?' he asked suddenly.

'Rock 'n' roll,' I replied. I think I denoted a sign of interest flash across his face. 'Look, more importantly, what am I doing here, and when will I be able to leave?' With a show of bravado, I added, 'If this is a joke, it's wearing a bit thin.'

'Leave?' He leant forward across the table. 'Are you off your rocker?'

With a voice one-part menacing, one-part kindness, he proceeded to tell me they had reason to believe that the Dixons were involved in a Conspiracy to Murder, and that if I didn't cooperate I would find myself embroiled in the whole case.

His words burned through my brain, and there were brightly coloured stars exploding before my eyes, spelling out the words like a firework display – *Conspiracy to Murder*. I repeated them two or three times standing in front of the solitary window, and suddenly the Thames seemed to stop flowing, and this lifeless room became a morgue.

Half a minute later and I was still unable to fully comprehend what was going on around me. I was dumbfounded. The sprockets of the film in my mind slowed down to a mere thirty-five frames a minute, and the mental picture was of a deep, dark and filthy dungeon; my hair long, white and tatty, and a thin, bony hand clutching a piece of hard, gnarled bread. The soundtrack was repetitious: fifteen years, fifteen years. That's what people got if convicted of this criminal act.

I turned back into the room and saw the face of my judge and executioner, who had uttered those terrible words. At that moment they had achieved what they'd set out to do. They had put the fear of God in me, so they could obtain a piece of the jigsaw that was missing. The door of my cell reopened and in they marched. Those twelve just men and true.

Wickstead pulled out a chair and plonked himself down on my right side, making a very sharp observation.

'You're looking a bit white and peaky, Bryan. Anything the matter?'

'Well, what do you think?'

I pointed towards my potential jailer.

'He just told me that you think I was involved in a crime that could carry up to a fifteen-year jail sentence.'

'No, no, Bryan. We're not suggesting that you're guilty of any crime. It's just that the people who came to see you are hardened criminals, and we have reason to believe they came to see you for more than just a drink.'

This had now gone far enough and although I was scared stiff I knew I'd done nothing wrong. What I wasn't aware of was how far the police were prepared to go, in order to get their convictions. I now started to resist.

'You're all crackers.'

And so I repeated the story of my visit to the East End, and the three of them coming to my office.

'Well, who threatened you then?' Wickstead asked.

'I don't see it as being relevant, because I never told the boys who it was that had been threatening me. I only told them that I might need their help one day.' Then I cut the conversation short, realising the mess I was getting myself into.

'Well, if you were being threatened, why didn't you come to us?'

Now here was the first logical question I'd heard, but I didn't have a logical answer.

'Why don't you just tell us the whole story?' he said.

At this point or probably much earlier, I should have done what they do in the crime novels and movies, and that was refuse to utter another word until I was in the presence of my lawyer. This simple request would have saved me all the trouble that I'd got myself into, but, in retrospect, it wouldn't have made such an interesting story. Having nothing to hide, I then told them the whole story, making it clear throughout that the Dixons knew nothing of who was threatening me, namely, the friends of the Bee Gees or whomever.

I was allowed to leave about an hour later. By the time I arrived back at the office, the only thing I had been charged with was the taxi fare home.

It was shortly after this that I learnt the Dixon brothers were not simply a couple of ordinary dudes who did a bit of housebreaking; they were more into arm and leg breaking. Such was their burgeoning notoriety that they were fast becoming the gang to fill the vacuum left by the Krays. This was the reason that the police wanted to nail them, before they got too powerful.

I remember Wickstead telling me a story about when the police had pulled in the Krays. They had sat in a room filled with the top officers in the land, around the same table. The Krays were so established in London at this point that the police were about to lose control. In fact, so assured were the twins of their invincibility at this meeting, they proclaimed that they would put away Detective Chief Superintendent 'Nipper' Read, of the Met's Murder Squad, before he managed to do the same to them. This was the justification for the police coming down so hard on the Dixon brothers.

It was some nine months later when the Dixon brothers and their mates were put on trial at the Old Bailey on assorted charges. I'd never actually seen the Old Bailey before, and it turned out to be a cavernous and austere building, where many a black cloth had been placed on a judge's white wig before the pronouncement of death by hanging. It was not until the second day of the Dixons' trial that the pieces of the jigsaw started fitting together.

The six accused were standing bolt upright in the dock, their physical presence almost bursting out like a soufflé in a hot oven. They had all spent the best part of the morning grinning and postulating, in constant communication with their briefs. By the end of a long morning, the Crown's case was beginning to wear thin and a sense of victory could be felt in the dock. Suddenly, to the amazement of the entire ensemble, the Crown announced its star witness.

In the box, six bodies stiffened, the air was electric and all eyes were riveted to a small wooden door that stood in the corner of the courtroom. It opened sharply, pulled with some force from within, and standing silhouetted in the doorway was the same figure that had more than amply filled the uprights of my office.

Pandemonium broke out in the courtroom and within two seconds of his entry two defendants had managed to get a leg or two over the dock before being roughly manhandled and squeezed back in like corks into a bottle. The judge started whacking his gavel up and down like a blacksmith with a wig, and having about as much effect – the commotion swept like a wave over the room. If looks could kill, if clawing hands could throttle, then our new witness would have been saying his prayers.

Thirty seconds had now passed and a new dimension was in play. It was not action now, but voices, which could be heard in an ever-increasing crescendo: 'You fuckin' bastard!' – 'Squealer!' – 'Grass!' The six in the box were joined by a dozen in the public gallery, all shouting obscenities as fast as their nervous systems could handle.

At about forty-five seconds, inaudible at first but then rising to a majestic soprano, was the voice of our judge, ringing out like a town crier, 'Order in court, order in court!'

Which surprised me somewhat, as I thought this sort of thing happened only in Hollywood films. After about a minute, two of the several briefs were searching their desks for the wigs that had slid from their heads in the chaos. Others were attempting to placate clients or the assembled relatives, while the clerks and several policemen were restoring order.

Finally, as a civilised dignity settled like a shroud over the ensemble, the raison d'être for this commotion became clear. The big one, the one that blocked out light, the one who stood in doorways and was now standing in the witness box, had turned Queen's evidence and was testifying for the prosecution.

I was to hear later that this supergrass had not behaved with the required etiquette and decorum when squiring a female member of the Dixon clan, and had been duly castigated. His motives never becoming quite clear, he had then turned from the hunter to the hunted. The evidence that he gave that day and in the ensuing days was to put all of his mates in the clanger for up to ten years.

I learnt that he was given a new name and number and, like many who'd travelled the same road before him, was to be relocated in some far-off and dusty corner of this earth – Australia being a favourite stop. It would seem that history repeats itself, or maybe the Australians just like ex-convicts. Of course, this was fodder for the national press, who had rightly covered the trial for days. The police now had what they wanted, I was both physically and mentally exhausted, and the Bee Gees and their management were not too happy.

I had been used by the police to catch a much bigger fish. No one was particularly interested about the threatening phone calls; they disappeared into the mist. The Bee Gees were back together and shortly afterwards recorded one of the biggest albums ever created, *Saturday Night Fever*, and it had really been just that. A Saturday night fever.

The police told me later that on the day I arrived at Tintagel House they had no idea who the third party was and without a third party there can be no conspiracy. However, after I had mentioned the Bee Gees, they had their third party. The police were trying to build a story as they needed to put the Dixons away and, fortunately for them, the big one achieved this.

The in-fighting with Robin Gibb did not terminate at this juncture, but at least from here on it was conducted with due legal process.

● ● ●

The Dixon Gang were not exactly the 'East End gents' that Bryan has recalled so fondly. The gang consisted of the brothers George, Alan and Brian Dixon, along with Mike Young, Mike Bailey, Leo Carlton and Philip Jacobs, who was their leader. Jacobs was a short man, who became known as 'Little Caesar', after the way he forcefully took over much of the Kray twins' pub and club protection racket. George and Alan Dixon had themselves been one-time associates of the Krays, before they had a falling out.

In July 1972, Jacobs and the rest of the Dixon gang were convicted at the Old Bailey of blackmail, conspiracy to blackmail, assault, grievous bodily harm and other kindred offences, and received prison sentences totalling sixty-one years.

THE MADCAP LAUGHS

While all of this was going on, Syd Barrett had disappeared and was living in a state of suspension. Within months of his departure from Pink Floyd, Syd had installed himself in the London Hilton hotel, on Park Lane. The room had three televisions, which were on constantly, plus a dozen guitars laying scattered around the room. Syd Barrett became the Howard Hughes of rock 'n' roll, running up a weekly bill that made us look like paupers. He had made a fortune and was now spending it at a rate of knots. By the end of 1968, Syd had recovered a certain degree of his health, and was enjoying a slightly more normal existence, although he was still prone to the occasional freak out.

One day his solitary existence came to an end, he ventured out and showed up at my office in Bruton Place. He had two things on his mind that day. The first was money and, secondly, he wanted to get back into rock 'n' roll and he needed a manager to look after his fast depleting affairs. So, I took over, and looked after him as best I could. A few weeks passed before Syd mentioned in passing that he'd written some new songs. I duly published these songs, which later made up the two albums *The Madcap Laughs* and *Barrett*.

One of the suggestions that had been bouncing around for some time was the idea of trying to get Syd to record an album. It would be a near impossible venture, but on the other hand, now was the time he should attempt it, as it was becoming abundantly clear that Syd might once again slip back into his dream world.

The songs he had written were wonderful and spoke of simplicity, with titles such as 'Effervescing Elephant' and 'Terrapin'. The obvious problem was the recording of these songs, because of Syd's short concentration span; in rehearsal he tended to sing a verse and then drift off into his reverie for minutes or even hours on end.

Anyway, EMI were very keen on making this album. Malcom Jones, head of its new Harvest label, agreed to produce it and on the appointed day in April 1969 we all arrived at Abbey Road studios and got started. The first day's production passed fairly peacefully with Syd working away in the studio; however, my worst fears began to materialise, because Syd's lack of concentration led to him randomly falling asleep, or just staring into space. One of the ideas that we used was to keep the tape running when Syd was in the studio, so that whenever he managed to get his act together, we could pick up a line, a verse, or maybe even half a song for posterity.

On one occasion, Syd was sitting on a three-legged stool in front of the microphone. We were observing him through the glass window of the control room, when halfway through the second verse of a song, we saw Syd slowly and surely fall asleep. As the last words came from his lips, his eyes closed for the third and final time, and Syd, the stool and the microphone went crashing to the floor. The amazing thing was that on impact, he didn't awake – he simply lay there on the floor, peacefully asleep, for the next thirty minutes.

This process was to continue for a further two or three weeks, and all credit must be given to the producer, Malcolm Jones, for his patience and understanding, and for producing one of the most outstanding albums, made under such duress. I am aware that Malcolm has a different take on the proceedings, but I was present at many of these days spent at Abbey Road and I witnessed the above first-hand. Who knows, the tortured and pained mind that created these musical gems may one day be likened to Van Gogh and his last desperate canvasses.

The two albums that were finally salvaged from these sessions have become two classics, in my opinion: *The Madcap Laughs* and *Barrett*. The first of these albums, *Madcap*, was released by EMI in January 1970, followed by *Barrett* in November of the same year. Eventually, EMI released Syd from his record contract about two years later. In fact, sometime after that I signed Syd to a new recording deal, but by then he had given up all interest in being involved in the music industry.

One of the functions that we were to perform for Syd was as a collector and distributor of his money. He was now, because of the incredible popularity of Pink Floyd, earning a considerable sum annually. Royalties were paid twice-yearly and it was about four months into one of these periods when Syd turned up one morning at the Lupus Music office to ask me if I could advance him some cash, which could then be deducted from his next royalty payment.

This posed me absolutely no problems. However, there was one hard and fast rule that had to be adhered to, because Cora, my PA, was a stickler for recording each and every cash transaction that took place. No matter how much money Syd borrowed at any one time, he would have to sign a receipt for the same.

Over the next six weeks, this borrowing became a regular process. Each time the same ritual – on handing over the cash, a receipt was obtained and signed by Syd. Weeks later, a rather large cheque arrived from Essex Music for Syd's royalties. The amount was more than enough to cover his advances. Cora rang him and told him of his good fortune, and that if he came in we would hand over the money.

When he eventually arrived a few hours later, I handed Syd the Essex Music cheque and asked him if he would reimburse me the money he owed. Unfortunately, at this point Syd suffered a memory lapse and adamantly denied ever borrowing or having any knowledge of the money that we had paid him over the last few weeks.

'But Syd, we've got signed receipts,' I said.

'No, no,' Syd insisted, 'I never sign anything these days, I never sign anything anymore.'

'Cora!' I bellowed. 'Show Syd those bloody receipts, will you?'

Each of the receipts were for between £100 and £500.

Cora produced a dozen or more receipts totalling in the region of £5-6,000. Evidently somewhat surprised, Syd seized the proffered invoices, and immediately retired into a corner of the office to peruse them, like some kind of absent-minded professor, checking his notes on the theory of relativity. Three or four minutes passed in silence when suddenly and triumphantly, Syd jumped up throwing his arms wildly in the air, waving the receipts like one of Admiral Nelson's flagmen.

'They're forgeries. These are all rotten forgeries!' he exclaimed.

I looked up from my desk.

'What the fuck are you talking about?' came my equally emphatic reply.

'These are all forgeries. You never lent me any money, and this proves it.'

Exasperated, I said, 'What proves what?'

'Well, look. These two receipts are signed in red ink and the others are in black, and I've never used a red pen in my whole life.'

I snatched the two receipts back. They were indeed signed in red ink.

They also totalled a mere £450 of the £5–6,000 that I had lent him.

'Syd,' I said, 'if I wanted to rob you, there are many easier ways of doing it, and it certainly wouldn't be for a measly four hundred and fifty pounds.'

After all, the cheque I was about to hand over to him was pushing £20,000. A few minutes elapsed and it appeared that he finally understood the logic of this. In the meantime, Cora had been looking on incredulously at this soap opera being performed before her eyes. Syd finally wrote me out a cheque and left.

The rest of the day passed pretty uneventfully, until about seven o'clock that evening. Cora and I were about to leave to have a drink in the Guinea, when we heard a terrible row, as bumping and crashing sounds cascaded up the stairs. In an instant, someone was pounding on the door of the office. I walked over, opened it, and there was Syd, swaying but standing.

In the same moment, I realised that he was in the process of directing his right fist, with some force, towards my unprotected chin. My left hand shot up to try to deflect it as he was lunging forward when, to my absolute horror, he sank his teeth into my hand. Before you could say *The Madcap Laughs*, he was biting straight through to the bone of one of my fingers. I actually quite liked my fingers – all ten of them – and the thought of losing one was not terribly appealing.

'Stop, Syd! Stop!' I cried.

But he didn't. By now I could feel his teeth penetrating through to the bare bone, and in that instant I decided that enough was enough, and with my free right hand, I dealt him what could only be described as a humdinger. His jaw dropped open, my finger was freed, and he collapsed, pole-axed, on the floor. In anger, I leapt on him, preparing to do some terrible damage, when Syd suddenly started laughing. Not a laugh of joy, but an ever-increasing pitch of hysteria. I froze, and poor old Cora nearly fainted.

We didn't know what to do. He simply lay there for a few minutes, bumping up and down on the floor, foaming at the mouth. Having recovered our composure, Cora immediately dialled 999 to call for an ambulance, before we heaved him up onto a chair. Syd sat slumped for a minute or two, hardly moving, before suddenly jumping to his feet and dashing out of the office.

As much as I loved Syd, this was obviously totally unacceptable behaviour. For the second time in my business career, a fracas had taken place. I'm delighted to say that from that day to this, it has never been repeated. The next day, I ruefully sent a letter to Syd, explaining that all management and agency agreements between us were hereby terminated, although the few songs of his that I had published would remain in place.

Syd proceeded to turn up on the corner of Berkeley Square and Bruton Place for the next six months. For hours on end, he would stand there gazing into the middle distance towards our office. The sightings became less and less until he finally disappeared. He only came back to our office once, when he asked Cora if I would change my mind and once again become his manager. That was the last time either of us saw him. To the best of my knowledge, he lived a quiet and retired life somewhere in Cambridge.

It was the end of a saga that had been sometimes desperate, but at the same time thrilling for me, and so another rock 'n' roll genius faded, or maybe not, into obscurity.

It was around this time that the whole world was getting extremely excited about the forthcoming Olympics, which were due to take place in Munich in 1972. There had been talk for some time about the Chinese playing a much larger part in this Olympics than ever before; the Chinese obviously wanting to prove to the world that they could produce great athletes, besides bloody good food and Confucius.

It occurred to me that China was not at this time a partner in the world copyright convention, which meant that any song sold or played within China earnt zilch in royalties. Also, it meant that any song written in China could be copyrighted in the West and owned by the publisher. Well, I was always on the look-out for something amusing and, in this case, possibly lucrative.

I hit on the idea that if the Chinese went to the Olympics, you could be damn sure they were going to win gold. If this was to be the case, then many of their athletes would be standing on the winners' rostrum shedding a tear or two as their national anthem was played – and where would the world's TV cameras be? Well, of course, watching the flag go up to the accompaniment of the country's national anthem.

Now, music attracts PRS payments, and with hundreds of millions of viewers watching, that's an awful lot of lucre. I don't know the exact sum, it would depend on the length of performance and how many viewers there were, but for sure it would be in the tens of thousands. I would also have been the only person in the world owning a national anthem.

I went to Chinatown and rummaged around second-hand shops until, lo and behold, I discovered a very old, decrepit 78 rpm copy of 'The East Is Red', the Chinese national anthem. I immediately had the music transcribed and on 23 April 1970, I copyrighted the piece of music and sat back to wait for the Olympics.

Imagine my chagrin when, two years later, the first Chinese athlete to attain gold stood on the rostrum and the band played – however, it wasn't my piece of music. If you can believe it, they had changed their anthem, which is probably just as well. It saved me from being chased by some geezer with a meat cleaver once they realised that I owned it.

● ● ●

When Syd Barrett was borrowing large amounts of cash from Bryan Morrison, he was spending much of it on new guitars. It became almost an obsession, until he had about thirty of them. One day, he mentioned to Cora Jackman that he was now living in the Penta Hotel, a massive new hotel opposite the West London Air Terminal on Cromwell Road. He told her, 'It's great there. You pick up the phone and ask for something and they bring it.'

When she asked how much it was costing him, he replied, 'Oh, I think I can afford it.'

Cora rented a flat for him in Chelsea Cloisters in Sloane Avenue for £20 a week and arranged for a van to collect all his guitars and other belongings from the hotel. When she saw Syd a few weeks later, she asked him how he was enjoying the flat. He said, 'It's great, Cora. I've got all my guitars in there. But I don't live there … I still live at the Penta!'

Barrett finally moved into his flat on the ninth floor of Chelsea Cloisters and stayed there from late 1974 until 1982, when he left London for Cambridge. Almost nothing is known about those years. In his excellent book, Syd Barrett: A Very Irregular Head, *Rob Chapman recounts how friends who tried to visit him there were often turned away, or found his living conditions so unsanitary and his behaviour so unsettling that they had to leave. It appeared that Barrett was isolating himself from his friends, his family, and the world.*

In 1982, he returned home to Cambridge to live with his elderly mother, Win, in her three-bedroom, semi-detached house in Cherry Hinton, a village four miles from Cambridge city centre. By then he had stopped using the name Syd and reverted to his real name of Roger Keith Barrett. After his mother's death in 1991, he lived a solitary life and renewed his schoolboy interest in painting, although he did venture out on his bicycle to go to his local Sainsbury's supermarket, or to the pub.

Barrett suffered from chronic stomach problems and he also developed type 2 diabetes. In May 2006, he was admitted to Addenbrooke's Hospital in Cambridge, where he was diagnosed with inoperable pancreatic cancer, and he died at his home on 7 July 2006, aged sixty.

It was only nine days before Bryan had his life-changing polo accident.

HAVE A CIGAR!

12

ART FOR ART'S SAKE

By 1970, in spite of my apparent disdain for money, I seemed to be enjoying its fruits, with a beautiful Grade II-listed, sixteenth-century manor house in Oxted, Surrey, and a pied-à-terre in London with all the various accoutrements. The only thing that I needed to complete the picture was a wife and family.

I suppose in the end it happens to all bachelors. The ever-constant regime of a new woman, a new bed, and waking up in the middle of the night in an icy state, not knowing whether you're on planet Earth or Venus. I remember once reading: 'A man's mind and body are not purged until he has woken up at least once with a woman by his side, whose name he doesn't know.'

By the time I was twenty-eight years old, I had experienced this once too often and I was now ready to change course.

I saw her in an advertisement in a magazine one day. This vision of beauty – a woman of such sexual poise, with sensual lips and a wonderful face, haloed by golden hair the colour of wheat. The advertisement was for Smirnoff vodka and she was astride a horse on a long beach. I became immediately besotted. Through friends in the advertising industry, I soon discovered who this paragon of beauty was.

Her name was Greta van Rantwyk and after about three months of manoeuvring we had dinner in a restaurant in Beauchamp Place. Everything was set for the birth of one of those great eternal love stories – the candles, the food, the wine. Everything was perfect, or was it?

There was one small detail that I hadn't counted on – it seemed she wasn't too keen on me. Later, I was to discover that she felt I was too flash. My black leather clothing, zip-up jacket and tight-fitting trousers, plus the black Aston Martin DB7 sitting by the front door, were simply too much. She was probably right; I was a bit flash.

I was not to see her again for quite some time. It was almost two years later when I was invited by some mutual friends to dinner in Bayswater and, as luck would have it, Greta turned out to be one of the dinner guests. This second meeting turned out to be far more successful than the first. By evening's end it was love, if not at first sight, then at second.

I was due to go to Rome for a wedding the next day, but was able to persuade her to join me there in four or five days' time. I intended driving to Rome in my brand-new Rolls-Royce, which I had bought as my dream gift for my thirtieth birthday.

OK, she was right. I was flash.

I set off next day on the Grand Tour, via the RN 7, stopping at the Hotel de la Poste, where Napoleon had stopped many years previously on the way to his various conquests.

Once in Rome, it didn't take long to get into the customs of this wonderful Italian city. In fact, on the first night of my stay in the hotel Parco dei Principi, I was to behold one of the great traditions of Italy – lifting radios from cars.

I had been told by the hotel management that under no circumstances should I leave my car on the road, or the outside car park, so on my first night I stored the black Rolls in the hotel's underground car park, which I was assured would be locked and bolted at 11 p.m.

The next morning, I was awoken by an over-excited member of the hotel staff, jumping up and down.

'Signor Morrison, excuza me, but your car in the garage – it eez smashed up. Pleeza come fast!'

I threw on a pair of jeans and tore downstairs, where I was joined by the hotel manager. I arrived in an underground car park filled with the crème de la crème of automobiles: Ferraris, Maseratis, BMWs and Mercedes and, of course, my Rolls. Shattered glass lay everywhere. Rear doors, drivers' doors, passengers' doors – all were open or askew.

Quarter-lights smashed, windscreens crushed – it was complete devastation; their interiors were now a mass of tangled wires and jack plugs, left dangling in the air without their radios. Wincing in anticipation, I walked over to my Rolls, and then I stopped dead.

For some inexplicable reason, instead of smashing the windows or prising the doors open, they'd merely cut the rubber surround off the windscreen and taken it out in one piece, before gingerly stowing it by the side of the car. Why, I have no idea – maybe even they couldn't rape this great piece of British engineering. The radio was gone, but I was able to have the windscreen put back within twenty-four hours.

What was even more amazing was that the thieves had not come through the steel doors, but through a ventilation shaft some twelve feet above the floor. My first baptism into car theft, Italian style.

Greta arrived the next day and after picking her up we hit the road for Portofino and the fabulous Hotel Splendido, where we had lunch in the beautiful quayside restaurant. The sea was a dark cobalt blue, flowers of all shapes and sizes danced and bent their heads in the gentle breeze, and yachts bobbed tugging on their umbilical cords that attached them to the quay.

She sat there, with her long blonde hair and that classical smile, the catalyst that created beauty for the day. I told Gret (as she was now called) that we would be married by December. She accepted and within twenty-four hours of our meeting, we had made a commitment to marry. All those thoughts for years about who she might be, what she would look like, the touch of her skin, the voice – indeed, would it ever happen? All these questions were answered in a matter of minutes. It seemed a perfect match.

We were married on 12 December 1972, and the reception was held in the Hyde Park Hotel, now known as the Mandarin Oriental Hyde Park. The one mistake that I made was having my stag night on the eve of the wedding. Of course, I went completely crackers for the whole night, finally falling asleep at half past six, only to rise a couple of hours later to prepare for my big day.

Come the evening, I was so tired I remember very little about our party, though I am told it was a great success. Greta was beautiful, intelligent, and making a fortune – what I didn't know then was that this apparent fortune was going to dry up the day after I married her, as she'd had her fill of the glamour of high fashion and photography.

She stopped working soon afterwards and the only monetary equation was not one of profit, but loss. Within months of that December day, I had to pay out a small fortune in back taxes for her. However, Greta was influential in changing the course of my business career. It was time for something to be completely different.

In the early seventies, I felt the music business was going through some kind of metamorphosis. It had started to lose its way, creativity was drying up, and few new artists were making it. We had entered a new era of the 'supergroups', individual artists of great proficiency who had already achieved fame or respect in other bands, and were now getting together to form supergroups.

The term took its name from the 1968 album *Super Session*, with Al Kooper, Mike Bloomfield and Stephen Stills. These bands made great music, like Crosby, Stills, Nash & Young, Cream, and Yes, to mention a few, but my interest had always been in finding new artists. As this source was now drying up, I found myself enjoying more and more the haven and the daily flow of NEMS, which was rather more interesting than the pursuit of unknown bands, who had ceased to exist. I must say that the last seven months I spent in 3 Hill Street bring back very fond memories.

Don Black, who wrote the lyrics to 'Born Free', 'To Sir with Love' and 'Diamonds Are Forever', among many others, constantly amused me with his quick-witted stories and one-liners. Don was a great friend of Vic Lewis, and manager of the singer Matt Monro, and he was often around as Vic went about his everyday business, with his artists, in his personal fiefdom. I was always the outsider looking in on his grand and opulent office, with his two pretty secretaries guarding first the outer and then the inner sanctum doors.

Vic loved his opulence and thrived on precision. He nearly always wore a well-cut, dark blue suit, or a blazer and flannels, with a tie of the finest silk. Tea was served punctually at 4 p.m., a habit that in all my years I've never seen portrayed so earnestly. It was served as it should be: Earl Grey, Orange Pekoe, Darjeeling or Indian, with fine bone china tea cups, teapots and milk jugs; a pat or two of butter lying like small yellow suns next to the perfectly produced scones and regimentally aligned slices of toast. All of this nestling on a fine crisp Irish linen cloth.

When taking his lunch or dinner, Vic would only patronise those restaurants where he was well known to the management. I had many a giggle when eating with him, while eying the obsequiousness that these waiters displayed. The finest food, finest wine and always tea, never coffee. The jokes, the stories, the reminiscing of his days as a bandleader in the fifties and sixties – this was the way I was to ride out the years of 1971 and 1972, the last years I was to be actively involved in rock 'n' roll until 1976.

I now craved something different. I was quite well off and had been quietly indulging myself in one of my principal passions, the collection of art and artefacts. I always get a particular kick when an unknown painter, whose work I'd bought for nothing years ago, becomes a star, or when I can use their success for a bit of one-upmanship. It didn't take long for me to turn this passion for art into a new business.

In 1972, along with Rodney Kinsman, my old compadré from the Central School of Art, and the art dealer Bernard Jacobson as our working partner, we set up a gallery in Maddox Street. It was to be called the Jacobson Kinsman Morrison Gallery. It was a beautiful space – dark mahogany wooden floors, high ceilings, and a rear gallery that had a vaulted glass atrium. The gallery specialised in modern prints. By the early seventies, more and more people were clamouring to buy good art, but the prices were becoming unobtainable. The natural progression was to buy limited edition, signed prints.

Of course, the art of the printmaker had been around for centuries and many great editions had been published, including 'The Vollard Suite' by Picasso and 'Elles' by Toulouse Lautrec, the latter being for me the greatest exponent of this movement.

So we rode the wave by selling modern prints by Hockney, Lichtenstein, Oldenburg, Caulfield, William Tillyer and Ivor Abrahams. For me there was one truly great print artist and painter of this period and that was David Hockney. I personally rate his 'Celia' from 1973 as one of the great masterpieces of art. The fluidity of his line for me matches the genius of Lautrec and Picasso.

So, with all this demand, an even greater profusion of screen prints, lithograph wood block, and every other medium was used to satisfy the growing avarice of the buying public. Inevitably, in many cases the currency was debased as more and more publishers put out even larger editions, sometimes up to as much as a thousand units. I remember seeing an advert in one of the Sunday colour supplements that boasted of a unique print, which was limited to only ten thousand impressions. It all started to get a bit like Germany in the twenties and the hyperinflation in the Weimar Republic.

The ultimate failure of the modern print market is all said with the benefit of hindsight. If it had been looked at logically, we probably wouldn't have started the gallery in the first place. In 1972, of course, we were not to know this, and so we went into the business 'gung-ho'.

One of the first important buying decisions we had to make was whether to invest heavily in any one particular artist. We all favoured Hockney, but finally we decided that Patrick Caulfield was our man.

I was visiting the office of the music publisher Freddy Bienstock. He had picked me up in his Rolls and we were driving around Berkeley Square.

Freddy was one of the most successful independent music publishers of the day, and his principal company was called Carlin Music. I remember him telling me on this occasion that he owned 56,000 songs – this was before he bought Chappell Music in 1984, which increased his ownership of songs by about 400,000.

'Bryan,' he said, in his slightly Eastern European accent, 'I have all these songs, but only twenty great ones. I should sell the rest and retire on my Evergreens.'

I had about 600 songs at this time and I think one great one, which left rather an imbalance in my mind, and gave me some idea of how far I still had to go to become a music publisher. About ten minutes later, sitting gazing around his office, my eyes suddenly alighted onto an abstract painting.

'That's nice,' I murmured.

'You like the painting?'

Yes,' I said, 'it's excellent. I've always loved Appel.'

He looked at me for a second with total amazement, before asking me how I was familiar with this little-known artist in England. I explained that I was an avid collector and had also studied art for five years.

'Well,' he said, 'I paid £30,000 for that, Bryan.'

'Did you Fred?' I replied. 'I've got a similar one that cost me £150.' I had purchased mine back in 1960.

His jaw dropped open and, momentarily at least, I had redressed the balance between his 56,000 songs and my 600.

Being a great lover of Patrick Caulfield, I owned at the time two of his paintings, including one of his masterpieces, a painting entitled 'Santa Margherita Ligure, 1964', which together with another of his paintings, 'Boats at Brindisi', ranked Caulfield, for me, as one of the great English painters to come out of the sixties.

There was in fact a less amusing story attached to my masterpiece. One day the Tate Gallery wrote to inform me that they were about to put on a major retrospective of Caulfield's work, and they asked me if I could lend them 'Santa Margherita Ligure, 1964' for this exhibition.

This was a difficult decision for me as I had looked after, loved and cherished this painting for more than ten years, moving it from pillar to post. In the end the painting was duly dispatched to the Tate, and nothing was heard for several weeks until the fateful day when I received a telephone call from them.

'Mr Morrison? Ramsbottom here.' (Not his actual name, but I've forgotten what it was.) 'Sorry, sir, but we have some bad news for you.'

A thousand different scenarios flashed through my mind as to what could have happened to my beloved painting and I realised that I was gripping the receiver very tightly.

'Well, actually, sir ...,' he stammered, 'we were photographing it propped on two easels, and it just slipped off and hit the floor!'

I should say at this point that the painting was not on canvas, but instead on a form of hardboard. I remember thinking that it was a bloody good job that the Tate wasn't around at the time of Leonardo or Michelangelo because if it had been there would be nothing left for posterity. The painting was damaged and I was duly paid out by the insurance company, but no amount of money could ever make up for the loss of my painting.

Years later I was approached again by the Tate, this time to borrow a picture by Peter Blake. Boldly, I took the plunge and lent it to them. I am glad to report that it came back in one piece.

Back at the Jacobson Kinsman Morrison Gallery, the next two years were gloriously full of exhibitions featuring everything from Art Deco jukeboxes and Toulouse Lautrec prints, to Californian orange-box labels. The interesting thing about the latter two exhibitions was that the Lautrec exhibition was one of the finest collections of an artist's work to be put together for decades. We had some thirty different prints on show and although the exhibition received extensive publicity I doubt if even three hundred people came in to see it. In 1991, the Royal Academy of Arts in Piccadilly put on a similar Lautrec show, the main difference being that hundreds of thousands of people poured in to see it.

By contrast, our orange box show was a sensation. Two American students ventured into the gallery one day, carrying with them three or four boxes of assorted orange-box labels from California. Back in the forties and fifties, colourful crate labels were one of the keys to marketing citrus fruit. At first, these labels only identified the contents and packer, but soon they became small advertising posters. A well-designed label with a distinctive slogan or image would attract buyers and ensure a profitable season.

Today these labels are considered among the twentieth century's best graphic designs and are highly sought by collectors of advertising art and local history. The kids assured me that they could procure a couple of thousand if needed and so we organised an exhibition.

Our humble showing got a very small mention in the *Observer* one Sunday.

The following Monday morning, we had a queue a hundred feet long outside of the gallery, almost beating down the doors to get in. Not only did we sell hundreds of these works of art but in the course of the exhibition literally thousands of people poured in through our hallowed portal.

Having recently visited the 1990 Velázquez exhibition at the Museo del Prado in Madrid, where I witnessed daily a queue that took six hours, with people four abreast stretching for half a mile, I can only assume that the general public's perception of art and its importance in our lives has finally personified itself. The intriguing thing is that all these people could have gone to the Prado prior to the exhibition, or after, walked in without a moment's delay, and seen probably eighty per cent of Diego Velázquez's work, as they are all owned by the museum. Once again, the power of publicity. Still, I have never seen such beauty, such foresight, and such individuality in my life as I did in that exhibition.

The Jacobson Kinsman Morrison Gallery finally closed its doors in the mid-seventies, unable to compete in a market where modern prints lay as thick on the ground as the ticker tape after a Wall Street parade. Today the wonderful space we once occupied in Maddox Street is a Chinese restaurant. I suppose the reader might think of me as a butterfly, as I flit from business to business. The reason for this, I suppose, is my passion to achieve the best, whether in music, art, fashion or latterly the polo club.

Never was there so much as a thought about selling an inferior product regardless of its potential. In those heady years, business was always about a passion to create, and never one that was money led; it was only a tool to be used to prolong the buzz of creativity. Given the same set of circumstances today, I would not change a single thing. I loved every moment of it.

The art gallery was not the only business venture that Rodney and I embarked upon together; many years earlier we had set up a modern furniture company called OMK Design Ltd.

I was the M and Rodney the K, and the third partner in this venture, the O in OMK, was Jurek Olejnik. We had all been at Central School of Art together. As I explained earlier, I had left Central School early to manage the Pretty Things. Six or seven months later, I was in the enviable position of having not only enough money to enjoy myself, but also some spare cash for investment.

It was decided in 1965 that the three of us would form this new company based on our initials OMK, which for some reason sounded Scandinavian, a country that dominated the furniture design scene at that time.

As I was the only one with any money, it fell on me to finance the company, with Rodney and Jurek being the designers. Our first office in Charing Cross Road was so small that either Rodney or Jurek had to stand up in order to let the other one pass by to get to his drawing board. The weekly outgoings of this little set-up were in the region of £100 (about £2,000 at today's prices). This enabled the fledgling company to produce chairs and furniture that now dominate many of the world's international airports, railway stations, police stations and public buildings.

In fact, I always smile when I arrive at somewhere like Kennedy Airport in the US to be greeted by acres of my furniture, then to be whisked into a car and hear one of my songs on the radio. It's always a great thrill.

Someone once asked me what I did for a living, and I replied that I was in the furniture and music business. 'Oh, musical chairs!' they replied. That about sums it up, I guess.

I suppose that my biggest influence on the company was financial support, combined with a new and flourishing business acumen and belief in my partners. Unlike the music business, where the most popular statement is 'Where there's a hit, there's a writ', in the furniture business this hardly ever happens.

However, on one occasion I remember receiving a call from Rodney, irate because Terence Conran's company was knocking off one of our designs. I rushed over to a meeting at the OMK offices to discuss this potentially major problem. The difficult situation was exacerbated by the fact that over thirty per cent of our business was at that point going through the various Conran establishments, including the newly emerging Habitat. It seemed rather unwise to begin legal action with one of our largest clients – potentially suicidal.

Rodney's view was that we could not afford to sue Conran and potentially upset the whole organisation; but my view was the opposite. Unless we insisted on them discontinuing, then they would surely go on and knock off all our designs within a year and we would have nothing. So a course of action was finally agreed upon, that we would sue them if they failed to stop.

Letters were sent and to our surprise they did stop, pulling the design from their stores. Some two years later, the managing director of Conran stores told me how surprised they had been that we had taken this line of action, as they knew they were by far our largest customer. I took that as a sign of vindication. From my first years at Central School of Art, I have always believed that Rodney Kinsman is one of the great furniture designers of our time, but I also believed that OMK had to protect the copyright of its designs at all times.

• • •

The Habitat stores carried on selling OMK products, such as their innovative T1 leather swing chair, for another fifteen years. Kinsman and Morrison bought out their partner Jurek Olejnik in about 1970 and Bryan was involved with the company for the rest of his life.

In 1972, OMK launched its 'Omstak' tubular steel frame stacking chair, which has sold more than a million and is still in production. It is now regarded as a classic of 1970s hi-tech design and is included in the permanent collections of twentieth-century furniture in the Victoria and Albert Museum, the Philadelphia Museum of Art, and other museums.

In 1982, Rodney Kinsman was commissioned by the British Airport Authority to design and produce a new seating system for Gatwick Airport. The 'Transit' seating system is now used in more than 100 airports and other public buildings. Since then, he has designed many other furniture projects, including the 'Trax' seating system in 1990 for British Rail Intercity stations, which has been installed in more than 300 airports worldwide and received a British Design Award.

Rodney Kinsman was appointed a Royal Designer for Industry in 1990 and he continues to lead OMK Design.

13

FASHION VICTIM

After Greta and I were married, I sold my mews house in Paddington and bought a maisonette apartment at 113a Old Church Street, in Chelsea. It was in a former artists' studio built in about 1910, and the house was on four floors, with double-height windows overlooking Carlyle Square. We had the top two floors, and the author Robert Lacey, a friend of mine for more than thirty years, moved with his wife, Sandi, into the lower two floors.

One day in 1973, Greta arrived home with a couple of new dresses that she had bought. She wanted to show them to me, so she put them on, and came bouncing into the drawing-room. In the same way that Marc Bolan's musical talent had socked me in the eye, here was a designer to compare with fashion icons like Yves St Laurent and Karl Lagerfeld, a designer of obvious rich talent. The line, the colour and the material were all new and invigorating. I'd never taken any particular interest in ladies' dresses before (other than taking them off, of course), but here was something completely original.

'They're fantastic, Gret, who designed them?'

'They're by a fairly new designer by the name of Bill Gibb.'

'He's not Scottish, with a beard, is he?'

'Yes, he is.'

'Well then, it must be the same Bill Gibb that I was at St Martin's with!'

'No,' she exclaimed, 'he's much younger than you.'

'Thanks a million,' I replied.

I was intrigued to see if I was right and a few days later I visited Bill Gibb's showroom in Knightsbridge; it was him alright. He had spent the years since leaving St Martin's working for various manufacturers and in 1968 had set up his own fashion house.

My foray into the fashion industry started a few days later, when Bill Gibb and his partner, Kate Franklin, invited me to dinner. During the meal, somewhere between the hors d'oeuvre and the main course, Kate asked me if I'd like to become their partner. They admitted that they had no management skills, or any idea of how to run a business at all.

At that time their business was very small, turning over no more than £30,000 a year, and there was obviously a lot of work required to make it into anything approaching a major fashion brand. They offered me fifty per cent of the company in return for my input, and I said I would have to go and think about it, which I did.

Like the idiot that I am, I came to the conclusion that it was more equitable to split the shares of the company three ways, between Gibb, Franklin and myself. This rash decision proved to be my undoing years later. But here was a golden opportunity for a new and exciting business. My thinking was, why not go into partnership with Gibb and promote him like a rock star? Build a market, create an international star through press, events and shows, and produce a perfume.

It had occurred to me for some time that what we needed in England was a fashion designer on a par with the greats in France. As these thoughts matured, I decided that the prime objective of building a name was not merely to sell 'frocks', as they are affectionately known in the trade, but to build a signature that could be used for a whole range of products, principally perfumes and cosmetics.

Not since the thirties had a great designer-named perfume wafted in essence from a bottle. The classic names such as Chanel, Givenchy and Dior. This was the ultimate goal, but it would be more than a decade before new names in designer perfume finally came into vogue, and it was a perfume bottle that would lead to the terminal demise of my relationship with Bill Gibb.

The other designer with a huge potential in the early seventies was Zandra Rhodes. Coincidentally, she and I had also been having conversations about the possibility of me becoming her partner. So I found myself in earnest discussions with the two fashion designers who were to dominate the English fashion industry. Oddly enough, in the fifteen years that followed, they were also the only two English designers to make any impression on the world scene. *Vogue* magazine eventually included Bill Gibb along with Yves St Laurent and Chloe as three of the top designers in the world, an accolade never conferred before on a British fashion designer. But this was all to come.

I felt that it would be easier to promote a man than a woman in the world of fashion, and Zandra had started talking to other backers and partners, so eventually the decision was made for me. One other thing had happened, though, which sealed my fate with Bill.

I was at one of the Paris fashion shows in the spring of 1973. I had gone there out of interest, to see what the whole thing was about. Marie Helvin, an ex-girlfriend of mine, was then the star supermodel. One of the many English fashion journalists who slavishly followed these shows was Lady Prudence Glyn. Lady Prue was the chief fashion writer for *The Times* newspaper and over the coming years she was to become a very good friend of mine. We were sitting in one of those cavernous show halls on a glorious spring day in Paris, when I ventured to ask her what she thought of Bill Gibb. She came back instantly with her answer.

'Bill,' she said, 'is the first designer in a decade not just to lower a hemline, raise a hemline or redecorate a frock, but is someone who can actually design a new detail or item.'

She hadn't really got the drift of what I was saying. I had been inquiring casually as to Bill's sensuality, presence, humour, disposition and general reputation in the fashion scene, but here I was being given an important lecture on what it was really all about. Lady Prue was not about to be railroaded, she merely ignored my redundant question.

'He designs,' she pronounced imperiously, 'a pocket. An entirely new pocket.'

'A pocket?'

'Yes, Bryan. In my view, he's the only innovative designer in England today.'

It was at that moment I decided, although he didn't know it yet, to go into partnership with Bill Gibb.

For the next few years I became involved full-time in the management and running of Bill Gibb Limited. The order of the day was entertaining, publicity and shows. Gradually and imperceptibly, the perception and persona expanded. Incredible fashion extravaganzas took place in every major city, from the capitals of Europe to New York. It was a world of fashion shows and beautiful models. Bill's models were always the most gorgeous, and the mainstays of his shows for the next four years included the stunning Ika Hindley; Lady Carina Fitzalan-Howard, who later married Sir David Frost; Hazel Collins, who from that day to this has never had a huge smile off her face; and, of course, the wonderful Dominga. These were only some of the superb show models we used in this period.

Colour, light and majesty reigned supreme. Soon buyers were coming from the four corners of the globe to acquire Bill Gibb frocks and we started to open our shops. The first opened in Bond Street, the next Madison Avenue, and then Athens. The renowned department stores Harrods and Harvey Nichols were also now selling our designs. We had arrived.

By late 1977, the two brightest stars in the firmament of English fashion were Zandra Rhodes and our Billy, closely followed by Jean Muir. I had been preoccupied for the last few months of that year pondering ways of catapulting Bill Gibb into the number one position. I knew it needed something very special, a huge PR number that would consolidate Billy as the undisputed top designer.

Soaking in my bath one morning, the idea came to me. I didn't shout 'Eureka!' but I was very excited. We would have a show in the Royal Albert Hall. It would be without question a first in English couture. Five thousand people, black tie, celebrities, in a fashion extravaganza with carriages at eleven. The Albert Hall, still the most prestigious venue in England, would be our showcase; the very same place where over a decade earlier I had promoted the Floyd to stardom. The words crazy, mad and insane were the first to come out of Kate Franklin's lips, while Bill was too dumbfounded to speak and stared without passion at his oversized shoes.

'Five thousand people? That's impossible,' Kate exclaimed.

Twenty minutes later, the corner was turned. Kate loved it and Bill went along for the ride, with oodles of apprehension. By the end of the day, Kate and I had planned the whole thing. It would be a retrospective of ten years of Bill's work, plus the forthcoming season. We would attempt to borrow back some of Bill's most beautiful creations that had been bought by the rich and famous over the years.

To make the evening a bit different, and more than a mere fashion show, I was also to arrange live music from one of my artists, John Otway. Wayne Sleep was going to dance a small ballet, and we would invite people such as Twiggy, Penelope Tree, Annie Ross, Marie Helvin and Antoinette Sibley to show their own dresses, with videos of those stars unable to attend. Her Grace the Duchess of Bedford, a great Bill Gibb collector, agreed to be present, and Gerald Harper, the actor, was to be the master of ceremonies. The date was to be 18 November 1977.

With my partners convinced and behind the idea, all that was needed was enough media hype to make the event a sensation. We all assumed that to sell five thousand tickets would be extremely difficult – up until this point, the largest attendance to a fashion show would have been no more than a few hundred people.

I had lunch with Beatrix Miller in early March 1977. She was arguably the greatest editor of *Vogue* magazine ever in the UK, an absolute ruler, and also one of the loveliest people I had met in the fashion business. My proposition to Bea was pretty simple. If she could guarantee a certain number of editorial pages – she agreed to at least ten pages of editorial – I would attempt to sell a certain number of pages of advertising. What ensued was a major supplement in the November issue, with over thirty pages dedicated to Bill Gibb.

After that, we only needed the help of a few of the national newspapers to get the ball rolling. Within hours of the tickets going on sale, at the then hefty price of twenty pounds, we sold out. It became literally the hottest ticket in town. The phone lines to the showroom were alive with calls from people in Paris, New York and Milan, all trying to squeeze themselves in on the last few remaining press tickets. With some satisfaction, I milked the hype to the last drop.

On the evening of 18 November, you could have cut the excitement and our fear with a knife. The Albert Hall was packed to capacity with 2,500 male penguins, along with their mates resplendent in evening attire, many in Bill Gibb. Backstage, thirty of the best show models in the world were about to strut their stuff. A huge video screen hung over the auditorium. Barbara Daley, the renowned make-up artist, was putting the finishing touches to the models' faces, while the choreographers were making their final adjustments, and then it was lights, colour and spectacle. The evening proceeded excitingly to its ultimate foot-stomping, standing, cheering conclusion.

Looking back, it is still probably the most important fashion show held in this country for thirty years, and the only time an English fashion designer has commanded the world stage. Pages and pages of publicity were to spring from this show, both nationally and internationally. So a tiny bit of the showman Mike Todd had been achieved; all those dreams of thirty years ago were coming true. The other innovation that we created was the start of London Fashion Week, which is now a huge success.

With all the components now in place – fantastic designs, glamour, international celebrity and a huge press profile – I set about achieving what was for me the pinnacle in the fashion industry. To secure a Bill Gibb perfume contract. At the time, there were only two or three manufacturing distributors capable of selling the product internationally and the company I wanted was Unilever: an international conglomerate with the money and marketing muscle to see our dream come to fruition. Several months were spent wining and dining individuals at the company until after much manoeuvring we had reached a conclusion on a contract.

It was a deal of staggering proportions, as far as we were concerned. Within two years of signature, we would be receiving up to a minimum of a million pounds in royalties, which over the next few years could become multi-millions annually. After that, with a fair waft and God's blessing, there would be incalculable riches, all for a mere signature.

At the closing board meeting in their offices at Port Talbot, during the completion of negotiations when these millions were being bounced back and forth like a ball at a Wimbledon final, I suggested quite innocently (well, not that innocently) that perhaps an advance of some sort could be payable on signing. Since getting Pink Floyd's first £5,000 in 1967 from EMI, one of the first advances ever paid to a rock 'n' roll band, this had become normal business practice, but this idea had obviously not permeated through to Port Talbot.

Twelve pinstripe suits holding an assortment of pens dropped them simultaneously onto twelve leather-bound white blotters and writing pads, placed at intervals around the large boardroom table.

'An advance?' the chairman repeated twice, his words barely audible above the grunts and tuts emanating from the assembled cast. I hastily explained that this was a pretty standard practice in the music industry, but this didn't seem to have much effect either. A dozen or so eyes started squinting at each other across the table.

It was at this moment that my intuitions from being in the music industry for the last eighteen years told me that I was on a loser, and I had some back-pedalling to do. My request for £50,000 was in moments scaled down to a more modest £5,000, a token gesture, I remonstrated. With all the points in place, it was agreed that the contract would be signed in three weeks' time. I returned to London in a jubilant mood.

My jubilation was to be short-lived. In less than a week, I had my illusions shattered. It was Easter Sunday and my great friend Robert Lacey, who amongst other accomplishments is a British historian noted for writing such books as *Majesty*, *The Kingdom* and *Ford*, took me out to lunch with his wife Sandi.

After the usual pleasantries had been exchanged, and once wine and food had been ordered, Robert's demeanour became grave. Robert is very good at being grave when he wants to be. The reasons for this were soon apparent. Two days earlier, he had been at a dinner with both Bill Gibb and Kate Franklin and had been astonished to hear them explaining in graphic detail the wonders of our soon-to-be-signed perfume deal.

Even more fascinating to Robert were the things that they had to say about me. My face fell as Robert told me that they had been complaining that I was 'already rich enough', having houses, ponies and beautiful cars, so why should I be eligible for a third of the profits of the perfume deal?

Ignoring the fact that we were equal shareholders in the company, they also intoned that I was a 'swashbuckler', stopped something short of calling me a thief but, nevertheless, suggested that skulduggery had taken place. All this, despite the fact that in all the years of running Bill Gibb Ltd, I had never taken one penny of salary, my partners having both taken out substantial amounts.

This was more than I could take. I was dumbfounded. Since my arrival on the scene six years ago, I had taken the company from a £30,000 turnover per annum to in excess of £2,000,000, built a huge reputation and now, with the crock of gold tantalisingly on the horizon, they objected to me having my fair share.

The next day was Easter Monday, a public holiday, so I couldn't find either of the rats anywhere. Steam issued from my ears, rage and revenge loomed foremost in my mind, and the whole day and night were spent waiting for the Tuesday morning, when I could see them in person.

The next morning, we sat together. Basically spineless, they would neither admit nor deny what had been said, but piped up that maybe they should have a bit more than two-thirds of the perfume deal. I gave up the argument after trying to rationalise with them for some time, and feeling as hurt as I've ever felt in the break-up of anything. I was forced to conclude, which I am sure made them very happy, that I was through with them. I felt like Julius Caesar must have done in his dying seconds, after being stabbed by his friend Brutus.

I gave them fourteen days to buy me out for two hundred thousand and release me from my guarantees with the banks, or I would wind the company up. They were crestfallen.

Bill couldn't accept that for a couple of hundred thousand pounds I was prepared to forfeit the millions that could potentially come from the perfume deal. It took quite some time to persuade him that principle came before profit, something I think that he never understood. As the years go by, I feel that less and less people understand this, a sad indictment of the world we live in.

Off they went to seek legal advice on this latest predicament. News soon filtered through that some smart arse was feeding them, what I considered, some very bad advice. Neville was the man who became their adviser in this whole sorry saga. 'Smart arse' suggested to them that the really clever thing to do would be to let me go ahead and wind up the company.

With this done, they would be in a position to buy back the name, and a huge stock of dresses and fabric, from the receiver for next to nothing; leaving me with the overdrafts, amounting to in excess of £500,000. Then they could start again with no debt, a brilliant name, and a perfume deal yet to be signed.

Bill came to see me after a week and yet again repeated his utter disbelief that I was prepared to give up everything for a point of honour, and have to shoulder the burden of debt that was rising steadily by the day. It was at this point, against my better judgement, that I offered Bill the last piece of advice I was ever to give him.

I pointed out one salient fact. I told him that we had spent the last six years building a fantasy, a dream in which every woman who put on a Bill Gibb dress felt like a queen. That the name of Bill Gibb was synonymous with esteem, wealth and glamour. I pointed out that when a woman bought a Bill Gibb dress for £1,000, she was spending £999 on the name and only £1 on the dress; a mere sack with a Bill Gibb label would take on a whole new look.

Therefore, if he allowed this company to go into liquidation, the subsequent publicity, however limited, would shatter the mirage like a piece of broken mirror. What woman at a party would throw back her tresses and mention the name of Bill Gibb after a liquidation?

'Take this course of action and your mark will disappear in a year,' I said.

Sadly for them, and I suppose for me also, they heeded me not. A group of successful businessmen were hovering in the wings, waiting to inject their money and expertise into this newly acquired 'clean machine'. The vultures were circling ready to swoop and feast – the banquet being between £300,000 and £400,000 worth of stock, a pending perfume contract and shops on three continents, plus a name of incalculable value. And so it was done. The company was wound up, I was left with a huge debt, and the revamped phoenix failed to rise.

Regrettably for Gibb and his new backers, only days after the announcement of the winding up, Unilever took the same view as me that the shattered image of Bill Gibb was not worth investing in, and they cancelled their contract. Within a year, it was all over. Their new backer, a prominent West End art dealer, had to close his gallery because of the accumulative and massive losses – up to a million pounds in that year – of Bill Gibb Ltd. The shops were all closed and the whole empire crumbled. What a terrible waste.

To add insult to injury, within eighteen months the American designers Calvin Klein signed a perfume contract with Unilever and they all prospered mightily through the next twenty years.

Besides the pain of losing something that I loved so dearly, I was now to suffer another form of retribution. The ever-so-friendly bank manager now screamed for his pound of flesh, and all my protestations, asking for time to pay off a debt that I surely owed, led to nothing. I faced the prospect of owing a small fortune to the bank and, as often happens in times like these, there was no cash available.

My first thought was to try to sell one of my publishing companies, the one that owned some Pink Floyd songs, back to the band. But their manager, Steve O'Rourke, sensing panic after hearing of my demise, attempted to clinch a better deal than was deserved. I'm not sure what I finally said to him, but I kept the company.

So it all went. Two years earlier, I had sold Merle Common House, my beautiful sixteenth-century manor house in Surrey, to pay off another debt. Now the magnificent studio house in Chelsea was gone, along with the cars, some of the paintings and most of the furniture.

On 16 January 1979, when I finally moved out of Chelsea and into a house in Barnet, north London, kindly lent to me by Ian Ralfini, then the managing director of Warner Bros and one of my best mates, all we had left was what we stood up in.

As we carried the last of our belongings out of Chelsea, I was standing by the kerb, having loaded something into a van I'd borrowed from OMK, when suddenly Jamie, my three-year-old son, ran down the steps of the house between two parked cars. I watched aghast as his little legs stretched to plant themselves on Old Church Street.

I screamed, 'Stop!' and he did, as a taxi travelling at forty miles an hour sped past his nose by about six inches. I may have been skint, but I am also one of the luckiest bastards in the world. This incident once again reminded me of the priorities of life. We didn't have much money, but we had plenty of life and boy did we enjoy it.

My new baby daughter, Karina, was born on the day we vacated Chelsea. Although I had lost all the material things, I was as happy as a sandboy. I had my dreams fulfilled, a beautiful wife and two kids, experience in bucketfuls, and a whole new phase of life to look forward to. There was one huge worry. Karina had been born two months prematurely and was fighting for her life in an incubator at Queen Charlotte's and Chelsea Hospital in Hammersmith. Although a frightening experience, I never once doubted her survival; even at a week old, I knew I was looking at a survivor.

The marvellous thing about Greta at this time was that she never, for one moment, complained. She was now facing being homeless with two young children and an out-of-work husband, but the style, smile and optimism remained. My thoughts turned to that age-old question: 'What to do next?'

I decided to look for a place to rent. I couldn't find anything suitable, but I found a delightful little cottage that was falling down. The roof leaked and the furniture was in the region of thirty years old, and I'm not talking antiques here. The place was in Wraysbury, near Windsor, and it overlooked one of the most historical sites in England, the fields where the Magna Carta was signed. I rented the cottage from a charming man named Robert Campbell.

With my family rehoused, I set about rebuilding my life once again. The prerequisite was to get my head together, lose some weight, and get fit. I was even roped into a fun run to raise money for a cancer charity. It was to take place in Hyde Park. I'll never forget walking out of the front door on the first night of my training and managing only about fifty yards before being overcome with exhaustion and having to stop. I marked the spot and next night did fifty yards more.

This process was repeated nightly through a very bleak and cold winter, until I was able to run between eight and ten miles easily. In the event, I completed about five laps of Hyde Park and raised almost £4,000 for the charity. As none of my friends or acquaintances believed I could run more than a few feet, they were over-generous in their lap donations, and by the third lap they were trying to buy me out of the competition, as it was costing them too much money.

Our rundown little cottage was to produce more fun and optimism than a man could handle, and I learnt how adaptable we could become. I remember having a dinner party there, with the usual pail and bowl positioned on the stairs to catch dripping water. Greta covered the stained settee with loose fabric, and candlelight burnished the room. My guests that evening, all polo-playing mates, included Sir Raymond Brown, founder of Racal Electronics; the billionaire businessman Galen Weston and his wife, Hilary; property developer Peter (later Lord) Palumbo, and lastly the captain of English polo, the mighty Howard Hipwood. We laughed and talked until the early hours.

It was a salutary lesson in friendships.

● ● ●

After the liquidation of his company in 1978, Bill Gibb is said to have viewed his hugely successful retrospective show at the Royal Albert Hall as an act of hubris; over-confidence inviting disaster and ruin. His fashion business never recovered its former glory and it collapsed again in 1980. Gibb was reduced to selling his designs by mail order to readers of Women's Journal *magazine. He was also seriously ill, and he died in January 1988, three weeks short of his forty-fifth birthday.*

Following his death, Twiggy described Bill Gibb as her 'knight in shining armour' and as 'a sweet, sunny farm boy in baggy corduroys, whom I absolutely adored'. There were rumours in several newspapers that he had been suffering from AIDS, but the hospital confirmed that he had died of bowel cancer after a long illness.

Gibb is now considered to be one of the forgotten heroes of British fashion. In the words of John Galliano, former head designer of Christian Dior, 'British designers are storytellers, dreamers, and I think this was really the essence of Bill Gibb.'

14

GOING UNDERGROUND

Although I had done nothing active in the music business since 1972, I had continued to run my publishing companies with Cora from the office at Bruton Place. Then, after four years, a single event happened that once again triggered my imagination.

I received a call in early 1976 from a young man called Malcolm McLaren. The name meant nothing to me, but he told my secretary that it was something very exciting to do with the music business. From memory, the call went something like, 'We haven't met, Bryan, but I know of your past successes in the music business and all of them were avant-garde and part of the new wave. Well, there's another wave coming and I'm managing the best band in the world.'

I asked him what they were called, and he replied, 'The Sex Pistols.'

I'm sure it's true to say that McLaren, like Brian Epstein, was one of the managerial catalysts that created rock 'n' roll in the sixties and seventies and, like Epstein, McLaren was a prophet preaching the impending revolution. He suggested that we might be able to do something together and would I go to see his band?

On 23 April 1976, I arrived at the Nashville Rooms on the corner where the Cromwell Road meets West Kensington, and was met by a very typical, smoky, stale-beer-smelling London pub. An assortment of bentwood chairs was lying in crazed lines about six rows deep and behind them stood a multitude of youngsters. Mainly, I seem to recall, standing around in old gabardine raincoats and tatty jeans.

After a delay, during which you could feel the energy in the room charging, the band emerged through the swirling smoke, and there they were, the Sex Pistols. My first impressions were that they looked dirty and shaggy. They looked like they had been sleeping rough for the last seven nights but, as they crashed into the first few chords, it became obvious that this was a new concept – fresh, spontaneous, aggressive and menacing, but totally unique. A far cry from the jaded supergroups of the early seventies. By the third song, I knew this band was going a long way and, with the surge of excitement at its peak, the looming menace snapped to outright mayhem.

I had noticed a couple sat near the stage who'd been squabbling throughout the opening of the set. Suddenly, out of nowhere, the girl stood up and started whacking the lad next to her. Arms flailing, teeth bared, she was ferocious. In the same moment, the band stopped mid-frenzied performance, whipped the guitars from their necks and flung them to the ground. Diving off the stage, they set about beating the shit out of the young man, who was still being attacked by this girl.

Chaos ensued, while the band's drummer was struggling to get off his seat and around the drum kit, so that he could enter the affray. It must have been at least five minutes before peace was restored; the band then clambered back onto the stage to continue their performance.

I should say here that, aside from being incredibly sorry for the young man concerned, I was becoming increasingly convinced that this was a new band who could break the mould. That was until a moment or two later, when Johnny Rotten started marching up and down the stage screaming Nazi slogans, goose-stepping and doing the 'Sieg Heil' salute. This display, albeit mock fascism, was beyond the pale for me, and any interest I had in this band immediately dissipated.

In retrospect, I should have given them more time, but my initial reaction was to recoil. Freedom of expression always seemed to be one of the great prerogatives of rock 'n' roll bands. Their message in the past had uniformly been one of love and freedom, so it was anathema to me to come across a band whose attitudes and postures appeared to encapsulate both fascism and evil. It wasn't pleasant, but it was undeniably powerful.

The influence that pop music has had on the world order is, I think, far greater than that of the politicians and other media. It was the English and American rock 'n' roll bands that rose like a gigantic wave crashing onto a thousand islands, flowing into every nook and cranny of the planet Earth. I'm sure it was fair to say that John Lennon's name was known by almost every man, woman and child on this planet. I knew the Sex Pistols were the green light for the new order. They were so unique in the seventies that they had to be the procurer of a new wave.

I went away from this gig feeling enlightened. I was now convinced that we were entering a new phase of music. Punk was in the air. There was to be a sea change and I wanted to be in the middle of the new maelstrom. I made a conscious decision to keep my eyes open for the newly emerging bands.

Nearly a year later, on the evening of 2 March 1977, I found myself in a pub near Hammersmith called the Red Cow. I had arranged to meet Chris Parry, a relatively new A&R man from Polydor. I had first met him a few weeks earlier and discovered that he too felt that a major musical change was about to happen. He was having a great deal of difficulty persuading the 'powers that be' at Polydor that changes were imminent and felt that a bit of muscle from me would not go amiss. So we kindred spirits came together on the night in question.

I've written here the quote from my diary that night after the show; a diary that I still have to this day:

We arrived about nine o'clock to find about a hundred young people between the ages of 16 and 23. Their hair was unusually cut 'short short', and to a man they all wore Burton or Hepworth black suits with thin black ties. They all danced as if on pogo-sticks. I think I've found the new Beatles, and they are going to be huge.

Looking back at this particular diary entry, it makes me chuckle. It seems more like a quote from Dr Livingstone's journal, on blundering into the celebrations of an undiscovered African tribe, than a gig review. The thrill of such an exciting discovery, though, was one I shared with him.

The band was a three-piece: guitar, bass and drums. They shrieked raw energy and were called the Jam. They were under starter's orders, the tapes were up; this then, was the start of another decade of British music. I must confess at the time that I believed the Jam could be almost as important as the Beatles. As it transpired, it was not the music of the Jam that restrained them, but Paul Weller's attitude to the media.

More of this later, but back to that night in March.

The Jam were managed by the lead singer's dad, John Weller. John stood about five-foot-six tall and probably four feet wide. He had been a bricklayer by trade, and he used his van to ferry the boys and their equipment to gigs. John was one of those great characters that rock 'n' roll throws up, and when he got agitated, he would stomp around like a bull in a record shop. There were no grey areas with John Weller.

Their performance made me determined to sign this band to a publishing deal, which I did. The morning after the Red Cow gig, I went to Polydor to meet with John and the band and showed them a publishing contract. Their reply was, 'Let's sign it now.' I suggested that they may want a lawyer to look over it, to which they replied, 'It's great, let's just sign it.' In my diary of that day, I actually stated how flabbergasted I was that bands never learn, always ready to sign without taking legal advice; fortunately for them they were in good hands, they signed, and there were never any complaints.

At the end of the day, the only thing that counted with John Weller was the money. Because of his initial lack of experience as a manager, it fell on me to act as adviser in this respect, which I was more than happy to do.

I started a brand-new company and as my son Jamie had been born just six months prior I decided to call the company And Son Music, and the Jam's copyrights were the first to be published by my new company.

Some ten years later, wanting to buy an office block in Bayswater, I suggested to Dick Leahy that maybe our very successful business should buy And Son Music off me for the then princely sum of £130,000. Dick thought this figure to be far in excess of what the catalogue was worth so, in order to prove him wrong, I offered it to EMI, who paid the asking price. Point proven, but catalogue lost – sometimes I think I am mental.

Anyway, Chris Parry signed the band to Polydor and, in May 1977, their first single was called 'In the City' and reached number 40. Their second single, 'All Around the World', nearly broke into the British Top 10 and the group embarked on a successful British tour. Chris and I had been proved right – the Jam looked poised to take on the world.

One of the reasons for signing the Jam was because nobody wanted bands like them in the music business. Many of my old acquaintances knew of the existence of these punk bands, some before I did, but those movers and shakers in their positions of power didn't understand their music and so I was able to sign them relatively easily. As it turned out there were others like them – the Clash and the Boomtown Rats – all waiting to happen, and boy, did they happen.

From 1977 onwards, the Jam's career flourished and grew. The one thing that was to hold them back internationally was Paul Weller's arrogance. It was more ignorance really, and it was to stop them becoming world-class players. It seemed that the more their popularity grew, the more stubborn Paul became. Sticking to his punk-rock principles, he was wary of press and playing the 'media game'.

◗ *George Michael performing live at the Odeon Hammersmith, London, in November 1983.*

Alamy

◀ *Andrew Ridgeley and George Michael of Wham! in 1984.*

Alamy

◗ *Dick Leahy and Bryan with Wham! in the early 1980s.*

⊙ Clockwise from top:
Her Majesty the Queen with Bryan and Wham! at the Guards Polo Club, Windsor. The Queen knew all of their hits.

Andrew Ridgeley with his American girlfriend Donya Fiorentino, 1986. 'Wham's Girl Donya Is Publisher's Lover!'

Bryan and Dick Leahy with a poster of the workshop production of their musical Matador *at Marriott's Lincolnshire Theatre, Chicago, Illinois, July 1989.*

Jamie, Greta, Karina and Bryan at the world premiere of Matador *at the Queen's Theatre, Shaftesbury Avenue, London on 16 April 1991.*

◉ *Stefanie Powers (right), the star of* Matador, *with American actress Pamela Sue Martin at the newly opened Royal County of Berkshire Polo Club, 1986.*

◀ *Greta, Bryan and Sarah, Duchess of York at Eliza Ferguson's christening, 1986.*

⬤ *Bryan and Prince Charles with Major Ronald and Susan Ferguson at the christening of their daughter Eliza, 1986. They were joint godfathers.*

Bryan in action at the RCBPC, 1988.

Mike Rutherford of Genesis, Kenney Jones of the Faces, Bryan, and Stewart Copeland of the Police, June 1988.

Captain James Hewitt (with hand on face) and Prince Charles at the Gulf War Day at the RCBPC, July 1991.

 Bryan writing his memoir at a beach house in Jamaica, 1991.

Bryan with the three-time world heavyweight boxing champion Lennox Lewis, 1990s.

Bryan on a motorbike at his office in Star Street, Bayswater, London in the 1990s.

Rose Lewis

○ *Clockwise from above:*
Bryan and HRH Prince Philip at the Guards Polo Club, 1990s.

The scoreboard at a private match between HRH the Prince of Wales and Bryan Morrison at the Guards Polo Club, 1990s.

Greta Morrison in an artwork by the British pop artist Allen Jones, commissioned by Bryan for her 50th birthday in 1995.

Prince Charles and Greta Morrison at the Prince of Wales Trophy match at the RCBPC, 1997.

 Jamie and Bryan Morrison with the Leos Trophy at the RCBPC, 1997.

 Bryan with Prince Charles at the Prince of Wales Trophy match at the RCBPC, 1998.

Jamie, Karina, Greta and Bryan in front of a ceramic mural by Leget at their favourite hotel, La Colombe d'Or, Saint-Paul-de-Vence, France, 2006.

Jamie Morrison in England polo team shirt at the Asahi British Beach Polo Championships, Sandbanks, Bournemouth, July 2014.

◀ *Jamie Morrison on the Royal Pavilion balcony at the RCBPC.*

▶ *Stefanie Powers, Greta Morrison and Jerry Hall at the Cartier Queen's Cup final at the Guards Polo Club, June 2015.*

Tony Ramirez/www.imagesofpolo.com

🔽 *Jamie Morrison in a polo match at the RCBPC in May 2019.*

When you become an international celebrity, certain things are expected of you. Even the most outrageous of acts finally has to sit down with a middle-aged television presenter, or a reporter. Paul never quite came to terms with the fact that his rebellion against the system could go only so far, he also needed that system to spread his message. Without television, radio and the press, the word could not be carried to the more remote corners of the earth.

I will never forget one such occasion on the West Coast of the USA, in April 1978, when the band performed at the Starwood, in Santa Monica. It also turned out to be, in my opinion, the demise of world conquest for the Jam.

The auditorium was packed to capacity and as the band appeared onstage, the audience went totally crazy. This was one of their first major gigs in America since they'd supported Blue Öyster Cult on a try-out tour a year earlier. We all knew after five minutes of watching this seething, hysterical mass of kids that we were about to crack the States. It was a repeat of the performance at the Red Cow, right down to the fans dressing as their heroes, except there were up to 5,000 at this one.

The concert finished, the band was slumped in corners of their dressing room, and acolytes were squeezing in through the half-open dressing-room door. All around, the air was electric. The sense of knowing that America was at our feet was as heady as drowning in a large vat of wine. Some time went by when, on my travels between the venue manager's office and the dressing rooms, I noticed a group of seven or eight people waiting patiently on chairs along a corridor. They had been there for about forty-five minutes to my reckoning.

I finally approached one of them, who introduced himself as a music journalist from the *New York Times*. He said he'd really enjoyed the gig and desperately wanted to interview Paul Weller, as he planned a big story about the new wave of English music. The others then introduced themselves and it became clear that a large and very important part of the US media was represented: *Rolling Stone* magazine, *Los Angeles Times*, various radio and TV stations. They were all in our clutches, waiting for us, ready to spread the gospel.

I explained that it would be impossible for Paul to do individual interviews, as we were in a desperate hurry to leave for our next gig.

'Perhaps,' one of them suggested, 'we could do a sort of mini press conference, which would take less of Paul's time, but achieve the same purpose?'

'Great!' I replied. 'Give me a minute and I'll put it together.'

I ducked back inside the boys' dressing room, beside myself with the news. The room was vibrant – after a gig like that, there is an immense feeling of 'Yes!' The roadies were busying themselves and a few new hangers-on were making their pitches.

'Paul, Paul.'

'Yeah,' came his response.

'Out there are several of the most important people in American media. They all loved the show and want to do a mini press conference. This is it, Paul. The one we've been waiting for. The big one!'

He stood up, shoulders hunched, and slouched down the corridor to where the press were waiting expectantly. He stopped in front of them, stood for a second stock still, and then in his usual fairly direct manner said, 'I've got more important fucking things to do than doing interviews with you lot. I should be signing autographs out there for my fans.'

Then he pursed his lips, spat on the floor and strode past them. Other expletives were heard as he made his way down the corridor to where some fans were waiting. My mouth dropped open. I looked at the assembled hacks, almost speechless, and mumbled something of an apology. At the same time, I realised that the Jam had possibly thrown away the best opportunity they were ever going to have, kissing goodbye to the USA forever.

This was to prove to be the case. They never had a hit in the States. It was a travesty, but one that I had seen occurring in different forms on so many occasions. In the case of the Jam, it was an unmitigated disaster, because here was a great band whose rawness and strength were supplemented by one of the great songwriters of the seventies.

I returned to England feeling totally depressed. I hated to see talent like that wasted. Over the next year, the Jam released the album *All Mod Cons*, which reached number 6 in the UK album charts, but they were still struggling to achieve their first Top 10 single.

Then, in the summer of 1979, I received a phone call from them one afternoon saying that they had finished recording their new album, *Setting Sons*, and that I should come down to the Virgin Studio in Shepherds Bush to have a listen. I arrived to find the usual discussion that comes at the end of a recording session. Everyone seemed to have a different favourite track that they were convinced should be the next single.

I settled down to hear the playback and was delighted to hear one great track after another; it was obviously going to be a strong release. And then it hit me, the stirring opening chords as 'Eton Rifles' blared out.

'That's it!' I shouted out. 'That's the one, it's a definite smash. It has to be the next single.'

A word with Chris Parry and it was to be. 'Eton Rifles' shot to number 3 in November 1979 and the Jam were on the map. What a song, what a record. It deserved to be huge and it was. Four months after this, their next release, 'Going Underground', went straight to number one in the charts, a rare feat in those days. In the years I worked with them, they had four number ones – 'Start!', 'Town Called Malice' and 'Beat Surrender' were the titles of the other three.

Their albums were also extremely successful and many of them reached the top ten on the album charts; *The Gift*, which was released in 1982, making number one. Shortly after this, Paul Weller in his wisdom decided to break up the Jam and pursue new ideas; nothing wrong with that, except that the band was never given full lease and they never achieved their full potential.

By the time of *Setting Sons*, Paul's songwriting had matured and combined social comment with pop sensibilities. His songs were quintessentially British and the subject matter struck a chord with their fans, who heard their feelings and frustrations echoed in the lyrics. I believe that his songs like 'Eton Rifles' and the haunting ballad 'English Rose' will become a part of pop legend.

During my time with the Jam, I had signed two other artists, although neither of them had the potential of the former.

One was a band called Secret Affair, who had a considerable amount of success and two Top 20 records – their lead guitarist, Dave Cairns, being one of the few artists I managed who was eventually to become a good friend of mine.

The other was John Otway. Although having achieved only one Top 30 record, 'Really Free', with Wild Willy Barrett, he was nonetheless one of the lovable eccentrics of the British music business.

His timing proved to be immaculate. Almost to the day his record reached number 27 in December 1977, his recording contract with Polydor terminated. So here he was – a big record, no contract. The most perfect place for a recording artist to be. The record company, on the other hand, found themselves in the embarrassing position of losing an artist at his most successful. John asked me if I would negotiate a new contract with whomever I chose, and Polydor was my first stop.

For John, it was one of the greatest deals ever. Polydor signed him to a five-album deal. He was paid a small fortune and it was no less than he deserved. He spent most of it in a few years. I asked him later what he'd done with all this money. John stood there in his odd socks and this black suit that had become shiny with the years, and his open-top white shirt. His reply to my question was very simple.

'Spent it. But it was sure fun.'

His first single after the new contract had been signed was called 'Geneva', and I suppose in a way it showed me how wrong you can be about a song. I thought this one was going to be a giant. It flopped and so John joined the ranks of yesterday's rock stars.

Another project that I really enjoyed being involved in during this period happened quite innocently. When lunching one afternoon with David Wigg, who was and still is one of the great music journalists, reminiscing about our golden days back in the sixties, he happened to mention that he had interviewed many, if not all of the huge artists of the day, and that at home in his attic he had boxes and boxes of taped interviews.

A man eager to embrace new technologies, he had foregone the shorthand notebook and recorded all his meetings with these idols. He said that he was about to jettison the lot and felt that, although they had historic value, he had absolutely no use for the tapes.

'Who have you got on these tapes?' I asked.

'I've got Bowie, the Who, Jagger, the Beatles ...'

'The Beatles?' I cut him short. 'What have you got on the Beatles?'

'Oh, hours of conversation on all sorts of topics with John, Paul, George and Ringo.'

'Listen, send me a couple of cassettes and I'll have a listen,' I said. 'I've got an idea.'

'No problem. I'll have them around to you in a couple of days.' Then, sensing that I obviously had a scheme whizzing around in my brain, he leant over and asked, 'Why are you so interested?'

'I'll let you know tomorrow,' was my reply.

Having heard the tapes a day or two later, I rang David back to explain my idea. If he had a load more material, in the same vein, we could put together a project and call it *The Beatles Tapes from the David Wigg Interviews*. David loved the idea, a small studio was booked, and we spent many enjoyable hours listening to these tapes and re-recording them to a releasable quality.

Between them they narrated the complete history of the Beatles from the early days in Merseyside, continuing right up until the mid-seventies.

Having put together an album with some instrumental versions of Beatles songs by the Martyn Ford Orchestra, the rest being oral interviews, I negotiated a deal with Polydor, and the double album package was released in July 1976, finally reaching a position of number 45 in the LP charts. It was a fun project and maybe it seems trivial today, but my money is on some of those records becoming real collectors' items in the decades to come.

After the collapse of the Bill Gibb fashion business and having had it all, at the age of thirty-seven I was now skint, boracic, up the Khyber and Donald Ducked. Having paid off all the debts, I was left owning one small publishing company, with a rather large overdraft hanging over it.

It didn't take long for me to decide to go back into the industry that I loved. I had this feeling that a radical change was about to take place and I wanted to be a part of it. I wanted to return full-time to the music business that had given me shelter and sustenance for the last seventeen years.

The lease had now expired on my offices in Bruton Place, so the first thing to do was look for a new office from which to work. I soon found the property I wanted with the prestigious address of 1 Hyde Park Place. The landlord offered me a five-year lease, but I told him I couldn't possibly entertain anything for that length of time. After some discussion, he insisted the minimum period he would grant was a year. Being extremely unsure of the future, I refused to sign anything longer than a three-month term with ongoing three-monthly options.

He finally acceded to this request and in the Christmas of 1978, Cora and I moved into the office, which was actually a residential flat. It was filled with all sorts of inconceivable bad taste, from floral sofas to worn and stained carpets, flocked table lamps, and pine beds of horrendous design.

The landlord insisted that anything removed would have to be replaced in perfect order, so I had the whole lot packed up and moved into storage, where it was to remain for eight years. Later, I estimated that the cost of storing it with Pickfords for this length of time amounted to more than four times the furniture's value, but I wasn't to know this at the end of 1978. I was only pleased to feel settled, so I could now get back on course.

• • •

The Jam's recording of 'Eton Rifles' was inspired by a 'Right to Work' march organised by the Socialist Workers Party, which had started out in Liverpool and passed through Eton College on its way to London. As the demonstrators marched down Eton High Street, they were heckled and jeered by several Eton pupils, causing the marchers to react angrily, and resulting in a street battle between the opposing sides. Paul Weller saw this as a typical example of British class war.

Years later, the Conservative prime minister David Cameron, an Old Etonian, proudly named 'Eton Rifles' as one of his favourite songs, because he had trained in Eton's combined cadet force, founded in 1860 as the Eton College Rifle Corps. Cameron claimed he had been a big fan of the Jam, adding, 'I don't see why the Left should be the only ones allowed to listen to protest songs.'

Weller responded with disbelief, telling the New Statesman *magazine, 'Which part of it didn't he get? It wasn't intended as a fucking jolly drinking song for the cadet corps!'*

CARELESS WHISPER

With Cora and I now well ensconced in Hyde Park Place, I decided to take on an A&R man – in other words, an artist and repertoire person. As with most titles, you don't necessarily get what you're paying for, and so too with A&R men. The main talent of a successful A&R executive is the ability to pick hits. To hear a piece of music or song and know instantly in his gut that he has found a tune or an act that will become well known and loved worldwide.

Anyone who has these 'ears' doesn't need to work for a record company. Their skills are rarer than moon rock on earth. There are probably no more than ten people in the UK who in the course of twenty years have discovered or have been involved with all the major new talent in this country.

As far as I've been able to ascertain over the years, the role of most A&R departments within the major record companies is to release anything that looks or sounds like a potential hit, then wait to see how it does. Witness the fact that every week in this country there are probably in excess of 150 singles released. Of these, maybe three per cent will make the Top 50 in a given week, which leaves ninety-seven per cent of these records basking like jellyfish on the shelves of the distributors or record shops.

Remember, each one of these records, almost without exception, has not only had advances paid, but has cost tens of thousands of pounds to produce; not to mention the money spent on promotion once the record has been released. All of this starts at the A&R man's desk, and yet for twenty years the same situation has existed. The reason for their existence is simple enough: the profits that are made from international artists, which are huge, more than make up for the losses from the non-selling records. Now a good A&R man could stop this rot, but the trouble is, if he's that good, why would he want to work for a record company? He could take his talent, sign a couple of artists, make a fortune, and retire to his Caribbean island.

So the quest for my A&R man was going to be extremely difficult. I was going to try to form my own A&R department. These chaps who sign the bands, who approve the finished master, who tell the marketing and distribution departments, as well as the thousands of others employed in a record company, that this record is going to be a hit. A small independent company, such as ours at the time, couldn't indulge in a three per cent hit rate.

Although I have never studied it in detail, I am sure that our own success rate was to be nearer the thirty to forty per cent mark.

Advertisements were placed in the music press advertising the position, and within a week over two hundred people had applied for the job. I set about interviewing a potential A&R person every twenty minutes. By the middle of the first day, I realised that although they were smart, some had degrees, and they could all talk without effort about the Beatles, the Stones, and the Mamas and the Papas, none of them told me what I didn't already know; so my line of questioning changed and a new tack was taken.

'Tell me what I don't know about the current crop of artists,' became my opening line. 'Tell me about yet undiscovered artists, records, and trends.'

This line of interviewing floored most of them within the first minute. A few struggled, but none told me anything new. On the second day, late in the afternoon, I was becoming bored and desperate with the whole thing, when in walked a cocky little bugger, about eighteen years old, by the name of Mark Dean. He had a sallow complexion, with brown curly hair. For the 120th time, and after an introduction, I asked him the same question.

'Tell me what I don't know.'

His reply was direct and slightly cocky. 'That's a doddle!'

Very cocky actually! By the way, a 'doddle' means simply easy, or no problem. He was right. In the next ten minutes, he was to tell me plenty of things that I'd never heard about artists, records, and movements that were churning around ready to personify themselves in the world record market. By the eleventh minute, he had the job and, although he was studying at a local polytechnic, he was prepared to leave and start immediately. His wage was paltry, some twenty pounds a week, but if he delivered there would be lots more to come.

He delivered all right. He found them and I would try to hook them, although, for one reason or another, I couldn't land them, but for the first time I had someone else with ears to help me.

Within weeks of starting work with me, Deano, as he was known, was chasing such bands as Adam and the Ants, ABC, Spandau Ballet, and Soft Cell. He was always there at the right place at the right time, and his amazing musical taste guided him. This was one guy destined to go far. Within six months, Polygram had offered him a deal as their A&R man with a figure in excess of £50,000 a year.

'Take the job, Deano,' I said, 'and good luck!'

Within another month or two, another company had tripled this offer. Within a year, Mark had become a star in the music business firmament – the boy with the golden touch. Like a bee in spring, he flew from flower to flower, each time drawing more pollen with which to fill his hive.

By 1981, he was at his peak, totally out of control, but loving every minute of it. It was in this same year that he achieved what was probably his crowning glory. Under the auspices of CBS Records, he was given his own label and a huge fund of money to spend on signing and promoting his artists.

Coincidentally, at this same time, I was to go into partnership with an old music business acquaintance of mine, Dick Leahy. He had recently sold out his music company interests and was looking to start something new. I had a great deal of respect for Dick's abilities. We went back many years, in fact he'd been Jack Baverstock's assistant and tea boy back in the old days when I signed the Pretty Things to Fontana Records.

We'd more or less cemented the idea of a future partnership a year or two earlier, when we'd decided to go on the relatively new Concorde to New York. In the early days of 1978, it was a dream machine and, from the moment of arrival at the check-in, the very best champagne was poured down your throat by the bottleful.

Before either of us had actually got on the aircraft, we were totally out of our minds, and little more than an hour later, or so it seemed, we were in a large limo careering across the rivet-studded Brooklyn Bridge in New York. It was during this journey to the New World, from centre to centre, that our plans were made to start a new publishing company, Morrison Leahy Music.

So Dick came in with me at 1 Hyde Park Place and we launched our new joint venture. A few months after his arrival, I received a call from young Deano.

'Got a few minutes, Brysey? Cos I think I got something very exciting to play you, and you would know.'

An hour later he arrived, bouncy and irrepressible. He had a grin from ear to ear and as ever was in a state of perpetual motion.

'Listen to this, listen to it. I think I've cracked it!'

He slid the tape into the deck. I pressed play on the £75 music centre – nothing very grandiose for me. The first two songs were fantastic: special songs, special voice. The third one was *the song*! Even as a piano demo, it had a class of its own. Lyrics, form and music, this was not just a song, it was destined to become a great Evergreen. These words were written in retrospect, but they are absolutely true. We knew then and there that we were listening to something created by the gods.

The song was a ballad, and its title was 'Careless Whisper'. Deano and I were ecstatic – we jumped up and down in anticipation.

'Who are they, Mark? Where did you find them? What's it all about?'

'They're two guys from near where I live. In fact, one of them went to the same school as me. They're called Wham!'

'What?'

'Wham!' He spelled it out, 'WHAM! Why don't I sign them for recording and you sign the publishing?'

Twenty-four hours later, they arrived. George Michael and Andrew Ridgeley. It's very easy after the event to say that you knew an artist or sportsman would make it big one day, but with these two it was obvious. They were dressed like dudes with their own style. Full of life, full of youth, unique, original, and special. We had to have this band. Mark had been instrumental in not only bringing Wham! to our attention, but initially in helping us to sign them. To that I owe him my eternal gratitude.

After Mark had left us and before my partnership started with Dick Leahy, I had signed one act in particular who I thought was going to be enormous. The band was Haircut One Hundred and, like Wham!, they were unique, both in Nick Heyward's songs and the image that they portrayed.

The first single that Haircut released in October 1981 was 'Favourite Shirts', which went straight to number 4, and this was followed by 'Love Plus One', which achieved the number 3 position. Two other singles, 'Fantastic Day' and 'Nobody's Fool', also made the Top 10. Their only album, *Pelican West*, which came out in February 1982, reached as high as number 2 in the UK Albums Chart and went platinum.

This was a band that could have taken the world by the seat of its pants and become enormous, if it hadn't been for the usual stupidities and acrimonious behaviour of its members. Songs like 'Fantastic Day' and 'Love

Plus One' flowed from Nick's pen. A sell-out tour of England was eclipsed by possibly one of the best gigs I've ever seen when they played the Odeon Hammersmith in June 1982 at the end of the tour. The audience and I went wild, absolutely wild. I was never more convinced that I had a truly international supergroup on my hands.

They were in the studio recording their second album in July of that year when the farce began. Within days of the record company announcing that a new album by Haircut One Hundred would be out in November, they'd taken an unprecedented 400,000 orders and the group had yet to lay down one track in the studio. Their future seemed huge and assured.

It didn't start with a kiss, but with a telephone call. It was from one of the band's representatives.

'We just want to tell you Bryan, that Nick didn't write all the songs for the new album. Well, actually he wrote all the songs, but we put passages in here and there and gave him ideas that helped to embellish them, and therefore we want some of his writer's share.'

'Oh no. Not that old hot potato.'

You see, there is nothing more horrendous for a band in their position, than seeing a real talent writing great songs two inches from their noses, and making a fortune doing it. This is deemed by the untalented to be unacceptable behaviour, and so the band was now in full cry, like a pack of hounds, trying to cut their pound of flesh from the gilded carcass.

A further week went by, until things started to reach fever pitch, and I was summoned down to Richard Branson's Manor Studio, near Oxford. They'd been holed up there now for over two weeks, and the murmurings and mutterings were becoming more audible than the tape playbacks. The record company was starting to get the shakes, as the order book was piling up to unprecedented proportions. So, in the second week of August, I arrived at the studio. The tapes in playback told the real story.

The essential ingredient of Haircut's records was gone. That freshness of sound captured instantly, like Chinese food cooked in a wok, was being eroded through days in the studio spent bickering about who had composed what or who had contributed those three bars that made up part of the song, which would give them some form of authorship, to eventually fill their greedy little palms with silver.

Although things were in a sorry state, I nurtured a hope that common sense would prevail. I spent a whole day cajoling, talking, and telling these idiots how big their future was going to be and the fortunes they were likely to amass. The one common thread to my theme was to 'leave Nick alone … let him write his great songs', as they were the source of the band's success. My pleas, it appeared, fell on deaf ears.

The rot had set in. The lawyers, accountants, and other non-productive acolytes buzzed like flies around a honey pot, but the one man they were isolating was the creative genius whom they needed, Nick Heyward. He eventually cracked and one morning in the middle of a session he came back from the country to my office saying that he could take no more and couldn't or wouldn't finish the album.

There was uproar at Arista Records. Although my dear old friend David Simone, who was managing director at the time, was worried, he maintained his normal jocular attitude.

'What are these fucking idiots up to?' he asked.

David rarely swore, so this was a major event. The explanation was simple – it was a story as old as the Bible. A story of greed, lust and power – and, like most of these stories, there's always someone who comes out the loser. Arista would lose, we would lose, but worst of all these seven musicians, who would brook no advice from me, who were on the threshold of their careers, were about to throw it all away.

My message was repeated *ad infinitum*, 'There is so much cake to be shared around over the next few years, what does it matter if Nick earns a bit more?'

Lennon and McCartney, Jagger and Richards and others had been encouraged and worshipped for their writing, not penalised for it. Even the looming threat of the dole queue had no effect on their sensibilities. Finally, with no other course of action left, the last throw of the dice was made and a meeting was called.

The meeting was to have very little to do with artistic endeavour. All altruistic considerations were forgotten. The 'suits' took over. In more than twenty years in the music business, this meeting was to be the high point in farce.

Gone was the passion of groups of musicians who took to the stage because they loved the blues, or who worshiped Elvis, the Beatles, or the Stones. Gone was the simplicity of picking up some cheap guitars and playing drums on a couple of old saucepans, or washboards. That freedom of expression, the lodestone of this fantastic industry. All of this talent and yet here we were on this spring day in the Royal Lancaster Hotel in Bayswater Road and it seemed to have come down to the same old thing: friction and fighting over money.

We met for a late breakfast in a private room. The entire band was there and, to my horror, each one of them was to arrive accompanied by his own myriad assortment of advisers, whether they be accountants, lawyers, or managers. The musicians took up posture more like boxers, with their trainers and managers standing either behind or at their shoulder.

My mind tried to conjure up the words to explain what stood before me. After a minute or two of thought, I found the categories for all of them. We had a posse of lawyers, a pack of minders, and a lament of managers.

As each round of conversation was ticked off, a huddle of repair and advice was given to each of the contestants by their seconds. I was reminded of that wonderful film *Zorba the Greek* when, on the death of the mistress of the house, the whole village set upon her goods and chattels, like so many locusts with so many hands, grabbing in sheer frenzy, but no one really coming out with anything.

At the end of three hours on that fateful day, all that was left of that potentially great band was a broken record lying shattered and unfinished on a studio floor. Haircut One Hundred were no more. The album that had promised so much lay unfinished, sitting in a large round tin, its destiny never fulfilled. Within months, most of the band was on the dole, or back in the jobs they'd hoped never to see again.

Nick struggled on writing and recording, but it was never to be the same again. Over the years in the music business, I have often wondered what goes on in a man's mind when, months or years after, the full gravity and stupidity of his decisions become a reality. That imperceptible moment in time when they realise they've blown it.

Fortunately for me, the cycle of rock 'n' roll appears to be constant, and it wasn't to be too long before that day when Deano telephoned me about another great new band.

It was now my and Dick's intention to sign Wham! regardless. However, as in most things in life, it wasn't as straightforward as I might have hoped. George Michael was eighteen years old, but he had a presence and understanding that belied his youth. What was extraordinary about him was that he knew then exactly what he wanted and where he was going. I've never in all my years come across an individual who was so resolute in his objectives, so prepared to sacrifice everything, if necessary, for what he regarded to be his destiny.

The negotiations with us were concluded within hours, but the finer points on one or two issues were to take days, which became months, during which the buzz from the duo started to emanate around the village of rock 'n' roll. Although several record companies had turned them down previously, they were now coming back with substantial offers, in most cases higher than ours. But George wished to sign with us and he was not about to be railroaded, even by higher financial compensation. He wanted our managerial advice, which came with the publishing deal.

Finally, all was settled, but for one crucial point. I'd insisted all along that the songs had to be signed to us for the life of copyright. George didn't see it this way – it was unusual in the eighties for a publisher to seek life of copyright. Nevertheless, that's what I wanted. Life of copyright means that each song written by a writer will be owned by the publisher for the natural life of the writer, plus fifty years after his death. This period of time alters from country to country. In America, for example, they currently have a retention of seventy-five years.

This particular point has aroused much contention between publishers, artists, and lawyers in the last few years, with the result that publishers have been throwing in the towel on this emotive issue; for the most part, publishers now accept retention periods from anything between three and ten years. I did not and do not share this view, as it is my belief that although I did not conceive the song, the work and effort that we put into making the song a success gives me the right of part ownership with the writer. I ask you also to remember, dear reader, that ninety-five per cent of the songs written are valueless within a few years of their recording.

It would be wrong of me to suggest that every publisher deserves life of copyright, because frankly most of them don't, but anybody who really works, promotes and busts a gut for a writer, deserves his just reward. George did not agree and proved to be as intransigent as me. It was during these negotiations that I became aware of the self-purpose and the total belief in his infallibility that any major artist must have.

I remember clearly the final 'make or break' day. It began with a meeting in the office of George's lawyer, Robert Allen, in Covent Garden. The meeting had started at about eleven o'clock, and I was due to play a game of polo in Cowdray Park at four o'clock the same afternoon.

So it started. The bone of contention being the only topic of conversation: life of copyright. George said no, I said it had to be. We talked for hours, neither of us willing to compromise or give an inch, no quarter given nor asked. Time was now running out and for the fiftieth time that morning I beseeched George to give us life of copyright.

'George, it's got to be a life of copyright.'

'No,' he replied adamantly. 'I want to retain the copyright.'

Robert Allen was sitting on the far side of the desk, and piled up beside him were rolls of papers, all tied with very neat red ribbons. Every now and then he nodded in acquiescence with one of George's comments. On several occasions, he interjected along the lines of, 'You know he's right, Bryan. No one else would be asking for life of copyright. Why, he could sign three deals right now with more money and five-year retentions.'

That was as maybe, but George wanted to deal with us, and we sure as hell wanted to deal with him. One hour melted into two, and the plastic coffee cups were soon taking on the look of a New York skyline. I looked at my watch. God! It was 2.30 p.m.

'Chaps, I gotta go. I'm playing polo at four o'clock in Cowdray Park, and I just can't be late.'

I can imagine the thoughts that crossed both George's and his lawyer's mind as this idiot prepared to leave the meeting unconcluded, especially to go and play a game of polo.

'George, I gotta go. Everything else is agreed. Why don't you just say yes to life of copyright?'

There was a long pause. He looked in succession at his lawyer, Dick, and me, and said, 'No. No deal with life of copyright.'

'Okay,' I moved towards the door. His lawyer was looking with some deep-rooted fascination at the top of his pen, Dick was sitting back reflecting on the moment, and George was resolute.

'See you.' I opened the door and stepped out into the particularly unimpressive hall. I stopped on the top step and thought, you have a writer writing some of the best songs you have ever heard. You're beaten but not bowed, now go back in there and do a deal.

All that remained now was to get the best terms available, so I turned around, pushed open the door and walked back into the room.

'George, give us "Careless Whisper" and the first album for life of copyright, and you've got a deal.'

Within a second, he'd nodded his agreement and replied, 'You've got a deal.'

With George, when he said 'Yes' to something, he always kept his word. One hour and ten minutes later, I was on a polo pony playing at Cowdray

Park, certainly not realising how important the day would turn out to be in years to come. Not signing George Michael would have been as bad as Decca turning down the Beatles. So the deal was consummated, and Wham! was launched.

In the early days, although George was the obvious musical talent, Andrew Ridgeley was also a star, besides being an extremely nice person. I personally think that Andrew was an important rock 'n' roll talent. His problem was always living under the greater star of George Michael. Frankly, performing next to someone of George's talent will always be difficult, but Andrew went for it and the young gun cracked it.

Today Andrew is a happy and contented man who lives life to the full and is as charming as ever. The history of their success is legendary. In a few short years, the boys from Bushey became international superstars with songs like 'Young Guns', the mighty 'Wake Me Up Before You Go Go', 'Freedom' and 'Last Christmas'. Then came the Evergreen, a song every music publisher dreams of owning, a tune that has been the most requested in England for over fifteen years, 'Careless Whisper'.

George was an instinctive songwriter. One of the stories about his writing, which has always amused me, was on returning late one night to Andrew's house. George reminded him that they had to leave early the next day for a TV show and that he would be round to collect him at nine o'clock or thereabouts. Before going to bed, Andrew wrote a note to his mother saying, 'Mum, wake me up before you go-go!' The note was stuck on an upright at the bottom of the stairs,

Next morning, George arrived to pick him up, read the note, and a chord was struck as he glanced at the words on the scrap of paper. Before the car had got three streets away, he had written the song in his head. So works the miracle of genius.

That was in the future. A lot was about to happen before those great heights were scaled. The first major problem came soon after Wham! achieved their first chart success. Mark Dean had been either unwilling or unable to pay the kind of royalties that a major act had come to expect. The bigger they grew, the more apparent became the discrepancy. No amount of discussion between the band and Mark could resolve the situation and it started to become dirty. I tried on several occasions to mediate, but to no avail.

George and Andrew decided that the only recourse they had was to attempt to break Deano's contract. In the first instance, CBS threw their allegiances behind Mark Dean as they were the mother label behind his company, but eventually and probably shrewdly they decided to throw their weight behind Wham!

During this period, both parties proffered all sorts of deals. One of these happened in the north of England, where Wham! were on an incredibly successful tour. After the gig, the whole entourage of record company, publishers, managers and hangers-on were assembled along a bar in the green room. At one end were Wham! and their friends, at the other Mark Dean and his mates.

A deal was put together between George, Andrew and me, which was to offer Deano three points on every record that Wham! sold, plus giving him an imprint. I walked up the bar to put it to Mark.

At this time, both George and Andrew were very keen that Mark should come out of the whole thing with a good deal, because they actually respected what he'd done for them in the early stages. They offered him a very decent royalty on all records sold, plus label credit on any future records bearing their songs.

Considering Mark's vulnerable position at the time, this would have been a very favourable outcome for him. It was becoming increasing apparent to the rest of us that unless he took a deal of sorts, he would more than likely end up with nothing. I spent a considerable amount of time explaining to Mark that in situations such as these, there was a time to attack and a time to retreat.

There was also a time to surrender with honour. One that would probably be worth hundreds of thousands of pounds to him annually. It seemed to me, and I insisted to Mark, that a fresh flag and a new piece of land was a better duchy than having to lose your entire kingdom. But Mark would not be persuaded, and he continued to sally forth until his eventual demise. Ultimately, he lost the contract, recovering no compensation, and ended up a very sad man.

At about this time, and unbeknown to us, the giant CBS corporation decided to put out an inferior recording of 'Careless Whisper' – one that had been recorded by George at the Muscle Shoals Studio in Alabama with the producer Jerry Wexler, some seven months earlier. It was a recording that Dick and I both felt did not have the feeling and charisma deserving of such a classic song. But here was the record company about to release this substandard version. George was horrified, for they were about to ruin one of the world's great songs. He pleaded with the 'powers that be', but to no avail. We too regaled CBS with the same request – again, with no luck.

After many hours' discussion with George, there appeared to be only one option left to us. It was similar to the one available to the President of the United States. Legend has it that on his desk in the Oval Office there sits a telephone with a red button, and that button can launch a nuclear attack. Always there, never used, but catastrophic if touched. The red button in music publishing is the publisher's right to veto the record company's rights.

These rights are invested in a simple piece of paper called a stat note. The publisher has complete power over the use of a song until after its initial release. Up until the point of that first release, the publisher may or may not grant a licence to a record company for a recording. After its release, there is nothing the publisher can do to stop a record company issuing another version of the song, unless there is a material change in lyric or composition.

In reality, publishers are only too pleased to have songs released and, in all my years in the music business, this was to be the first and only time I have used this weapon. With no further options and with the absolute belief they were putting out the wrong version of the song, Dick and I said 'No deal'. We would not grant them a licence for 'Careless Whisper', which was a bit like David fighting Goliath, except in this case we didn't even have a sling. Goliath roared, because they wanted it so badly. But as with all good fairy tales, in the end the poor little defenceless bugger won out against the giant.

To say that our relationship with CBS deteriorated over the next months would be a gross understatement. However, a year or so later, all was forgiven when the new version of 'Careless Whisper' went to number one in virtually every corner of the globe. And so we were brought once again into the firmament of CBS and instead of Goliath smiting David, we broke bread as one, as the Yanks would say.

Mark Dean finally lost Wham! and to the best of my knowledge has spent the last few years working in record companies in England and America. I don't know if he is still cheeky and bouncy, but my guess would be that I would find him a bit more subdued than I did twenty years ago.

● ● ●

George Michael always remembered exactly where he was when he first came up with the idea for 'Careless Whisper'. He was only seventeen and sitting on a bus and as he handed the money over to the bus conductor, he heard a tune in his head, which was the iconic saxophone line in the song. He wrote more of the melody in his head on the bus and then developed the song over the next three months.

In his autobiography, Bare, *George Michael described how he wrote the lyrics with his friend Andrew Ridgeley and they were inspired by two girls named Jane and Helen. A year earlier, when he was sixteen, George had been dating both girls for a couple of months, and he felt guilty in case the first girl found out about the second. She never did, but 'Careless Whisper' was about what might have happened if she had done. He explained: '"Careless Whisper" was us dancing, because we danced a lot, and the idea was – we are dancing ... but she knows ... and it's finished.'*

Surprisingly, George was dissatisfied with the song. He told the Big Issue *in 2009, 'I'm still a bit puzzled why it's made such an impression on people ... is it because so many people have cheated on their partners?' He went on, 'It's ironic that this song, which has come to define me in some way, should have been written right at the beginning of my career when I was still so young. I was only seventeen and didn't really know much about anything – and certainly nothing about relationships.'*

'Careless Whisper' was released as a single in July 1984 and topped the charts in about twenty-five countries, including the UK and the USA, where it was later named Billboard's *number one song of 1985. It went on to sell more than six million copies.*

16

WHAM! BAM!

One of the essential ingredients of the music business world is the annual pilgrimage to a trade fair by the name of Midem, which usually takes place at the end of January in Cannes, in the South of France. I had first travelled the road to Midem in 1967, the second year the event ever ran. It was an inglorious affair then, but it did have the seeds of future greatness and by the mid-eighties it was the only world music business event worth attending. Anyone who was anyone would make the journey to Cannes.

I have to say that some of the best poker games I ever played were during our jaunts there. In order to attend this annual jamboree, you required the constitution of a horse. You had to be able to take up to five nights of crawling into bed with the dawn, a few hundred quid up or down, gained or lost, from the casino or one of the numerous poker games.

In the early years, the one thing you would notice in Cannes at this trade fair was the shortage of good-looking young women. There were women, of course, but they were the type you would see as you staggered back down La Croisette at 4.30 in the morning. Large numbers of pretty women spread evenly along this piece of prime Riviera beachfront. They were the hookers all down for the week from Paris.

I remember the drill. Having skirted these ladies and arrived back at the Carlton hotel, it was a quick sleep and then up at 8.30 a.m. to repair down for breakfast in the restaurant. After a breakfast with assorted music publishers and record executives, then it was off to the Palais des Festivals, where in a six-by-ten-foot room I would have a dozen or more meetings.

One of my never-to-be-forgotten memories is of sitting in one of those tiny booths in the Palais, the second or third time that day that I had played someone the new Bee Gees track 'How Can You Mend a Broken Heart'. It was due to be released within a month or so, and I must say we were very proud of it. All of a sudden, my meeting was interrupted by a ferocious rapping on the door and moments later this little man burst into the room, slightly out of breath.

'What was that record you were playing?' he demanded. 'I heard it through the walls. Oh, and sorry for the rude interruption, my name is Eddie Kassner.'

Coincidentally and quite inconceivably, I was in the presence of the man who had some thirty years earlier published the artists that sent me on this voyage of discovery. It was him, the publisher who owned 'Rock Around the Clock' – lucky chap.

'Which record did you hear?' I asked

He began to hum a pretty good version of 'Broken Heart' in response to my question.

'You must mean this,' I said, enjoying the moment as I played him the first few bars.

'That,' he declared, rising to his full height of five feet four inches, 'is a worldwide number one.'

Like old Dick James, these boys weren't lucky. They were music men.

Incidents like this made the interminable lists of appointments bearable. Your eardrums would be blasted off by the end of the day. Not only with the music that you were listening to directly, but also a cacophony of other sounds coming from an assortment of other little boxes spread all over the Palais.

At 1.30 p.m., it was off to lunch for a large bowl of mussels, followed by a lightly cooked Chateaubriand, and a delicious bottle of wine, while all the time talking music. The journey back to the box involved slapping at least twenty people on the back, shaking more hands than Nixon during a presidential campaign, and then once more unto the breach for a dozen more meetings.

After talking shop all day, it was then off to join half the world in either the Carlton or the Majestic bar, where the serious business of drinking and fun was about to begin. Then it was a bath and out to dinner, where the fun continued, until you finally slid gratefully between the crisp, clean sheets in the early hours, only to start the whole process again after a few hours' sleep.

If you could face five days of this, while keeping a smile on your face and a buzz in your heart, then the business of rock 'n' roll is for you.

At Midem 1986, Dick Leahy and I were happily ensconced in one of those traditionally French suites; stuffy Louis XV furniture, four-poster beds and gilt everywhere. The suite was five floors up on the corner of the Carlton hotel, with an unparalleled view of the dancing and exquisite Mediterranean Sea. Wham! was at its peak. We had just achieved the number three position as publishers of the year, and we were flying.

Andrew Ridgeley had been living in Monte Carlo with his very, very pretty girlfriend, Donya Fiorentino, and they were coming over for dinner that very night. Dick and I had spent an hour or so downstairs in the Carlton bar, mixing both the spirits and the company. The place was packed and the tempo increased, each person trying to be heard above the other, while new arrivals filled gaps in the bar that hadn't existed half a minute before. I must confess that I was giving it plenty – a music business euphemism for trying to talk up a deal.

At about 7.30, Dick had had enough and went upstairs to change while I continued pouring Kir Royales down my throat at 100 francs a glass, like a man possessed. Sometime later, pushing and squeezing through the multitude, there was Dick again. He arrived at my elbow, and it was obvious by his lack of composure that something drastic had happened.

'Come on,' he said, and almost dragged me from my seat. Something was definitely amiss. We hustled through the crowds towards the lift, picking our way between great writers, great pretenders and a great deal of very pissed people. The silence and proximity of the lift brought Dick and me face to face.

'You've got a big problem, Brysey. I've just been on the phone to Pat in the office back home and she says the *Sun* newspaper is printing a front-page exposé tomorrow morning with the banner headline: WHAM'S GIRL DONYA IS PUBLISHER'S LOVER.'

Dick paused, probably noticing the frown around my eyes, which he interpreted correctly as meaning that those last few words had not been comprehended.

'And the publisher is you!'

'Me? Donya's lover? You gotta be joking! I mean, one can dream, she's young and stunningly beautiful and with a body like, well one of the best I've seen. But no, not me, Dicky-boy. I'm not that stupid, besides I like Andrew too much to even think about it.'

'Well, Brysey, they've got a story and you've got a problem!'

At that moment the lift came to a stop, decompressed an inch or two, and the doors opened onto our floor. The next sixty minutes were mayhem.

'I don't give a shit if they print it or not. If they do, I'll sue them for a fortune. But on the other hand, the die is cast, the damage done. Try explaining that one to the wife, kids, and family. And how about, "Honestly, Andrew, I didn't make love to your beautiful young girlfriend!"'

I was becoming embroiled in a farce. The awful thing was that I couldn't see the funny side of it. The news from the *Sun* was that I'd been seen in Donya's company at many an exclusive watering-hole and a close friend of Donya's had confirmed the affair. There's always a 'close' friend, or an intimate source, that is so close that they're prepared to sell their friend up the river.

Far more damning, the *Sun* insisted that they knew with all certainty that I had, and I quote, 'a love-nest' with Donya in Chelsea. Each time I think of these words now, I fall about in almost unstoppable fits of laughter.

Imagine the scene: sitting in this fifth-floor suite, the Mediterranean ebbing and flowing beneath me, in one hand a glass of champagne, surrounded by that mock Louis XV French hotel furniture, and in the other hand a telephone.

From out of the mouthpiece of this phone appears a writhing and spitting green serpent with those bulbous red eyes and those thin, sharp, long white teeth. As he spits forth his venom, he tries to devour me.

This, my dear friend, was the scene in my suite at the Carlton hotel. Those bastards at the *Sun* were about to turn my world upside down with a pack of lies. As I was protesting my innocence, in walked Andrew and Donya. I threw the phone back into its cradle, swallowed yet another glass of champagne in one hit and approached the lovebirds, arms wide. After a few minutes of pleasantries, Dick and I excused ourselves and headed for the 'war room', which in fact was my bathroom.

'Speak to Tony, speak to the lawyers,' Dick said. 'You've got to stop this rubbish from coming out.'

Several phone calls and thirty minutes later, the strategy had been formulated. My lawyers would fax the *Sun*, refuting all of the charges laid down by the paper. Also, if they continued and refused to desist in their action, they would be the subject of a huge libel suit.

Having completed the legal part of the problem, for the time being, I now had to ring Greta and explain that if in the morning the *Sun* newspaper was delivered to her by either friend or foe, and if by any chance the headline of said 'rag' bore the words BRYAN MORRISON AND DONYA IN CHELSEA LOVE-NEST, she shouldn't jump to conclusions, as the other five million readers of the *Sun* undoubtedly would, because the whole thing was garbage and lies, which could be explained in the course of time.

However, I still had to deal with a more immediate problem of my two guests sitting in the next room waiting for me. How to explain to Andrew that it was all a pack of lies, because I knew if the story came out, the world's press would descend on us like a flock of vultures. By my sixth glass of Moët drunk in about thirty-five minutes, I walked somewhat unsteadily into the drawing room where Dick, Andrew and Donya sat talking, and I attempted to explain the saga to them.

Andrew laughed his head off and Donya went potty with mirth. I didn't quite know how to take that. I wasn't that bad looking, was I? When I got through to Greta some hours later and told her the story, her comment was 'How exciting,' and she was also completely unfazed.

The editor of the *Sun* obviously had second thoughts, too, because the feature never appeared, and yet something inside my head wouldn't go away with regards to this love-nest.

Back in England a week later, I was in my office surrounded by all the usual suspects. They were in animated discussion regarding my brush with infamy.

'What I don't understand is how they got this bee in their bonnet about a supposed love-nest.'

To a man, the ensemble shrugged their shoulders. No one had any idea where this had come from. At that moment, the office receptionist appeared. She had obviously picked up the drift of the conversation.

'Bryan, didn't Donya take the lease of her flat in the name of Bryan Morrison Music Limited?' she asked brightly.

With that, the penny dropped. *The Times* crossword had been cracked by the least likely person. Donya had arrived in England and wanted to rent a house or flat but because of the problem with sitting tenants she found it impossible. The only way to overcome this problem was a company let and, not having a company of her own, Donya had asked me if she could take the lease in the name of one of mine.

'Sure,' I'd replied, 'no problem. You can use Bryan Morrison Music Limited.'

We can only assume that the estate agent who drew the lease had misinformed the *Sun*. Being aware that Donya was living there, and it was in Bryan Morrison's name, they had put two and two together and made ten.

Another story that I often chuckle over was the fortieth birthday party of an old mate of mine, Gary Farrow, one of the top PR men in the business. Gary loved a star and he looked after a great number of them, including George; he also happened to be one of the funniest raconteurs in the music business.

Anyway, his party was held in Berkeley Square at Morton's, a private members' club with a first-floor dining-room that overlooks the square.

The place was buzzing. There weren't many of us, possibly forty or fifty, but everyone, with the exception of me, was a star – George, Elton John, Nick Faldo and more – and a great deal of fun was had by all. At about midnight, Gary came over to where we were sitting and asked if George and I would like to go to Annabel's night club. Annabel's has been an exclusive night club for the rich and famous since the early sixties and is situated in a basement under the Clermont Club casino, on the other side of Berkeley Square from Morton's.

'Gary, we can't go to Annabel's because George doesn't have a tie on and they have a very strict door dress code.'

'Brysey, George can get in anywhere; I'll fix it anyway.'

Gary returned a few minutes later, a huge grin on his face: he had done the business. 'It's all fixed, let's go.'

Once again, I pleaded, 'Gazza, they won't let him in.'

'Brysey, a grand says he gets in, let's have a bet. One thousand says he gets in without a tie.'

Now I'm not a betting man and anything over £100 is a huge bet for me; however, the glow of the evening and the champagne left me confident.

'OK, a grand with you, the same with George.'

Handshakes were exchanged and we sailed forth to the club. For some reason long forgotten, Gret and I got into our car to travel all of fifty yards to Annabel's, followed by the boys. Their car drew up and the two doormen stepped smartly forward, two or three steps across the pavement, and George and Gary were ready to descend. As one, they both looked back at me, with Gary putting up one finger, not as some crude gesture, but to remind me that £1,000 was at stake.

They descended the steps into the club, and I sat there in my car with a sinking feeling. I'd just done two grand in cold blood; suddenly I didn't fancy rocking and rolling down there.

'Let's go home, Gret.'

But I wasn't set on throwing in the towel quite yet.

'Wait, let's give it five minutes or so to see if they re-emerge.'

Seven long minutes later it was over, they were in and I was out – out of pocket, that is. So off we drove, a lesson learnt that you can win, but also lose. However, the next day didn't bring the expected phone call from Gary asking in his hilarious way for the readies, which made me think something was possibly amiss.

Two days later, a polo-playing mate of mine, Warren Scherer, was arranging a fortieth birthday party at Annabel's for the next Friday night, when he was surprised to hear the manager say, on seeing my name on the guest list, that George Michael and I had been turned away three nights previously. He said that George and his manager Bryan Morrison could not get in because of the dress code, but what the manager of Annabel's found strange was that instead of leaving immediately, the two of them chose to linger on a bench downstairs, but outside of the club, for about twenty minutes.

With that piece of news, I went into fits of laughter. The two of them down there being refused admission, but not daring to come up for twenty minutes because they would lose the bet and two grand. No one could have guessed they would be caught out in that way, but they were, and the sequel to the story is that I am still waiting for the readies.

It was always George's dream to go solo from the inception of Wham! The duo was the vehicle to achieve this, it was a fun-packed ride, but as their worldwide popularity grew, so did the need to have full-time management. George finally asked Dick and I if we could find him a full-time manager. I was not interested in the gig personally, so I said I'd see what I could do. At this time there was an eager, up-and-coming manager by the name of Jazz Summers, whom I'd known for several years. He was currently managing a couple of small bands, but was as keen as mustard to get on.

'Bryan,' he said, 'I want to manage George, introduce me to him.'

'Jazz, you don't have any major management experience.'

But even then, Jazz was not one to take no for an answer. His persistence knew no bounds and finally after a week or two I said, 'Jazz, go and find a partner who's had experience in the music management business, and I'll introduce the pair of you to George.'

Bugger me, a few days later Jazz appeared with his new partner, Simon Napier-Bell. Mr Napier-Bell's chief claim to fame was that he had managed the Yardbirds and later Marc Bolan in his early days, although I was unaware of this at the time of our meeting. What was obvious was that he had been around for quite some time and he knew the ropes.

Well, I had promised Jazz a meeting with George if he could find a worthwhile partner and here he was, so introduce them I did. I have to admit I didn't think they had the remotest chance of convincing George, but I was wrong – it was instant karma, and they became the managers of George Michael and Wham!

It was a meeting of minds that was not to last too long – from memory, only a couple of years. The time spent with George worked wonders for Jazz, however, who within a few months was managing another artist by the name of Yazz, who had a number one hit with 'The Only Way Is Up', and he has since become a major player in the world of rock.

Talking of Wham! reminds me of a polo event that they attended. Through an emissary, I learnt that the Queen had heard that I was managing and publishing Wham! and that she would like to meet them. It just so happened Greta was in the process of organising a party at the Guards, so the boys were invited. To my amazement, on greeting them, the Queen knew all of their hits and spent a great deal of time listening to their exploits.

The ending of my relationship with George in 1991 came out of the mess caused by him wanting to leave Sony Records. The ongoing trauma had been going on for months; George felt that Sony had failed in their duty as his record company, and the dispute escalated to an impending breakdown of their relationship.

A meeting was called in my new offices at 1 Star Street, a four-storey, former post office building in Bayswater, and all the main honchos were there, lawyers, managers, publishers and press agents.

After an hour or two of discussion as to the rights and wrongs of George's decision, which was to break ties with Sony, we were all asked one at a time for our thoughts, and to a man, we all agreed with George. Sony had failed to promote fully his second solo album, *Listen Without Prejudice Vol. 1*, and therefore deserved to lose their contract.

The course of action to be taken was to terminate the Sony Records contract. When my turn came to give my opinion on the morality and indeed the legality of the deal, I was of the view that morally George was wrong, he had a perfectly legitimate contract with Sony, and I believed that they had, with the tools of promotion that were available, done a very good job in the past. My views were not shared by the others, in particular George, and this meeting and contrary opinion proved too much for George and heralded the end of our relationship.

After that particular meeting, I was put out to grass; the fact that I was proved right in the long-term mattered little – what the man wants, the man gets. Has my view of George changed? No, not really, he was an incredible artist and a prolific writer. I still stay in touch, although rarely, with Andrew, who I have to say is probably one of the most successful retirees of rock 'n' roll, and a happier man I have yet to meet. His days are spent surfing, reading and, more importantly, enjoying his life. George, I don't know much about his life these days: I hope he is happy, he certainly helped to enrich mine.

I have to mention three or four amusing little incidents that I will always remember about the years with George and Andy. The first, and in no particular order, was the 'Wham! The Final' concert at Wembley stadium on 28 June 1986. Fortunately, or unfortunately, I was in yet another polo final, but with some deft manoeuvring I arranged to take a helicopter with the family from the polo club to Wembley Stadium. I asked the boys, with more than a hint of sarcasm, that if I was running late could they hold the gig until the helicopter was spied flying across Wembley.

That day was awe-inspiring; 100,000 people crammed into what looked like a small bowl from the air. I had sought and received permission to land on a small square of grass beside the police station a hundred yards from the stadium and, as we circled above, the stage was empty save for the odd roadie and their equipment. We landed and ran towards the stadium like people possessed, up the stairs and into the royal box and, just as we hit our seats complete mayhem broke out; not I hasten to add because I had arrived, but because Wham! had hit the stage.

The other memorable incident of that day was a lone pigeon, which had been circling the stadium for some time. Now I have to remind you that there were about 100,000 people present that day, but it was to me that the pigeon made its offering. It was short and sweet, and accompanied by a plopping sound – a dive, a hit, and I was covered in shit.

A year earlier, in January 1985, the boys were on tour in Japan, and the big night was going to be at the Budokan arena in Tokyo, a gig that couldn't be missed. The only flight that Dick and I could get arrived in Tokyo only one and a half hours before curtain-up. Thankfully the plane landed on time, a black limo was standing by, and within minutes we were speeding towards the Budokan – everything was perfect and on schedule.

I was savouring the thought of my ten-day trip to Japan, the first time besides working that I was going to see some of the more non-tourist aspects of this incredible country, to witness first-hand the real Japan, and spend some time on one of my favourite subjects, the samurai.

We arrived at the arena with seconds to spare, the curtain went up and once again the boys strutted their stuff. It was mind boggling and the show was brilliant. It had been arranged that we would all have dinner afterwards in this fantastic little restaurant in Roppongi, which was no more than a three-sided bar surrounded by stools. In the middle of the square sat two samurai warriors, swords in their scabbards, and in front of them lay a wonderful array of fish, meats and all kinds of exotic food. At a signal from one of the kimonoed waiters standing behind us, the swords would flash, and a fresh-looking salmon would be sliced into delicate leaves in the blinking of an eye.

I was like a cat who got the cream. I'd been to a great gig, and now I had two samurai and a huge heap of delicious food in front of me. I liked Japan and I couldn't wait for the next days. Alas, my dreams were about to be shattered. On the way to our hotel, I started to feel increasingly ill and, once we had checked in, I staggered with help to my room and straight into bed.

The next time I left that hotel room was ten days later, when I climbed into a car and was whisked straight back to the airport. I never did discover what struck me down so instantly, nor did I live my Japanese dream. So much for international rock 'n' roll.

Sadly, I was also to miss one of the most unique tours any band has ever contemplated, Wham!'s groundbreaking tour of China three months later. Of all their gigs, this was the one I most wanted to attend, but days before leaving for China, Greta's father, a wonderful ninety-four-year-old music professor, Harry van Rantwyk, passed away. The band went east and I went west to Montreal to pay my last respects, which brings me to the third part of this particular trilogy.

The Whamamerica! tour of the USA started in late August 1985. It was to promote their *Make It Big* album, which ended up selling more than four million in the States. On 30 August, we were in LA, Wham! had just played a concert at the Hollywood Park racecourse, attended by over 25,000 people, and as usual it had been a huge success. George suggested that the four of us – George, Andy, Dick and me – go out partying, and the chosen venue was Johnny Gold's Tramp's Club.

We arrived late and after some fun and games, we left at about 2.30 a.m. I was directly behind George, when suddenly this vision of beauty obstructed his path, with a rose held in her hand; she was stunningly beautiful, possibly one of the best-looking women I've ever seen.

I ushered her out of George's way and was struck by her fabulous perfume, which only added to the aura of an angel. I looked back at her momentarily

– the long dark hair, perfect body, skirt cut above the knees, and a really stunning pair of legs, supported by a pair of stilettos that only added to her statuesque beauty.

George and Andy were both in the limo but as I was about to join them she manoeuvred between the open door and the interior of the car. In that instant, George looked at her, then at me and shook his head so, grabbing her, I slowly eased her back out of the car.

'I'm sorry, darling, not tonight.'

She said nothing, but turned and walked a few yards to a parked car, not any parked car, but a drophead Rolls, dark chocolate brown, and standing by the passenger door was a chauffeur straight out of a James Bond movie: boots, button-up jacket and peaked cap. As she approached, the door was respectfully opened, this moving vision climbed gracefully into the car, and within seconds she was gone, which I have to say was a damn shame.

● ● ●

One of Simon Napier-Bell's other claims to fame is that he co-wrote the lyrics to the song 'You Don't Have to Say You Love Me'. In 1965, Dusty Springfield heard an Italian song called 'Io che non vivo (senza te)' at the Sanremo Music Festival and asked her friends Vicki Wickham, who booked the acts on the ITV pop show Ready Steady Go, *and Napier-Bell, a TV commercials producer, if they could write some English lyrics for her.*

After having dinner out together, they listened in Wickham's flat to an acetate recording of the song in Italian, and came up with the opening line, 'You Don't Have to Say You Love Me', but then they had to take a taxi to the Ad Lib Club. By the time they arrived about half an hour later, the lyrics were almost finished. Afterwards, Napier-Bell complained to Wickham, 'I don't like this lyric-writing business, it messes up the evening!'

Dusty Springfield released her recording in March 1966 and it became her most successful single, reaching number one in the UK and number 4 in the US. The song later became an international hit for Elvis Presley and has been covered more than sixty times by other artists.

17

ANOTHER ROCK AND ROLL CHRISTMAS

One of the more bizarre moments in my music business career came about in 1984. This particular incident should have made the Guinness Book of Records.

It had been a pretty typical Monday morning in October. From my vantage point at 1 Hyde Park Place, overlooking the park, I was made particularly aware of the onset of winter. The lofty oaks were turning into a pyramid of bronze, enhanced in their beauty by the copper, yellow and fading greens – a vast swathe of colour stretching across Hyde Park. Each area of tree stepped in front of the other, like some multi-scenic stage set, where the only way of creating the optical illusion of depth was by layering the props. Yes, winter was on its way.

The thoughts of winter led me to stomach-warming feelings of Christmas, which in turn led me to thinking about festive songs and carols.

Suddenly, *donner und blitzen*! I dashed away, but only as far as the nearest telephone. Within thirty minutes, I had rung a dozen songwriters asking each the same question.

'Do you by any chance have an unpublished Christmas song?'

Each time the answer came back as an unqualified, 'No!'

My inquiries had started at about 12 noon and, by 1.30 p.m., I was washed up. I thumbed through my telephone book looking for other names of writers who might be able to conjure up that elusive song, but to no avail. The clock ticked to 2.30 p.m. when, out of the blue, one of the writers whom I had phoned, Mike Leander, rang me back.

As a writer, arranger and producer, Mike had enjoyed huge success in the sixties and seventies with many smash hit songs, and unbeknown to me, he would later feature quite prominently in my life.

The essence of Mike's phone call was that since speaking to me two hours earlier he'd had the gem of an idea for a new Christmas song.

'Give me an idea of the melody.'

Mike sung me the first part of a song.

'Sounds good to me,' I said.

'Great, I'll work on it for another hour or so. Would you be interested in hearing it at about four o'clock this afternoon?'

'Sure, let me know when you're ready.'

He arrived a few hours later, beaming from ear to ear.

'I've got it. I hope you like it.'

He hummed the tune, showed me a partly finished lyric and asked me if I would pay a couple of hundred pounds to get a demo of it done that very evening. 'Yeah, go for it,' I replied.

On the Tuesday morning, Mike played me the demo and we both knew that we had a hit. Now all we needed was a singer. With this, Mike came out with a wonderful suggestion, well, wonderful at the time. He had written many a smash hit for Gary Glitter in the early seventies. Gary's career had been in a bit of a slump of late, so it seemed like the perfect combination. We whisked the demo immediately round to Gary Glitter, and his answer was, 'When can we do it?'

The studio was booked for 7 p.m. that evening and by early morning the next day – less than thirty-six hours from its conception – we had a finished master that we all knew would be a huge success.

On Wednesday morning, I went to see David Simone, who was then the managing director of Arista Records, and a deal was quickly struck.

And so, a piece of pop history had been made. A song that had existed only in someone's mind was now written, recorded, with a finished master, and a deal struck for its release all within forty-eight hours.

The record was released a month later and, by Christmas 1984, Gary Glitter's record, 'Another Rock and Roll Christmas' had reached number 7 in the charts. The song has since gone on to become a perennial Christmas favourite and has sold in excess of 4,500,000 units worldwide.

It was always a dream of mine to put on a musical on the West End stage, but finding the right subject was always going to be the problem. One day Mike Leander came to see me with the idea of a musical based on the life of a great Spanish bullfighter called El Cordobés, who had become a superstar in the sixties with his audacity in the bullring, his smouldering good looks, and his stylish haircut, which led the press to refer to him as the fifth Beatle.

My imagination was sparked by all the potential elements of Spain – flamenco dancing, heat and dust, Don Quixote and the bullfight. They were all there and, combined with Spanish music, it seemed too great an opportunity to miss.

Mike had started writing the musical with his lyricist, Eddie Seago, in 1983. I sat and listened to a few of his demos. They were absolutely fantastic. One song in particular, 'A Boy from Nowhere', sounded like a masterpiece, with the potential to be a signature tune, like 'My Way' had become for Frank Sinatra.

A few months later, Dick Leahy and I, along with Sony Records, became the principal investors in this new musical, which was to be called *Matador*.

The first thing the show needed was a star. The female lead had to be in the mould of the fifties film star Ava Gardner, who had lived and loved the bullfight. Who better than my great friend Stefanie Powers. Stef had even studied to become a *novillero*, a junior bullfighter, and knew more about the blood lines of Spanish bulls than most aficionados.

We had considered Tom Jones for the lead. He would have been perfect for the part of the matador, as he was already an established star and would have attracted many thousands of customers. But we needed the bullfighter to be in his late teens and, although Tom has always looked younger than his age, even he would have struggled to convince the public that he was under twenty-one. The leading male role was given to John Barrowman, a little-known actor at that time, but one with great potential.

However, Tom did perform a number of songs on the concept album that was released in 1987 – my favourite of which, 'A Boy from Nowhere', went to number 2 in the charts. It also went a long way to re-energising Tom's career at that time.

On the night *Matador* opened at the Queen's Theatre in 1991, I took the Duchess of York as my guest. It received polarised reviews from the critics, some glorious and some damning; however, I thought it was wonderful. Its main aggressor turned out not to be the critics, but the Gulf War. It changed the plans of many thousands of tourists who were, and still are, the backbone of the British theatrical industry.

The war started one week before our opening night, when it was too late for us to stop the process. Without this international incident, which stopped American tourists in particular coming to London, we might have had 'sold out' signs up every night. But it was not to be, and sadly the show closed after only three months.

Despite losing a small fortune, one of the best aspects to come out of the show was *Matador* winning a Laurence Olivier Award – British theatre's equivalent to an Oscar – for best choreography. It was for an absolutely terrific sequence, featuring a dancing bull made up of seven Spanish dancers.

The music still lives on and, hopefully, one day it will return to the West End stage.

● ● ●

Mike Leander is best known as the producer and co-writer of eleven consecutive Top 10 hits in the early seventies for Gary Glitter, including three number ones. 'Another Rock and Roll Christmas' was Glitter's final hit in 1984, before his subsequent imprisonment on sexual abuse charges.

In the sixties, Leander had worked as a producer, arranger and songwriter for some of the biggest stars of the day, such as Marianne Faithfull, Billy Fury, Lulu, Shirley Bassey, Van Morrison, Roy Orbison and Gene Pitney. In 1964 Atlantic Records invited him to work with the legendary Ben E. King and the Drifters in the USA, where he had an immediate number one hit with 'Under the Boardwalk'. He also scored, arranged and produced the soundtrack for the film Privilege, *starring Paul Jones.*

In 1967 Paul McCartney asked Leander to write the orchestral score for 'She's Leaving Home' on Sgt. Pepper's Lonely Hearts Club Band, *because the Beatles' producer and arranger George Martin was busy working with Cilla Black. This was said to have caused Martin to be genuinely upset with the Fab Four, although he did produce the recording using Leander's score. This made Mike Leander the only orchestral arranger apart from George Martin to work on an original track by the Beatles.*

18

THE GAME OF KINGS

I consider myself extremely fortunate to have always been in the privileged position of having businesses that were my passions as well as fun, ever since I was seventeen years old. I have never had the dread of waking up on a Monday morning to undergo another dreary day at the office and to suffer another week of misery and drudgery. Instead, I've had the pleasures of music, design, travel and meeting many interesting people. As important as these were to me, they were eclipsed by something even greater. The passion of polo. A game of such intensity, skill, bravery and presence of mind that everything else pales into insignificance.

If you have never seen a game of polo, there are four players on each team and a match is divided into seven-minute 'chukkas', with an interval of three minutes between each one. The object is to score goals by hitting the ball through the goal posts. All this while riding a horse.

Polo's uniqueness is a singular problem that separates it from virtually every other sport. That being the mind of the horse. Every other ball sport is played with the feet firmly (or nearly always firmly) on the ground. Imagine hurtling at nearly thirty miles per hour towards a small white ball some three inches in circumference, while your opposite number has the absolute right to ride into you at not more than forty-five degrees, sometimes hitting you with such force and ferocity that both horse and rider can be knocked through the air for up to three or four feet.

At the same time as this is happening, your eyes are glued to a ball that sits some five feet below you. All of this while positioned up and out of the saddle, arm pulled back as if a bowman of England, ready to execute the perfect arc at a ball that you are travelling towards at around the speed limit on an urban road. At the moment of impact, another opponent on your nearside shoves his stick towards the mallet or ball. As the sticks meet, the

181

intensity and sound is like the sharp crack of rutting deer locking antlers.

Sometimes the impact of the stick will send your opponent's mallet head at speed up your 51-inch cane, the only obstacle in its way, onto your gloved hand. Knuckles are torn, but still the mallet head travels upwards in its 360-degree arc. The forearm is the next to feel the weight of the bamboo, and if you are very unlucky, this whole process of the swinging mallet, which has lasted no more than one and a half seconds, will end up grinding itself into your face or helmet.

If at this point you have missed the ball, it is imperative to throw your body weight backwards onto the haunches of your mount, while applying slight pressure from the hands, plus a deft touch with the right or left boot and, within six yards, a good polo pony will have stopped, pirouetted, and thrown itself once more into the affray. Only then, with the pain and sheer power, will you understand what it is like to be at the epicentre of the game of polo.

Another moment to savour is when for seven and a half minutes you become entwined and bonded with the horse as one, never aware of the separation between man and beast. Truly the centaur in Greek mythology.

I saw my first game of polo on a balmy day in July 1972, and my heart burst, overwhelmed. I had found what was to become a lifelong passion. Within a day of witnessing my first game, I was chatting to one of the great characters of the game, Billy Walsh. But it soon became obvious that the only time he spoke, or recognised you, was if you had the misfortune to be thrown or fall off your mount.

I remember the first time this happened to me. We were perhaps ten minutes into a ride, and I was beginning to feel, at my third attempt, that I was getting the hang of riding American style. Suddenly there was a slight movement to my right, possibly a small deer or rabbit. This imperceptible movement was nevertheless picked up by the big brown eyes or ears of my horse. This sent him into an immediate change of leg, followed by a two-foot yaw to the left. I was left momentarily hanging in space, where a fraction of a second earlier my saddle had been. I hit the ground hard, but any pain was immediately overridden by the total embarrassment that I now felt, sprawled on the ground.

As word reached Billy up the line – there were sometimes thirty or forty horses on these rides – he reined in his horse, turned and slowly meandered back to where I lay in a bundle on the ground. Getting up on one knee, I looked up at the colossus towering above me, like the statue of the Duke of Wellington.

'What are you doing on the floor, boy? We're not picking daisies, are we? Get up immediately!' he said, in his beautiful Irish lilt.

With that, he wheeled round and continued the ride. I grabbed at the reins being held out to me and with great difficulty managed to plant my foot in the stirrup. I spent the rest of the ride skulking alone, the last man in the pack. However, I learnt a salutary lesson that day, which was don't fall off a polo pony – always go down with the ship.

The next five years of my polo career were spent at the small, but charming, Ham Polo Club in Richmond. Indeed, it was here in my first official game that I completed a feat that I have never been able to surpass, and one which I am sure is unique. In my first game, from the very first throw-in, I took the ball from position one straight up the pitch, and scored within about fifteen seconds of the game starting.

The number one position is usually given to the least competent member of the team. In all my years of playing polo, and despite having achieved one of the best amateur handicaps in the country of three goals, I have never got near to repeating this performance.

However, perseverance and fortitude were to pay off in the ensuing years. Although it took me too many years to realise that, in order to become a good polo player, I needed to play with, and watch, the best in action. Having the aspiration of wanting to be three or four goals, I stayed for too long in the cradle of Ham. I had started late, at thirty years old, and in order to achieve the handicap I wanted, time was of the essence.

The moment finally arrived when I had to go up from the Second to First Division. The big city was beckoning me, and the Guards Polo Club was where the action was. Here, during each day of the season, many of the world's greatest players could be found, dancing on their beautiful ponies while showing their honed skills to perfection. The press and media over the last decade would have you believe that the only reason players joined the Guards Polo Club was to rub shoulders with Prince Charles, and other luminaries, which up to a point is true. However, most players join clubs for one main reason, because they are besotted with the game of polo.

In 1977, my chance came to join the number one club in England, though my membership in that first year was granted on the proviso that I played only mid-week. This was due to a certain amount of congestion at the weekend.

The anticipation of playing at the Guards Polo Club was killing – the only problem was that on arriving for my first chukkas, I discovered that I was playing with players of my own calibre, although there was a smattering of one and two goal players. Being a zero at the time, this was still quite appealing, but it didn't stop me from looking ruefully up to Number 3 ground, where the big boys were having their practice chukkas.

The 1978 season arrived, and so did I. The polo fields were cut to perfection after a wet winter and an early spring. The ponies stood side by side, glistening in the lines, their bodies rippling with strength and power like the athletes they are. Black, red, yellow, blue – a multitude of leg and tail bandages, wrapped tightly to protect the mount from the blow of stick or ball. Grooms were making last minute adjustments to tack, while down the line, two ponies reared, gnashing teeth, and kicking out at each other with their front legs; the grooms jumping up to grab the head collars to placate the anxious steeds.

We were in about the fourth week of the season. The five-minute hooter sounded and the valiant warriors, both player and horse, were getting ready for action.

'I'll take Honey first,' I said to Diana, my groom, and one of my best-loved horses was eased backwards out of the pony lines.

I rode onto the field to practise, spending a couple of minutes stick and balling – that is, warming up with horse, stick, and ball. Because of my total absorption at this point, believe it or not, I was totally unaware that I was still smoking a rather large cigar.

I was certainly unaware that I had made the worst transgression in recent Guards' history. Running off with a player's wife was totally acceptable; stealing polo boots, sticks, or another team's professional player was unacceptable, but riding onto a polo pitch with a lardy clenched between one's teeth was unthinkable.

Suddenly, a sound like thunder rang out and seconds later the words came down in waves rolling out across three polo fields, a distance of some nine hundred yards.

Looking up towards Number 3 ground, I saw a horse and rider charging across the fields towards us. Eight players stopped, mesmerised, as the rider drew closer, all the time keeping up a steady gallop. They came to an abrupt halt eight feet from where I stood.

It was him, God personified (at least at the Guards Polo Club). It was Major Ronald Ferguson, the father of the future Duchess of York, sitting there deep in his saddle, his riding boots glistening in the sunlight and, judging by the withering stare he was giving me with those huge bushy eyebrows, he was none too happy with me. I had the feeling that within a few seconds I was not going to be happy either.

Although I had been to the club earlier that year, I hadn't been within fifty feet of the major and had never even spoken to him and, for his part, he had certainly never lifted a stone to find me squirming about underneath it. His words came out slowly, concisely but powerfully.

'Are you stupid? Are you totally stupid?'

He had a way of pronouncing stupid, the 'stuw' and the 'p' and the 'id' were all said with supreme definition.

'Get off my bloody polo field and get that awful thing out of your mouth immediately!' he bellowed.

By this time, the major was standing up in the stirrups, pointing in several directions at once. Now, not many people had witnessed the major in full flow, and let me tell you that it was an awesome sight. For out there on those hallowed grounds, he was the lord over all. Princes, industrialists, moguls, and generals – all would quake and get back into line when the major poured scorn and derision on them.

'Ah ... it cost me a fiver,' I said, trying to be funny and hoping to diffuse the situation a little. 'I'll go and smoke it over there.' I pointed in the general direction of the horseboxes.

'Morrison!' he roared. 'It is Morrison, isn't it? If I see that bloody thing on any of my polo fields again, you're out!'

That's when I fixed him with my favourite 'go fuck yourself' stare, shrugged my shoulders, turned my horse, and exited the pitch puffing wildly on my cigar. The enemy's charge had been met, the attack parried and no wall had been breached. Within minutes I was playing chukkas, and nothing else of any consequence happened.

A few of my fellow players did point out to me, though, that I was probably now in big trouble with the 'powers that be'. One or two even suggested that I could be blackballed. Suddenly I wasn't feeling so cocksure.

I arrived on the Thursday as nervous as hell, and scanned the chukka sheets to see in which ones I would be playing. There was some slight trepidation, because I had this negative feeling that maybe I wouldn't be playing at all, and to my horror my name was nowhere to be seen on the sheets for fields 5 and 6, the grounds for low-goal players. It seemed the major had struck. I had been routed, and no prisoners had been taken. My polo career had finished before it ever started, my world had fallen in.

'Morrison! Bryan Morrison!'

The voice of Ginger, the assistant polo manager, rang out from some distance away, breaking my gloomy reverie.

'Come here!' he called. 'Come here quickly.'

I ran the fifty yards or so to where he was.

'Hurry up, guv, hurry up!' he said, pointing towards the Number 3 ground. 'You're up there playin' with the big boys today.'

I immediately rushed back to the pony lines, grabbed both horse and stick and rode up to the Number 3 ground, where seven players were assembled. The first to greet me was the Marquis of Waterford, who then proceeded to introduce me to Prince Charles and a whole bevy of aristos and high goal players.

'Where would you like to play?'

'Erm, anywhere,' was my reply.

'OK, you play at number one.' That was it. I had arrived.

Years later, I asked Ron why. Why had he invited me to play with the big boys in spite of my faux pas?

'Bugler' (that was his nickname for me), 'I haven't got the faintest idea.'

The nickname had been bestowed on me one afternoon. I had just finished playing a game in which I represented the British Army against the Indian Army. The other seven players all being soldiers, not merely soldiers but generals, brigadiers, colonels, all the way down to a lowly major. It was prize presentation time, and the commentator first called the visitors, 'General Singh, Brigadier Kumar,' and so on. Then it was to the British contingent, all officers, until he got to me. There was a sudden silence, followed by, 'Bugler Morrison.' I'd made it, my first commission in the British Army.

Ronald Ferguson hit the headlines in 1988, when he was 'discovered' by the *News of the World* using an exclusive health club and massage parlour called the Wigmore Club, and subsequently through his affair with a young lady by the name of Lesley Player. It was a photograph of him leaving this salubrious venue that led to his being ostracised by many of his friends, but what rankled him most was that many of the same friends availed themselves of this very establishment.

Shortly before the story broke, Ronnie and three of his mates decided to take me there on the night after my fortieth birthday; they figured a good sauna and massage would be just the pick-me-up I needed. I can say, hand on heart, that, if it was a brothel as described in acres of newsprint after Ronnie's capture, I certainly saw nothing of it. I was not propositioned or offered any of the services that I was later to read about.

Perhaps I am being totally naive, but it was no different from any number of sauna and massage parlours that existed in London in the seventies and eighties. It appeared to be no more than a boys' club, where you could have a good sauna and massage; and, knowing the man as I did, I believe that he had absolutely no interest in prostitution.

Ronnie and I were invited with eight others to a very grand stag night in one of the top London hotels. The party was held in two of its incredible penthouse suites, and it was stocked to the gills with the finest of everything: vintage champagne, Scottish smoked salmon – it all flowed. The ten of us were just finishing our hors d'oeuvres when there was a knock at the door and two or three beauties entered, to be followed over the next ten minutes by a baker's dozen. By the time the main course arrived, the table was empty but for two individuals, and all manner of things were happening in the adjoining rooms.

Now I don't want to give the impression that I'm some sort of goody two shoes, because I am not; live and let live is the motto. I dislike intensely the shooting of game, but I don't in any way condemn those that get enjoyment from it, and the same with ladies of the night – if you enjoy it, fine, but it's not for me.

So, I decided to opt out discreetly. As I walked out, there must have been six girls sitting on various chairs and sofas, searching their nails for some small blemish or other. I strolled up the corridor and had pushed the button for the lift when I heard my name being called.

'Bugler, wait for me.'

It was Ronnie, who marched up to me with a big grin on his face.

'Aren't you staying and having some fun?' I asked.

'No, Bugler,' was his reply. 'That kind of thing's not for me.'

Seconds later, the two of us were in the street, on our way home. Ronnie was a much-maligned man, which is sad, because he was proper. He would be the one you would want to be with in the trenches, you could depend on him with your life and, to this day, he is one of the only real men I have known – and believe me, I've known many.

In 1986, I attended the christening of Sue and Ron's daughter, Eliza. The Prince of Wales and Princess Diana were present, as Charles and I were to become joint godfathers of Eliza. A few hymns were sung and I became aware of this rather lovely baritone voice, coming, as it turned out, from Prince Charles. After the ceremony, I remarked to the Prince that he should make a record, as he had an extremely good voice. In fact, I suggested we should make a Christmas charity record. He laughed and said, 'Why not?'

I think I may take this up with him someday.

Some of my favourite memories of the Guards Polo Club are of playing with Prince Charles. I had started playing in matches with his Windsor Park team in the late seventies. Prior to one of these games, we were sitting on chairs and the bumpers of cars, strapping on our kneepads in preparation for the game. I was as usual puffing on a large cigar, when the Prince enquired as to why I always smoked just before we played.

'I don't know, sir, maybe it relaxes me,' was my reply.

'Bryan,' he said, 'I was given a box of cigars by Fidel Castro; they are his personal cuvee, would you like them?'

Like them? I would have killed for them! Imagine a cigar smoker being offered a cigar rolled especially for Castro, being passed to the Prince of Wales and then on to me?

I said, yes please, and Prince Charles said he would bring one the next time we were to meet on Thursday.

True to his word, the Prince rolled up on Thursday, cigar in hand.

'Try this one,' he said, 'I know you only like certain cigars.' With that he handed me one of those precious stogies. That evening, utter confusion reigned – I couldn't smoke this piece of history, it would be sacrilege. But what to do? Should I say it was a good cigar in an attempt to get my hands on the box? God, life is difficult.

On the Saturday, Prince Charles asked if I had enjoyed the cigar. I couldn't tell a fib, as much as I might have wanted to.

'Er, no, not yet, sir, but I will.'

'Well, let me know when you have; if you like it, I'll give you the box.'

I never did smoke it. To this day, that cigar sits in my trophy cabinet; however, it lies there with quite a few of his fellow cigars, because Prince Charles, being the wonderful man that he is, never forgot and did send me the rest of the box, plus extras.

It was shortly after the cigar story that I was playing with the Prince and he had an accident that was of both our making. We were both charging flat out, chasing a loose ball, when, for whatever reason, I didn't see him. The next thing I knew, my horse smashed into the Prince's, just in front of his saddle, and the result was that he went flying over the horse's head to land face up on the ground. He lay there still, arms and legs prone, eyes closed.

Within seconds, the players and umpires had formed a circle around him, with one of the umpires and a player scrabbling off their horses to be of assistance. The Prince lay there motionless for at least thirty seconds, although it seemed like a lifetime. Suddenly his eyes opened up and a small smile crept across his face. Ronnie, who had been umpiring the match, looked up at me and said, 'Bugler, I thought you'd bloody well killed the future King of England!'

Fortunately, I had managed to avoid a trip to the Tower or, even worse, being beheaded. Prince Charles was up on his feet within minutes, none the worse for wear, and, oh yes, we won the game.

Shortly after this incident, I had noticed a white ambulance that barely seemed to hold itself together. It was always there, parked at the end of Number 1 or 2 grounds on a Sunday afternoon, with the back doors open. It was a bit of a mystery, and one day I asked Prince Charles if he knew anything about it.

'Oh yes, it belongs to a wonderful man by the name of John Prestwich, who's been on an iron lung for years and he just loves watching polo.'

My interest piqued, I wandered over to the crumbling ambulance. There were two people in it when I arrived, a vibrant woman in her forties, sitting next to this person with the eyes of the ancient mariner. He was lying prostrate on what looked like a metal camp bed. Sticking out of his chest was a rather large tube, which meandered its way to an instrument that looked a bit like the bellows a blacksmith might use. These bellows were constantly in use, creating a hollow breathing sound that filled the space in the van.

The man's piercing blue eyes peered into my soul.

'Hello, I'm Bryan Morrison. I play polo here.'

'I know, I've been watching you,' was his reply. 'Come and sit down here.' His eyes looked to the right, but his head did not move, remaining motionless. I stepped up into his world and eased myself into the jump seat by his bed.

'The name's John, John Prestwich, and that's my wife, Maggie.'

And so started a twenty-year friendship that is still one of the most important in my life. Here was a man who possessed a will of iron, the strength of character and a determination, under the most dreadful of circumstances, to witness the world - to understand and comment on man's goodness and inequality, to read, listen and grow - all the time encased in a body that is so racked by polio that he cannot move an arm or leg or even a finger. His only communication is through his vocal cords.

John is the oldest and longest surviving person to inhabit an iron lung. He was struck down at seventeen years old, while a vibrant, young merchant seaman. At the time of writing, he has spent forty-eight years in permanent and total paralysis and yet he is an inspiration. I have never seen him, even in his darkest moments, without a smile on his face. On more than one occasion I have visited John with a world of problems on my shoulders. I arrive able to laugh, feel, run, walk, jump, stand and sit; I drive a car, swim, dance, and have the ability to do everything. And yet, when I sit with him, he is the master, the wisdom, the strength. I leave shamefaced and problem free.

● ● ●

Bryan used to tell a story that summed up why he loved playing polo. It was in 1979, during the collapse of the Bill Gibb fashion business, and he had spent all morning in a meeting with four accountants, two lawyers, and several bank managers and their representatives. At 2.15 p.m., almost on his knees after all the arguments and questions, he announced that he had to leave, as he was off to play polo. At that point, none of the assembled suits could understand how he had any money to put petrol in his car, let alone to play polo.

He headed quickly down the M4 towards Windsor, travelling at breakneck speed in his red Ferrari, in an effort not to be late for the match. Keeping seven players waiting was deemed unacceptable. He roared through the park gates with only a few minutes to go and came to a halt in a cloud of dust, just as the other players in his team were walking or cantering onto the pitch.

He threw on his boots, kneepads, gloves and helmet, as the second hooter screamed for the start of the match. His teammates were now beginning to get angry. The zips on his boots would not close, and as his frustration grew, he realised that he had taken two left-handed gloves from the boot of his car. With the anger, the morning, the high-speed driving and the pettiness of gloves and boots that did not work, his brain felt like it would burst.

He shouted, 'Give me a pony. Quick, quick. That one will do!'

He thought, how can I go on and play like this. He was a total mess. But as his left foot hit the stirrup iron, in the precise moment that he swung up into the saddle, the darkness cleared and the light poured in.

Two hours later, he was sitting on the bonnet of his car, throwing back a cold beer.

He told later how this small incident was of great importance to him, because it illustrated exactly what polo had given him over the years, besides the friendships, the physical activity, and the power. It was a game that rationalised his attitude to life.

19

A FIELD OF DREAMS

The years at the Guards Polo Club were amongst my happiest. Annual tours became the norm, playing for English or quasi-English teams. Probably the most memorable of these was playing in Chile with the captain of the English team, Julian Hipwood, and another English player, Lord Charles Beresford.

The Chilean people and their country were both magnificent, the memories a thousandfold. One in particular was of a small club in the foothills of the mighty Andes. We were probably only ten to fifteen miles away from the base of the mountain, yet the heat on the pitch was in the region of 115 degrees. This was to be further intensified by the heat generated by horse and rider during a frantic seven-and-a-half-minute chukka.

At the end of the first chukka, my head felt like a volcano that was about to explode. I rode to the sidelines and as my feet hit the ground I grabbed for the bottles of water on a nearby table before throwing myself under the only bit of available shade, which turned out to be a kind of rustic bus shelter, topped off by a sheet of rusting, corrugated metal.

Sitting there, dehydrated and exhausted on the ground, it was a minute or two before I finally took my head out of my hands and looked up, and there stood that towering mountain range where, in spite of the all-consuming heat, the peaks were glistening with snow. The effect was a bit like an Irish coffee: white and cold on top, but underneath brown and as hot as hell.

As well as Chile, polo has taken me to France, Belgium, the Caribbean, India, Australia, South America and Pakistan. It was in America on another of these trips where an incident happened that I would probably rather forget. We were due to play the Texas State Side at medium goal polo. The hospitality was fantastic. Parties, barbecues, and dinners – all were laid on for us. After beating a Southern American team in a friendly match, our stock rose even higher, and on the third day we were invited to be the guests of honour on something the locals called a night ride, which from what we could gather comprised of lots of beer, wine, women, song and, oh yes, horses and candles.

Before telling the next part of the story, I would like to say that I was not drunk or legless; I was plain stupid. We met first for drinks, warm hot toddies and beer, before setting out for the stables and horses. All were lined up along a tall fence. There were probably in excess of 120 horses with their riders in various degrees of readiness. It seemed to be more of a posse than a ride. Each rider carried either a candle or an oil lamp with which to light our way into the badlands.

'Mount up and move 'em out!' came the order across the still night air, and lights danced left and forward: the US cavalry was on its way. Within thirty seconds, the flank of horses took on the appearance of a huge man-made firefly. I applied slight pressure to the mouth of my steed, at the same time squeezing with my legs. This action normally brings some kind of response from the animal beneath me, but nothing moved. Urgently I squeezed again, this time pulling the reins straight across to my left side, and his left shoulder. No response. I kicked even harder.

'Come on, move, move!'

The more I screamed at him, the more high-pitched my voice became. I was now getting frantic. The firefly was fast disappearing in front of me, and I was in danger of getting left there on my own. Here I was, the great polo player who wasn't even able to get his horse to walk. This mount wasn't going anywhere. All my renewed efforts achieved absolutely nothing, not even the slightest twitch.

With panic setting in, I strained my eyes into the fast fading light, but the four or five horses that had been at my rear were now some distance ahead. Their lights were dwindling with each passing step and, horror of horrors, Johnny Kidd, one of the English players, was rapidly being eaten up by the darkness. I was alone, marooned in a sea of blackness, unable to make the beast take a solitary step forward.

'Johnny, Johnny!' I shouted into the darkness. 'Come here. Come look at this.'

Under the circumstances, there was very little else I could say.

'Johnny,' I repeated, and suddenly from out of the blackness he appeared.

His legs almost touched the ground as he rode – Kiddy-boy must have been six foot six in his bare feet. He looked like an up-market version of Don Quixote. One thing I always remember about Johnny Kidd, and it is a thought he should be happy with, is that whenever I get a mental picture of him, I always envisage him with a warm smile grinning from ear to ear.

'What's up now, Bryan?' he inquired.

Leaning forward over my 'dead' horse's ear, I cautioned Johnny to talk quietly, and said, 'I can't get this fucking pony to move.'

He leant his six-foot-six frame forward and peered at my mount, and then went into near uncontrollable laughter that shook him from his head down through his body, right to his boots. Even his horse rocked as his mirth continued. He recovered momentarily after about forty seconds, which allowed me time in which to enquire as to what was so fucking funny?

His words hit me like a bolt in the cold night air.

'Try taking the head collar off. Or untie the horse from the wall. It might go then!'

With that, he went into a new round of total hysterics, which nearly caused him to fall off his horse. I could have died. All I wanted to do at that moment was to disappear into that rich Texan soil. Thank god it was pitch black. Johnny and I quickly worked out a deal that was especially weighted in his favour. Silence does not come cheap.

Mind you, I did see the funny side of the whole affair as lamps in hand we cantered into the darkness to seek out and join the glimmering trail.

One of my dreams, albeit a remote one, was to build a new polo club. A club with style, humour and, above all, great polo. Too many times in the past, my ideas about facilities in other clubs had fallen on deaf ears; I was always suggesting ways in which I believed they could be improved for both players and members, but my views were not always shared. However, in the back of my mind, there was always this tiny thought of what could be.

By now, Greta and I had moved with our two children to Bartlett House, a Georgian house with stables and paddocks in Holyport, near Maidenhead. Early in the spring of 1986, I was faced with the dilemma of having a horse that needed to be schooled, but the paddocks around the house were very wet and unusable. I remembered a player at the Guards Polo Club, Norman Lobel, who had a purpose-built riding track at his house situated somewhere between my home and the Guards. I rang Norman and asked if I could bring my horse over to use his track for half an hour.

'Sure,' he replied. 'Help yourself.'

I had been schooling the horse for about thirty-five minutes and was preparing to leave when he approached me.

'How's it going?'

'It's one that I bred. It's green, but it's got possibilities,' I said.

I had met Norman casually at the Guards, where he was a player, but up to this point had never spent any time with him. A few more minutes drifted by, spent in conversation about horses, players, and the coming season. Finally, the time to depart arrived. My groom loaded up the pony and I bade Norman farewell, thanking him for his hospitality. I was leaving his drive, when I remembered that I had seen a 'For Sale' sign at some stables about a mile down the road from him. My son Jamie, then ten years old, had pointed them out to me.

'Do you know anything about the property that's for sale down the road? The one with the stables?'

'Yes,' he said. 'My brother and I went to see it a couple of weeks ago. We weren't impressed. The land's in a terrible condition, basically the place looks like a junk yard.'

'Well, I'm going to have a look anyway,' I said. 'It's on my way home.'

'I'm doing nothing,' he rejoined. 'Would you mind if I came along?'

The place was very much as Norman had described it, although the stables, which had been built at the turn of the century, still maintained a certain charm and dignity, in spite of their decay. The rest, however, was a mess. Two or three large ugly sheds were being used for all manner of storage, including a dozen or so old Bentleys and Rollers.

A couple of thousand bales of rather mangy hay, which had lost all of its freshness and life the season before, lay piled high. The bales on the bottom were mouldy and black through rainwater that had seeped through the roof and walls, and birds' nests and long dark rats' holes were in abundance.

Worse, much worse, was to come. The fields surrounding the stables were wrecked and broken. Undernourished grass lay yellow, feeding off a soil so dead that it could hardly throw up a buttercup or daisy, let alone a good crop of hay. There were broken trees and filthy ponds full of overgrown weeds and algae, while a veritable army of rotting tractor parts and plough shears lay scattered around like the wasted vehicles of war. Then we came across a totally dilapidated cattleshed, with old cow dung two feet thick inside, though, judging by its current state, no self-respecting cow had been near it for years.

And yet, as I stood there amidst all this dereliction and decay, I sensed it had magic. It sat on its own, forlorn in this wilderness, waiting for someone to remove the dustsheets of time, so that it could live and breathe again. But wait, what was this? From where I stood amongst the waist-high weeds and bracken bushes, I could see through the mangy trees on the other side of a large, listless pond, the remains of a racetrack.

'You know, Norm,' the words slipped out idly, but with great anticipation. 'I reckon it's about 150 to 200 yards to that fence.'

Norman looked at me, shrugged, and said, 'So what?'

'I'll tell you later,' I said, then paced in large, looping strides the distance from the cow shed to the far rails, picking my way between large rabbit warrens and squelchy, slippery ground – 180 yards. I couldn't believe it. Suddenly the dream was becoming clear. If north to south was 180 yards, then east to west must be in excess of 500 yards. That was it. This was to be the Number 1 polo field, and the cow shed would be the Royal Box. In that moment, I knew exactly what had to be done and how to do it.

'Bryan, Bryan?'

I looked up at Norman, who was standing beneath a 200-year-old oak tree, right in the middle of my polo field.

'What exactly are you doing?'

His words brought me out of my reverie.

'I'm going to build a new polo club. The first one in England for donkey's years, and it's going to be right here.'

'What do you mean a polo club? You couldn't turn this place into a field with decent hay, let alone a polo club.'

'Norman. I'll fill those ponds, cut down those trees, level this ground, and—'

My words were cut short. Norman had zipped across the distance that separated us, faster than I had seen him move all day. He was now right in front of me.

'Can I be your partner?'

'What? No, no, I don't want any partners.'

'Bryan, I want to be your partner in this polo club.' I looked at him for a long, hard minute. Why not? Anyone who wanted to start a polo club had to be crackers, so why not two of us?

'Bryan, look, I've got two sets of goal posts at home, and dozens of polo balls. What more do we need?'

We shook hands and the fun began. Less than twenty-four hours later, at midday on Sunday, I was to be shaking hands yet again. This time, it was to be with the vendor of the land. By the Tuesday afternoon, it was signed, sealed, and delivered. After the first rush of blood to the head reality took over. Suddenly the sheer enormity of the task became obvious.

This was not merely a case of cutting down a few trees and moving some soil around with a tractor. Oh no. This was proper landscaping. We needed earth-clearing machines as big as buses – the ones they use on motorways – and drainage machines that had vast lengths of plastic pipe perched on top, like a giant cotton reel. This was going to be huge.

Ochre-coloured machines pushed and shoved thousands of tons of soil every hour. In fact, 15,000 cubic metres of topsoil was moved, while 20,000 metres of subsoil was shifted to level the area. We laid 17.5 kilometres of plastic pipes to drain 1, 2, and 3 grounds. We used 120 tons of lime, 10 tons of red slag, 8 tons of fertiliser, 3.5 tons of grass seed, and 1,000 tons of fine sand.

Each working day for six weeks, the contractors burned hundreds of gallons of diesel in their machines. But this was only the beginning. We would also need two miles of fencing, two hundred horse boxes, a riding track, clubhouse, tennis courts, and don't let's forget the bar.

We started work in May, only to be pulled up days later by the local planning officer, who advised us that we needed planning permission to turn a field that had had horses on it into a flat field that was going to have horses on it.

I simply could not believe that we would need permission to do this. Enquiries were made, and the process seemed simple enough. We had to put advertisements in four local newspapers announcing our intention to build a polo club. The planning officer pointedly assured us that if no letters of disagreement were received at the end of a period of three weeks, we would be granted immediate permission from the dedicated powers (the chief planning officer). However, if there was even one letter of complaint, it would go before the combined planning committee in August.

This was potentially a major disaster for us, as it was imperative that the grass seed be sown by the end of September, and the groundwork alone would take up to four months. In simple terms, it meant that if for any reason we had to wait until August, we would be set back a full year. However, with no option but to comply with the council's request, we duly placed our advertisements in the papers, and the machines stayed idle.

Three teeth-grinding weeks passed and the council received no letters. On the twenty-first day, my architect rang the council, who confirmed that as no letter of complaint had been received, our permission would be granted.

The very next morning, the twenty-second day, we had our first piece of major publicity on the new project. The headline rang out: PRINCE CHARLES' FRIEND OPENS NEW POLO CLUB. The story read that the club was destined to become the 'Annabel's' of English polo (the article was also accompanied by a not-too-bad photograph of Prince Charles and me). Included in the feature was a mention of where the club was going to be situated. The next day, the council received three letters of protest automatically.

Then all hell broke loose.

Our architect received a phone call from the chief planning officer saying that because they had now received these letters our application had to go before the committee in August. The council was now in the process of changing the rules in the middle of the game. I must have telephoned the planning officer thirty times in the next two days, trying to get an appointment, but to no avail. They were all too busy.

On the third day I left a message with his secretary saying that I was coming to see him at 11.30 the next morning, and would wait there at the council offices as long as it took for him to grant me an interview. I arrived the following day dressed in a black pinstripe suit, black shirt, and a garish pink tie. Within thirty minutes, I was sitting in the office of our chief planning officer.

After the usual pleasantries had been done away with, I asked how the council could change the rules to suit themselves.

'Well,' he explained, 'the letters arrived a day or two after the twenty-first day, and er--'

'Not good enough,' I interrupted. 'You made the rules and we complied by them, and now I want you to grant us permission.'

Twenty-five minutes had now passed and an impasse had been reached. The council had reneged on our agreement and they were not about to step down. I stood up, walked to the door, turned back and said, 'Based on the information received by my architect, from this council, I signed a contract for £1.5 million with a contractor to build my polo fields and unless I receive permission to build within twenty-four hours I will have no recourse other than to sue the council for this amount plus punitive damages.'

'You can't do that,' was his incredulous reply. 'You can't sue the council!'

'Just watch your letter-box, and you'll see what can and cannot be done.'

Before I had taken another step, our man asked if I would mind waiting in the outer office for a moment or two. He then adjourned to a separate office. Four minutes later, we had our planning permission. In the years since this occasion, our relationship with the council has improved no end and although I have asked the question several times no one has been able to explain why they did what they did.

We cranked up the diesel engines and those great earthmovers moved forward, devouring all that stood in their way. Everything went well for the first six weeks, until the first of August. I remember it as if it were yesterday. The heavens opened up and as the Bible said, 'the rains smote the Earth'. For twenty-eight days in succession, it poured. The fields became a sea of wet, clingy clay, machines stood idle, and men scratched their heads. A miniature Flanders field.

By day fifteen, I was almost a nervous wreck. Every morning, I awoke hardly daring to open my eyes, or to bring my head from under the sheets to hear the incessant pitter-patter of raindrops on windowpanes. By the twentieth day, I actually started developing an ulcer, for we still had one and a half months' work to do and if that seed did not go in there would be no polo the following May.

The word amongst those who knew in the polo community was that we had no chance of playing in May anyway, because the grass would not have taken by then. Oddly enough, the only person from the hierarchy of polo at this time who had shown any sign of putting his name to the project, or helping in any way, was Prince Charles. As far back as mid-June, in conversation one afternoon, he asked to hear all about the project and said that he would love to join. Because of this, he became the first member of the Royal County of Berkshire Polo Club.

The grass seeds went in at the end of September and by the following May the fields lay there green and bright. Norman, Michael Amoore (our polo manager) and I mounted three horses and rode onto the pitches. We galloped, turned, stopped and repeated this for twenty minutes. The grounds were fine. On the first of May 1986, the first chukkas were played.

With the groundworks completed, our minds turned to other issues such as running this new polo club, and the one thing that polo players need more than anything are polo ponies. Around ninety-five per cent of all polo ponies playing in England originate from Argentina, the reasons being twofold.

Firstly, the vast number of ponies available there, which are used as working horses for separating cattle and sheep on the huge pampas;

secondly, they were bred from the American quarter-horse and the English thoroughbred. The English thoroughbred gives them speed out of the box and the quarter-horse gives them stamina and turning ability on their hocks – the two essentials in the making of a good polo pony and, indeed, a working horse. Also, and quite importantly, the price, as breeding a pony in England is extremely expensive, because they need three to four years of training; something ponies in Argentina get every working day.

So it was to Argentina we went.

● ● ●

Major Ronald Ferguson always maintained that he had used the Wigmore Club 'for massage only ... and by that I mean a totally straight one' and as 'a kind of cocoon where I could shut myself away for an hour and think.' Later it was alleged that the News of the World had actually been targeting a senior politician who was also a member of the club, and Ferguson had simply been caught up in the tabloid's sting.

In his autobiography, The Galloping Major, *he revealed that his biggest disappointment was the reaction of Prince Philip: 'I was deeply wounded by Prince Philip's refusal, as President of the Club, to discuss it with me. I made repeated requests to see him, and appointments were made which were subsequently cancelled.'*

He left the Guards Polo Club after not being re-elected as deputy chairman, and went to work for Bryan at the Royal County of Berkshire Polo Club, while he continued to be Prince Charles's polo manager, scheduling his matches and looking after his ponies and equipment.

This relationship ended in 1993, after further tabloid revelations about an affair with Lesley Player, a young businesswoman with whom Ferguson had organised a Ladies' International Polo Tournament. His position with Prince Charles was terminated abruptly in a letter from the Prince's private secretary. Ferguson complained later, 'After serving him faithfully and unquestioningly for twenty-one years, I was appalled by the way it was handled. The Prince of Wales did not have the guts to send for me and tell me straight to my face.'

Soon afterwards, Ferguson told Bryan he would also have to leave the Berkshire. After the Major died in 2003 at the age of seventy-one, Bryan added this postscript to his original manuscript.

● ● ●

Ronnie's problems were twofold: he became the father of a princess, and his naivety. It is well documented how he wrote to a national newspaper asking if he could purchase the original cartoon of him coming out of the massage parlour; at the time he had done nothing wrong, as far as he was concerned. To compound his naivety, he wrote the letter on Guards Polo Club paper, which was not simply naive, to use his favourite phrase, it was plain 'stupid'. It cost him his position in the club, and later his role as Prince Charles's polo manager.

Having left the Guards, possibly the biggest disappointment in his life, Ron came to work for me as the sponsorship director of the Royal County of Berkshire Polo Club. Ronnie was the most successful sponsorship director we have ever had. In fact, so successful was he that at the start of his second season with us, I had to ask him to cut down on the number of sponsored days he was bringing in. The reason for this being very personal, as it was expected for the chairman of a major polo club to turn up suited and booted each time a major day took place.

In his first year, Ronnie came up with about fourteen days. This may not seem like a lot, until you consider that the main sponsorship day was a Sunday. The heart of the season runs from the end of May until the end of July, so poor old Brysey was on duty, suited and booted in shirt, tie and suit virtually every single weekend from 11.30 a.m. till 4 p.m. So I asked Ronnie to cut down in his second season to give me a breather, but before he had got into his stride Lesley Player arrived on the scene.

When the story broke, the press ran riot; there were dozens of paparazzi outside my house, the Polo Club was overrun: they were everywhere. What better than the father of a princess having an affair, truly his annus horribilis? Ron finally came up to me and said, 'Bugler, this can't go on, I'm sorry, it's having a dreadful effect on your club. I think I'd better go.'

So Ron left. He retired to Dummer, if not a broken man, then very disappointed. He didn't deserve it, he was unique.

When my daughter Karina was born prematurely in 1979, weighing only 2.5lbs, the hospital was in total stress as one of the important parts of her incubator was malfunctioning and they couldn't find a replacement. I mentioned it to Ron later that evening.

At 4.30 in the morning, I received a phone call from him to say he had been scouring the whole of Hampshire and the South and that he had finally managed to procure this new part that we required. He then delivered it to Queen Charlotte's and Chelsea Hospital in Hammersmith. This he did of his own volition and it took him the best part of a night.

Ronnie Ferguson was a true friend, someone you could rely on in adversity. Sure he bellowed, but he had a heart of gold. His youngest daughter and my goddaughter, Eliza, is today a beautiful young woman and is a constant reminder to me of a man that I literally loved.

HAVE A CIGAR!

(20)

REACH FOR THE SKY

At the time of our visit to Argentina, the Falklands War had finished three years earlier. Our Argentine polo-playing friends had not been allowed to come and play in England since that time, for obvious reasons. In addition, our assumption was that the Argentine public were not too happy over there with Englishmen, either. However, several of our friends said that they were getting on with their lives and would love to see us. So off I went with Norman Lobel and Michael Amoore on our quest to buy horses, saddles, blankets and tack.

I have to say, true to their word, we found no animosity, albeit that we spent all our time with our polo-playing friends. Horses were cheap, with few international buyers since the war had deterred them, so we had a field day.

I remember taking a taxi one day from Buenos Aires out onto the Pampas, to look at horses. Most of the roads were dust tracks, with huge great holes eroded by the relentless beating sun and the torrential tropical rains that make up the varied climate of Argentina.

Four of us were squashed like sardines into this old taxi, alongside the driver. It soon became clear that the only way to survive this rugged terrain was to put on our polo hats to protect our heads, which were continually smashing against the roof of the taxi as we plunged into the deep crevices of the road.

The taxi leapt forward under the driver's instructions, veering sharply to the left, and suddenly there was a puncture. Out we jumped and within minutes the tyre was changed. Then we were off again, until a few miles later we veered sharply to the right. For a while the car struggled along, veering this way and that, but with no air-conditioning we were soon shedding pounds in our baking sauna.

All of a sudden there was another puncture. Again the driver managed to repair the wheel and we were off once more, all the time veering sharply from left to right. An hour passed by – although it seemed like an eternity – when we had a third puncture. This time repair was useless as we had used his two spares.

Stuck with no tyres, we sent our lone Spanish speaker to hitch back to the nearest town to try to find a new tyre, or help. After all, he spoke the language, but, more importantly, he was in our employ so had no choice. After some time, he hitched a lift from a passing vehicle and disappeared in a ball of dust.

Norman and Michael tried talking with the driver through hand signals while I settled down on the ground, shaded in part by the side of our taxi. In the far distance, I spotted a small wooden shack with smoke rising from its chimney so I decided to go and have a closer look. A few minutes later, I found myself facing what can only be described as a scene from the Steinbeck novel *The Grapes of Wrath*.

Inside this lean-to building was a rough-hewn wooden bar where a beautiful young Argentine goddess, a vision to behold, stood adorned in a white dress, grubby with the chores of the day. Surrounded by her children playing in the dirt, she meticulously tried to clean the floor with a broom while her overweight sloth of a husband watched through half-closed eyes from behind the bar.

While contemplating this picture, I became aware of the most delicious smell of cooking. Several large juicy chorizo sausages were simmering gently in a large black pan so I ordered, in my poor Spanish, a chorizo and a cold beer.

To this day, I can tell you that I have never eaten anything more divine. I walked back out of the door and shouted to Norman, beckoning them over, 'Norm, I've found an oasis!' How they produced ice cold beer in these conditions was beyond me; the old generator outside must have worked overtime to produce such a cold, delicious drink.

While we had been in Argentina, Norm's brother had been in Brazil. The day before we left Argentina, Norm received a phone call from his brother to say that he had just got out of jail, having been inside for over twenty-four hours. As he was leaving Brazil, he had been stopped because it turned out he had a forged airline ticket. He was eventually released the next day. However, our tickets had been purchased from the same agency in the UK and he wanted to warn us that we might have a potential problem.

It is one thing being stopped with a forged ticket anywhere in Central America, but it was quite another to be English and stopped in Argentina only three years after the Falklands War. With this thought in mind, I decided that we would draw the airport staff's attention to the fact that we might be victims of forged tickets, before any further issues could arise.

At the check-in desk, I informed the young attendant that I had reason to believe there might be something wrong with our tickets and could she please check them.

She returned shortly afterwards with a smile on her face.

'Mr Morrison, these tickets are fine,' she informed me. 'Shall I check you in?'

'Please,' I replied.

Minutes later, we progressed through passport control and immigration. At the departure gate, we had approximately fifteen minutes to wait before boarding.

'Well, Norm,' I said, 'two weeks in Argentina with no incidents, no arrests and we are heading home!' High fives all round.

Across the tannoy came the words 'London Heathrow', and soon we were boarding, arriving at our seats and stowing our bags in the lockers along with our jackets containing passports, papers and wallets.

I literally collapsed into my seat, the emotions of the day and the trip making me extremely tired. Seconds later, with seat belts fastened, we awaited take off. The cabin doors were closed and the plane moved forward ... but only a yard or two, and then suddenly it stopped.

Half a minute later and rather ominously, the door opened once again. In stepped two soldiers with machine guns slung over their shoulders. They walked through the cabin, pausing at a stewardess who was now out of her seat and looking very worried.

I was watching them extremely closely, when suddenly one of them mouthed the words, 'Señor Morrison'. I couldn't believe it. After some seconds, the stewardess led them towards Norman and me.

'Señor Morrison?' This face peered down at me from above. 'Can you pleeze come with us.'

'No, you don't understand,' I pleaded, with more of a wish than belief. 'We are going to London.'

The words were repeated. 'Mr Morrison, pleeze come with us.'

Those two machine guns told me that resistance wasn't possible. So up we got, shoulders hunched, and we followed them. At the door of the plane,

I remembered that my wallet and passport were still in my jacket in the locker above.

'Hang on, I need my jacket, it's got my passport and wallet in it.'

His next words were the most ominous of all.

'It is not a problem, señor, you will not be needing them.'

That was it. I was convinced that they had come to get us. Were we about to be abducted? With a soldier at each side, we exited the plane, proceeded through customs and back out through passport control without a pause. My panic was slowly creeping up.

Suddenly there was a door in front of us with a porthole-style window in the centre. As we got closer, I could see that we were about to enter the main airport complex. In that split second, I was sure there would be a couple of green Ford Fairlanes parked outside, with a posse of suited security men wearing dark glasses inside them, waiting for us.

The two soldiers went through the door first, leading the way to an escalator that led down towards the main concourse and certain imprisonment. Sweating profusely from the heat and fear, I turned to Norm and said, 'At the bottom of the escalator, run – we are in the shit.' I was now absolutely certain that we were being abducted. Moreover, the escalator was taking us further down towards the mouth of the dragon.

I started to shout, 'Run, Norm, run!' when a crisp voice suddenly pierced my consciousness.

'Bryyyan! Norrrman!'

I looked past the soldiers towards the bottom of the escalator and there, ten feet in front, was Bernardo McCormick, a great Argentine friend, standing nonchalantly with a huge smile on his face.

We hit the bottom of the escalator and the two guards stepped aside, while Bernardo rushed forward, giving us each a huge embrace and a big hug.

'Hey. I am sorry, I get caught in the traffic, and I just had to say goodbye.'

Say goodbye, I thought, what's he talking about?

That was when the full impact of what had just happened hit us. We were convinced that we would be dead within hours, or at least tortured, and here was Bernardo, who had managed to stop an international jet airliner (how, I do not know) simply because he wanted to say goodbye.

In Argentina, when you know the right people, you can do anything.

The emotion and happiness at seeing his face overwhelmed us. We laughed and almost cried for minutes before Bernardo said something to the guards, who then escorted us back up the stairs and through security, passport control and customs. Once back on the plane, the looks we got from our fellow passengers were of total bemusement and impatience, after all they had been waiting for us for at least thirty minutes. Minutes later, we took our seats and once again we were on our way, covered in a huge blanket of relief.

While on the subject of aircraft, I must recount this story.

One day a mate of mine rang me up and asked what I was up to.

'Not a lot,' I replied. 'Why?'

'I am taking my helicopter up to Northampton and I thought that you might like to come for the ride?'

Some time passed before this ear-splitting noise, somewhat reminiscent of a helicopter sequence from *Good Morning, Vietnam*, split the air.

Seconds later, a large red Hughes 500 helicopter touched down with the delicacy of a woman's hand embracing a length of silk. This piece of silk was slap bang in the middle of the lawn behind my house.

Crouching low – as they do in the movies – I half ran and walked towards the machine. A hand waved me round to the front and within seconds I had heaved myself, not too gracefully, into the co-pilot's seat. Brian, my friend and pilot, was gesticulating at once from his ears and head towards my ears and head. Earphones I thought, or rather headphones, as I was to learn soon afterwards. Seconds later I was there, seatbelt tightened, headphones on, listening to a voice that sounded as if it was at the bottom of a well, rather than a few inches away from me.

'You alright?' the words came over the airwaves. Once again remembering the old movies, I responded with the thumbs up.

Sitting there, the garden and house loomed large. Suddenly and effortlessly we were gone. Within seconds the house that encapsulated my life looked no bigger than a postage stamp stuck on an envelope, and we were off on our great adventure. Ten minutes into the flight, Brian made a suggestion that seemed to reek of total madness.

'Do you want to take control? Do you want to fly it?'

'Are you kidding?' was my somewhat dubious reply.

'Just take the stick, not too much movement, give it a try,' he said.

My first reaction was to hold the stick as if I was hanging onto a piece of wood attached to a doomed raft in the Pacific Ocean, which was about to sink.

'No, caress it, hold it gently.'

Magically I heard the words, 'You have control.'

At this point, there was one thing I needed to do and that was to inform the pilot that I had control.

'I have control.'

For five minutes, I flew that beautiful machine and loved it. An hour later, having been to our destination, we were flying along the Thames at 1,500 feet, when once again, Brian over the RT said, 'Do you want control?'

'Yeah, I'd love to.'

'You have control.'

'I have control,' I repeated.

Everything was fine for the next two minutes. Then suddenly there was a massive jolt and the helicopter shook as if we were in a twin-tub washing machine. We were not exactly hurtling towards the earth, but we were descending pretty fast.

In that exact moment, over my headphones, I heard the words, 'Mayday! Mayday!' Two words associated with real danger.

I turned to look at Brian, who was pronouncing the third 'Mayday!' – it was us.

This whole experience lasted no more than thirty seconds before I realised that we were really in trouble. My hands left the stick with the acceleration of someone letting go of a white-hot poker. The vibrations were intense, we were skewering downwards. Seconds became an eternity and an eternity disappeared in seconds.

We were in the shit.

Don't ask me how, probably because he is a fantastic pilot, we landed safely. Within moments of our distress call, the airwaves were buzzing with the knowledge that an aircraft was down. An hour and a half later, we were back at base to be met by a plethora of people. Gold and silver braid was everywhere.

It turned out that the Hughes 500's rotor blades were susceptible to stones being thrown up from the ground during rotation. I don't know if this problem is particular to the Hughes but in order to protect the leading edge on the blades they had bound them with strapping. This strapping had torn and blown open, so creating turbulence in the blades' rotation. The wind and the rain of the day had done their job to exacerbate the problem.

'Are you OK?' I was asked

'Yeah, I am fine. Tell me, what are the chances of a helicopter crashing?'

'Oh, one in five million,' came the reply.

'Good, is there anywhere that I can learn to fly, having just enlarged the odds to one in ten million?'

That is how I turned up a week later at Wycombe Air Park, based at the former RAF Booker airfield, near High Wycombe in Buckinghamshire, to learn how to fly a helicopter. After taking more than forty lessons, and despite the fact that on my final exercise I strayed into military airspace and a live firing zone above Salisbury Plain, I completed my training. To everyone's disbelief, a few months later my full helicopter private pilot's licence arrived in the post.

About six months later, I was invited to Malaysia by one of my great friends, HRH Prince Abdullah ibni Sultan Haji Ahmad Shah, better known by a nickname I gave him years ago, 'The Prince of Peace'. He is the eldest son and heir of the Sultan of Pahang, the third largest state in Malaysia.

There were many amazing incidents during the trip, and the first was on the evening of our arrival. We had been invited to dinner with the rest of his extended family, who between them accounted for half the royal family of the region. The venue was a hotel restaurant owned by the Prince, where we were taken to a very large private room at the back. There were in the region of twenty-five of us sitting down and, as per usual, the hospitality was unrivalled.

The meal finished and Abdullah decided that we should go back with him to his palace, so he and I exited our private room together. The main restaurant had possibly seventy diners sitting at various tables, and most of the diners looked to be locals. As we stepped into the room a few heads turned, followed by the sound of chairs being pushed back on a marble floor, and before we had moved halfway across the restaurant virtually all the diners were lying prostrate on the floor. It was surreal.

The door opened to the main lobby where dozens of people were going about their business, some sitting and talking, with porters heaving suitcases, bell boys carrying small message boards with tinkling bells, concierges, management, check-in girls – the normal mêlée of a busy hotel lobby. At the main exit, thirty yards in front, were about thirty people standing motionless; they looked like some sort of greeting party. Within ten seconds, I felt like Gulliver walking through dozens of small people – it was either that or a war zone.

From my right the Prince whispered, 'Just look ahead and keep walking.'

By now every person in that lobby with the exception of a couple of Europeans, who looked like lone trees in a denuded forest, was on their belly or at least in a prayer position. It was the most unbelievable sight. The party dead ahead were on their knees, and the whole lobby was now on the floor. Then three or four of the welcoming party rose, greeting the Prince with huge affection, we climbed into the awaiting cars and were gone.

Where was I? Oh yes, the helicopter story.

As part of our trip, the Prince had arranged for us to spend two nights in the middle of the jungle in a camp. He'd told Greta and me that a large craft would take us up-river to our camping site. 'Don't worry, the boat will be well equipped.'

I noticed a glint in his eye when he said this, but I thought no more about it.

A couple of his chaps took us in a 4x4 to a small landing by the side of this great river, my eyes darting here and there looking for the *African Queen* to take us up-river. All I could see, however, were some rough-hewn, canoe-like craft; not, I thought, a boat fit for a prince.

'Where's our boat?' I enquired.

'That's it there,' a boatman said, pointing to a dug-out tree that was floating by the jetty.

At that moment, I could just picture the Prince's glee back at the palace, imagining my horror as to what was about to happen. Now I knew what that glint in his eye was for. This called for the British stiff upper lip that has mastered thousands of different situations, such as the eating of lambs' eyes off a pile of couscous – yes, I've done that as well, in a sheik's tent in the Sahara Desert.

With the maximum amount of poise, Greta and I climbed into our piece of floating bark for the commencement of our journey. It rained, it shone, and it was magnificent. Two days later, however, the thought of a warm, comfortable bed was beckoning to me.

An excited guardian of the jungle informed us that they had received a radio message that the Prince was sending a helicopter to pick us up. A boat took us across the river, and after a short hike we came to a very small clearing where ten minutes later the helicopter dropped out of the sky. Greta sat in the back, as I had been invited by the pilot to sit by his side, headphones were donned, and within seconds we were airborne.

A minute or two passed before I was aware of the pilot talking about landing back at the palace in Pahang. I pressed the intercom, 'Excuse me, but we are supposed to be going to Kuala Lumpur.'

'Oh, let me see.'

After a rapid conversation in Malaysian, he confirmed that our destination was in fact to be KL. We were at this time flying over dense jungle with no sighting available, so out came the pilot's map, board, rule and so on. For the next minute, he attempted to fly and at the same time rework his chart.

I pressed the intercom again. 'Why don't I fly it, while you fix your charts.'

'You fly it? What do you mean?' he replied disdainfully.

'I have a licence to fly a helicopter, I just passed a few months ago.'

He stared at me for a second or two, then came those magic words, 'You have control.'

I flew that beautiful machine for the next hour, sometimes going to within twenty feet of the jungle canopy, until dead ahead, the captivating and delightful city of Kuala Lumpur came slowly into view through the shimmering haze. We slid effortlessly across the city to the airfield, where, I say modestly, I made a perfect landing. It was a really great thrill.

The Royal County of Berkshire Polo Club was now in top gear, and one of the most interesting occasions was a day conceived by Ronnie Ferguson and, I believe, Captain James Hewitt, who was a friend of Princess Diana. The Gulf War had been over for a few months and Ronnie and I had been talking about the various troop commanders that we knew who had taken part in the war, when it occurred to us that there must be enough of them to make up a couple of polo teams. Arthur Denaro and James Hewitt, to name just a few.

So we decided to have a celebration of the event. Prince Charles was invited to play, along with the top military brass, a few Desert Rats, some tanks and possibly even a fly-past by some Tornado fighter jets – just a small day!

For organisational reasons, the event had to be on a Tuesday, a question of logistics. However, there was a problem with Tuesday, which was that the Joint Chiefs of Staff had always met on Tuesdays in London since Wellington beat Napoleon at Waterloo.

Somehow we managed to get them to break with tradition for our event. For the first time in over 150 years, the meeting was cancelled so that all the Joint Chiefs, as well the Secretary of State for Defence, the Right Honourable Tom King MP, and the Commander-in-Chief of British Forces in the Gulf War, General Sir Peter de la Billière, could be present at our Gulf War Day. Ronnie's idea was to raise £250,000 for charity on this day, and the date was set for Tuesday 16 July 1991.

We were blessed that day with beautiful warm weather. Four huge Desert Rat tanks stood satanically on the four corners of Number 1 polo field, standing out starkly from the lush green fields. God, they were evil. They had arrived the previous day on the biggest transporters I have ever seen. Looking at them, I would not like to have been the enemy.

The teams were made up of the 7th Armoured Brigade, the Desert Rats, against the 4th Armoured Brigade, the Black Rats. Prince Charles, being Colonel-in-Chief of the 5th Royal Inniskilling Dragoon Guards, was made the captain of the 7th; while Captain James Hewitt of the Life Guards, who served as a Challenger tank commander in the Gulf War, was the captain of the 4th.

The Royal Box was adorned with the great and the good. The Duchess of York, Ronnie's daughter, was also present, having agreed to present the prizes to the winning team, and so too His Majesty King Constantine of Greece.

The Band of the Welsh Guards took to the fields in all their sound, colour and pageantry, to begin the day's celebrations. Then, out of the azure blue sky, suddenly dozens of parachutes from the Red Devils display team appeared and, as if being funnelled from above, all landed within yards of the Royal Box.

From the east, a deafening roar shook the ground as about a dozen Tornado fighters screamed overhead at one thousand feet, followed by displays from the Sharks helicopter team, the Queen's Colour Squadron, and the Household Cavalry standard bearers.

The two teams fought out a fast and furious match, which was won by the 4th Armoured Brigade. The day was a huge success and went a long way to achieving Ronnie's target of £250,000 for the charity. The comment from most of the players afterwards was that playing in the game had been more nerve-racking than going to war.

I am sure they were only joking.

● ● ●

This is where Bryan Morrison finished his original manuscript in late 1991. Ultimately, he decided not to have the book published the following year and it was put away in a drawer, where it has remained ever since.

On Sunday 16 July 2006, Bryan was playing in a friendly match with his son Jamie at the Royal County of Berkshire Polo Ground, when his horse tripped and Bryan was thrown to the ground, where he lay unconscious. He had landed on his head, causing severe brain injuries. He was taken to Wexham Park Hospital, near Slough, and then transferred to John Radcliffe Hospital in Oxford.

Sadly, Bryan never regained consciousness and he was to remain in a coma for more than two years. He died aged sixty-six after contracting a virus on 27 September 2008, at the Holyport Lodge Care Home, near Maidenhead.

Looking back on his extraordinary life, Bryan Morrison once said, 'I'm a very fortunate man. All my businesses are my hobbies – I love music, I love design and I love polo. But if you want to know what I rate as my greatest achievement of the last decade, I'll tell you. It's got nothing to do with horses – it is learning how to fly a jet helicopter.'

EPILOGUE

After Bryan Morrison's original memoir ended in 1991, he continued working from 1 Star Street in Bayswater, managing his four music publishing companies, Bryan Morrison Music, Morrison Leahy Music, Snapper Music and Lupus Music as well as developing The Royal County of Berkshire Polo Club.

Over the next three decades, as the size of the membership of the Berkshire grew, so did the facilities, so that the club now includes seven polo fields, the UK's first all-weather polo arena, a stick and ball field, stabling for more than 200 horses, two tennis courts, a croquet lawn, a gym, clubhouse, Royal Pavilion, and a polo academy.

The gold and silver Prince of Wales Trophy, designed by society jeweller Theo Fennell, has become one of the most prestigious high goal tournaments in the calendar, attracting leading players and celebrities from around the world, and is now in its 34th year and is still held at the Club. The annual Polo Festival held in August is the largest festival of its kind in the UK, and other major events of the season include the medium goal Eduardo Moore Tournament; the John Prestwich 8-12 Goal Challenge Trophy; the Julian and Howard Hipwood Trophy; and the John Houghton Open Tournament. The club is also the Official Home of England Polo and now plays host to the prestigious Hurlingham Polo International.

Since his father's death in 2008, Jamie Morrison has become the Chairman and CEO of the Royal County of Berkshire Polo Club. He is an accomplished polo player himself, having started playing the sport at the age of twelve. He represented England Schools from sixteen years through to the senior team, and also won two gold medals at the Federation of International Polo's European Championships. He is a former England polo captain and he has been on two England tours, including test matches against South Africa and Argentina, amongst many more accolades.

Jamie's aim is to develop the club's commercial strategies to cement the stature of the Royal County of Berkshire Polo Club as a world-class polo, events and equestrian facility, which pushes the boundaries for generations to come.

ACKNOWLEDGEMENTS

The publisher would like to express their grateful thanks to the family and friends of Bryan and Greta Morrison for their help with editing and publishing this memoir.

Special thanks to Jamie Morrison and Abby Newell for entrusting us with the original manuscript by Bryan Morrison, and for their continuing support and encouragement. Thanks also to Karina Audeh, David Gentle, Bernard Jacobson and Cora Barnes, for their help in answering all of our questions about names, places, dates and times, and many thanks to Phil May for his personal recollections of The Pretty Things.

Finally, thank you to all of the team at Quiller and particularly to Barry Johnston for his skill in editing the original manuscript and to Guy Callaby for his design.

SELECT BIBLIOGRAPHY

Blake, Mark, *Pink Floyd: Pigs Might Fly*, Aurum Press, 2007.

Buckler, Rick and Ian Snowball, *The Jam*, This Day in Music, 2018.

Chapman, Rob, *Syd Barrett: A Very Irregular Head*, Faber and Faber, 2010.

Ferguson, Major Ronald, *The Galloping Major*, Macmillan, 1994.

Gambaccini, Paul, Tim Rice and Jonathan Rice, *British Hit Singles* (8th ed.), Guinness Publishing, 1991.

Harrison, Ann, *Music: The Business* (7th ed.), Virgin Books, 2017.

Jones, Lesley-Ann, *Ride a White Swan: The Lives and Death of Marc Bolan*, Hodder & Stoughton, 2012.

Mason, Nick, *Inside Out: A Personal History of Pink Floyd*, Weidenfeld & Nicolson, 2004.

Michael, George and Tony Parsons, *Bare*, Michael Joseph, 1990.

Napier-Bell, Simon, *Black Vinyl, White Powder*, Ebury Press, 2002.

Napier-Bell, Simon, *You Don't Have to Say You Love Me*, Ebury Press, 2005.

Pearson, John, *The Profession of Violence*, William Collins, 2015.

Rees, Dafydd and Luke Crampton, *Guinness Book of Rock Stars* (2nd ed.), Guinness Publishing, 1991.

Sandoval, Andrew, *Bee Gees: The Day-By-Day Story, 1945–1972*, Retrofuture, 2012.

INDEX

Note: Titles in *italics* refer to albums, those in `inverted commas' to song titles.
Women are under their maiden name, as in the text.